GUIDE TO
NEW YORK CITY
LANDMARKS

GUIDE TO NEW YORK CITY LANDMARKS

NEW YORK CITY LANDMARKS
PRESERVATION COMMISSION

Introduction by
BRENDAN GILL
Foreword by
MAYOR DAVID N. DINKINS
Compiled by
ANDREW S. DOLKART

Marjorie Pearson, Project Director

The Preservation Press
National Trust for Historic Preservation

The Preservation Press
National Trust for Historic Preservation
1785 Massachusetts Avenue, N.W.
Washington, D.C. 20036

The National Trust for Historic Preservation is the only
private, nonprofit organization chartered by Congress to
encourage public participation in the preservation of sites,
buildings, and objects significant in American history and
culture. Support is provided by membership dues,
endowment funds, contributions, and grants from federal
agencies, including the U.S. Department of the Interior,
under provisions of the National Historic Preservation Act
of 1966. The opinions expressed here do not necessarily
reflect the views or policies of the Interior Department.
For information about membership in the National Trust,
write to the Membership Office at the above address.

Printed in the United States of America
96 95 94 93 92   5 4 3 2 1

Library of Congress Cataloging in Publication Data
Dolkart, Andrew.
    Guide to New York City landmarks/New York
    City Landmarks Preservation Commission;
    introduction by Brendan Gill; foreword by David N.
    Dinkins; compiled by Andrew S. Dolkart; Marjorie
    Pearson, project director.
        p.   cm.
    Includes index.
    ISBN 0-89133-166-2
    1. New York (N.Y.)—Guidebooks. 2. Historic
sites—New York (N.Y.)—Guidebooks. 3. New York
(N.Y.)—Buildings, structures, etc.—Guidebooks.
I. Pearson, Marjorie. II. New York (N.Y.) Landmarks
Preservation Commission. III. Title.
F128.18.D65 1992
917.47'10442—dc20   92-10790

Designed and typeset by J. Scott Knudsen, Park City, Utah
Maps by Brian Goeken and Christopher Jenks, New York,
New York
Printed by the John D. Lucas Printing Company,
Baltimore, Maryland

Front cover: The Chrysler Building's well-known spire
looms in the background, framed by one wall of the
Flatiron Building. Grapple hooks attached to the
Flatiron's cornice were used during cleaning.
Back cover: Central Park West's skyline overlooks a
peaceful setting with Bow Bridge in Central Park. Both
photos: Caroline Kane

CONTENTS

New York City, known around the globe as the capital of the New World, is often imagined as a perennially new city, a place epitomized by what our Brooklyn poet Walt Whitman once called its tear-it-down-and-build-it-up-again spirit. Yet New York is also one of the oldest cities in North America, founded more than three and a half centuries ago. From its modest beginnings as a 17th-century Dutch trading post at the southern tip of Manhattan Island, New York has grown into a metropolis occupying hundreds of square miles spread over five boroughs, with a population of eight million people living and working in close to a million buildings. Some 19,000 of these buildings are now protected by the New York City Landmarks Preservation Commission; more than 900 are individual landmarks, and the balance are within 55 historic districts.

The diversity of our landmarks is stunning. They range from Pieter Claesen Wyckoff's Flatlands home of the 1650s to Frank Lloyd Wright's Guggenheim Museum of the 1950s, and from the Empire State Building to Louis Armstrong's house—from mansions to model tenements, from Broadway theaters to local movie houses, from the Eldridge Street Synagogue to St. Patrick's Cathedral, from libraries and firehouses to City Hall. They include parts of the physical plant that makes this vast city habitable: a steel viaduct for the subway system; a stone gatehouse for the Croton water system; and bridges that join the disparate components of the island city into one enormous whole. Colonial cemeteries and cast-iron street clocks; Victorian parks and modern skyscrapers; rides such as the Wonder Wheel, the Parachute Jump, and the Cyclone that once made Coney Island urban America's favorite playground—all of these are special to New York City, and all are landmarks.

The city's historic districts include communities in all five boroughs. In Brooklyn, neighborhoods in the brownstone belt—Brooklyn Heights and Stuyvesant Heights, Clinton Hill and Cobble Hill, Park Slope and Fort Greene—are complemented by turn-of-the-century planned suburbs such as Prospect Park South and the old commercial precincts around the Fulton Ferry landing. Manhattan's districts encompass the narrow streets of Greenwich Village and the cast-iron buildings of SoHo, the Beaux-Arts mansions of the Upper East Side and the twin-towered apartment houses of Central Park West,

City Hall, City Hall Park (Joseph-François Mangin and John McComb, Jr., 1802–11), with the Municipal Building, 1 Centre Street (McKim, Mead & White, 1907–14), in the background. Photo: John Barrington Bayley

and the quiet brownstone streets of Harlem's Hamilton Heights and Strivers' Row. Longwood and Mott Haven in the South Bronx and Riverdale in the North, Hunter's Point in Queens and Seaview in Staten Island—all these and more are among the treasures that New York honors and protects through its landmarks law.

Landmarks are often cited as incentives for tourism, and surely the millions of visitors to our city, called by some the capital of the world, come to see the buildings and places which we know as landmarks and historic districts. But the chief importance of New York's landmarks is for ourselves, for New Yorkers. Within our communities, landmarks—whether individual buildings or entire historic districts—become sources of neighborhood stability, self-worth, and pride. They are the monuments, great and small, which serve as the touchstones of our civic identity—the irreplaceable places without which New York becomes a different, and a poorer, city.

As mayor of New York, I invite all New Yorkers, and all friends of this city, wherever you may live, to visit our landmarks: to learn about our history, to learn about our treasures, and to learn about our people.

DAVID N. DINKINS
Mayor
City of New York

The landmarks of which Mayor David Dinkins writes so eloquently in his foreword survive not by chance, but because some 27 years ago a number of concerned citizens, perceiving that the architectural and historic heritage of New York City was threatened in many cases with mutilation, and in other, more desperate cases with outright destruction, brought about the establishment of an official New York City Landmarks Preservation Commission. The board of commissioners is composed of New Yorkers of appropriate professional backgrounds—architects, urban planners, real estate professionals, and the like—appointed by the mayor. The chairman of the board is a paid city official; the other commissioners, 10 in number, serve without pay, at meetings and hearings that often require them to manifest an exceptional measure of what Mayor Fiorello LaGuardia used to call patience and fortitude.

Chrysler Building at night with the Queensborough Bridge in the background. Photo: Andy Freeberg

Assisted by a small, well-trained staff, the commission exercises its powers of designation with deliberation and discretion, acting much as a good neighbor might do in identifying individual properties and even whole districts whose worth has hitherto gone unrecognized and unprotected. The staff also offers expert practical advice as to the rehabilitation of endangered structures and the new uses to which they may be put. The commission often works alongside the New York Landmarks Conservancy, the Municipal Art Society, and other local philanthropic organizations that share its goals.

At first glance, the mandate of the Landmarks Preservation Commission might appear to be limited to matters of brick and mortar, but in a broader sense it can be said to embrace a civic amenity not visible to the naked eye—the psychological good health of millions of anonymous New Yorkers. The densely woven fabric of a city, especially that of a city long settled and bearing the stamp of many generations of ambitious builders, is a source of emotional nourishment to its inhabitants. Whether we are conscious of it or not, we draw strength and reassurance from all those evidences of the past that bear witness to the successful outcome of struggles not unlike our own, undertaken in times that must have seemed every bit as difficult as those we face today. It is not too much to say of the buildings, streets, parks, and monuments that we have inherited—and not merely the best of them, mind you, but the most characteristic—that they are indispensable to our well-being. Silently, as we dwell among them, they help to make us aware of ourselves as members of a community.

It is for this reason, rising above others of a more matter-of-fact nature, that the citizens of New York do well to cherish the Landmarks Preservation Commission. For the commission embodies from day to day the noble precept of John Ruskin, who, in answering the question of whether it was expedient to preserve the buildings of the past, said at once and with passion, "We have no right whatever to touch them. They are not ours. They belong partly to those who built them, and partly to all the generations of mankind who are to follow us. . . . It may hereafter be a subject of sorrow, or a cause of injury, to millions, that we have consulted our present convenience when casting down such buildings as we choose to dispense with. That sorrow, that loss we have no right to inflict."

BRENDAN GILL
Chairman Emeritus
New York Landmarks Conservancy

This guide includes information on all individual landmarks, interior landmarks (which by law must be accessible to the public), scenic landmarks, and historic districts designated by the New York City Landmarks Preservation Commission from October 14, 1965 (when the commission made its first designations), through the end of 1991. The entries, written by the architectural historian Andrew S. Dolkart, briefly explain the architectural and historical significance of New York City's landmark properties (as of December 31, 1991, 904 individual landmarks, 83 interior landmarks, 9 scenic landmarks, and 55 historic districts.) The information has been collected from the commission's Research Department staff under the direction of Marjorie Pearson. Errors in earlier editions of this guide have been corrected (for example, names inaccurately assigned to properties at the time of designation have been emended), and newly discovered information previously unpublished (for example, the accurate historic names of many buildings) has been incorporated.

Listings have been divided among New York City's five boroughs: Manhattan, Brooklyn, Queens, the Bronx, and Staten Island. Governors, Liberty, and Roosevelt islands, which are under the jurisdiction of the borough of Manhattan, appear in a chapter of their own for easier reference. Within Manhattan, geographical subdivisions have been made based on street boundaries differentiating major areas. Within each section entries are listed in alphabetical order. The landmark's historic name is followed, when applicable, by other names associated with the property. Buildings without specific names are listed by address; these are alphabetized according to the name of the street (such names include the words *East* and *West*). In a few cases, where use of a historic name might lead to confusion or where a later name is much better known, the landmark is listed under its common name (for example, Fordham University, rather than St. John's College; Castle Clinton, rather than West Battery). Buildings named after individuals are alphabetized by the person's last name. Buildings such as theaters and churches are alphabetized by their specific proper names (for example, Church of the Incarnation is found under *I*; Theater Masque is under *M*). Individually designated landmarks that are part of a larger complex are listed under the name of the complex (for example, Low Memorial Library is found under Columbia University). All property names and addresses have been cross-indexed to facilitate identification.

Architects associated with the original construction and any relevant additions to the property are cited at the beginning of each entry along with dates indicating the widest determinable span of work, from design to completion.

Information about architects associated with relevant restoration or rehabilitation work, and the dates of such work, has been incorporated into the text.

Please note that the New York City Landmarks Preservation Commission does not own or operate any landmark properties. A listing in this guide is not an invitation to visit: permission must be obtained from the owner or occupant. In many cases, landmark properties are private residences, and the reader is asked to bear in mind that the owners' privacy must be respected. The entries indicate which properties are museums or otherwise open to the public; visitors to these properties are, in many cases, charged a fee. Interior landmarks, indicated in bold face in the text, are customarily open to the public. Depending on the nature and use of the space, a ticket may be required or a fee charged.

The New York City Landmarks Preservation Commission recognizes that ongoing research on the city's architecture and history will continue to bring new information to light about designated landmarks. The commission would be pleased to receive such information directed to the attention of its Research Department. Corrections of errors that may have inadvertently crept into this edition of the guide may also be addressed to this department.

This new and greatly expanded edition of the commission's guide to New York City landmarks would not have been possible without the leadership of Laurie Beckelman, Chair of the New York City Landmarks Preservation Commission. A grant from the Andy Warhol Foundation for the Visual Arts funded the work of Andrew S. Dolkart in compiling and writing the guide entries. Other funds were contributed by the New York Landmarks Preservation Foundation and Joseph E. Seagram & Sons, Inc.

Many of the commission's staff made exceptional efforts. Essential encouragement, support, and enthusiasm were provided by Joan R. Olshansky, Chief of Staff. Members of the commission's Research Department, under my direction, conducted research, resulting in the designation reports that form the basis of the guide entries. In addition, Marion Cleaver of the department compiled the index. Valuable on-site building information has been obtained by members of the commission's Preservation Department while working with architects and property owners. Special recognition goes to the late Alan Burnham whose work as director of research, assisted by Ellen W. Kramer, resulted in earlier editions of this guide. Thanks to Shirley Zavin, who, while a member of the commission's Survey Department, contributed extensive new information on the landmark buildings of Staten Island. Carl Forster, Caroline Kane, and Janet O'Hare provided photographs. Many owners of landmark buildings and other interested parties, too numerous to mention individually, have provided additional information.

Last, thanks to The Preservation Press, in particular, Buckley Jeppson, of the National Trust for Historic Preservation for publishing the guide in this new format. Terry Adams and Virginia Read gave valuable editorial guidance. We anticipate that this new edition, a truly comprehensive look at the city's landmarks, will reach a much larger, and nationwide, audience of readers and building lovers who, if they haven't already, will want to come and experience the diverse architecture we have to offer. New York City, certainly a major part of our national heritage, welcomes all.

MARJORIE PEARSON
Director of Research

MANHATTAN

THE BATTERY TO FULTON STREET

Bowling Green Fence, Bowling Green Park (1771). This simple iron fence was erected in 1771 to protect a statue of King George III. Although the statue was destroyed in 1776, the fence survives as a unique example of pre–Revolutionary War craftsmanship in New York City.

Castle Clinton, now Castle Clinton National Monument, Battery Park (Lt. Col. Jonathan Williams and John McComb, Jr., 1808–11). Originally built on an artificial island off the Battery, and referred to as West Battery, Castle Clinton—so named in 1815—was one of a series of forts, including Castle Williams (see p. 239) on Governors Island, erected to protect New York Harbor. Although the design of the brownstone fort is often attributed to John McComb, Jr., he was probably responsible only for the entrance. After becoming the property of New York City in 1823, the former fort served as a theater (Castle Garden), an immigrant station, and an aquarium, before it was restored by the federal government in the early 1970s.

Chamber of Commerce of the State of New York, now the International Commercial Bank of China, 65 Liberty Street (James B. Baker, 1900–01). This imposing Beaux-Arts building was erected by the chamber of commerce to symbolize its importance in New York's commercial life. The marble structure, occupied by the chamber until 1980, was restored in 1990–91 as part of its conversion into a bank.

Federal Reserve Bank of New York, 33 Liberty Street (York & Sawyer, 1919–24). The massive rusticated walls of the Federal Reserve Bank, constructed of stone in two colors, symbolize the strength of the Federal Reserve system and the impregnability of this building, which stores a significant part of the world's gold reserves. The Florentine palazzo form was chosen by York & Sawyer for its association with the Medicis and other leading Renaissance families whose fortunes were made, at least in part, from banking. The iron detail was crafted by the master iron worker Samuel Yellin of Philadelphia.

Church of the Transfiguration (Episcopal), also known as the Little Church Around the Corner, 1 East 29th Street (1849–50, 1852). See p. 64. Photo: Carl Forster

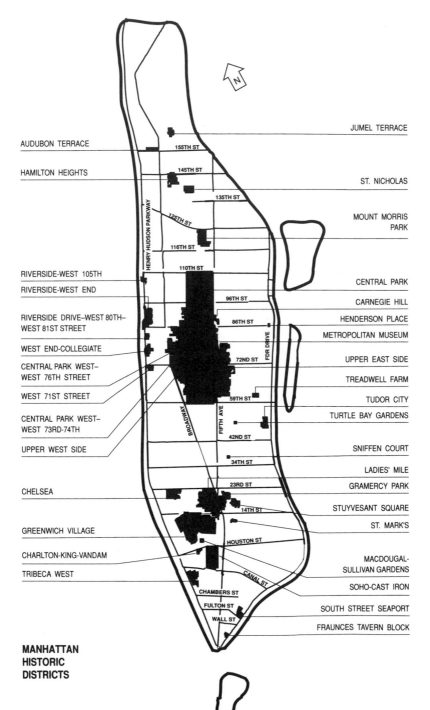

N

JUMEL TERRACE

AUDUBON TERRACE

155TH ST

HAMILTON HEIGHTS

145TH ST

ST. NICHOLAS

135TH ST

HENRY HUDSON PARKWAY

MOUNT MORRIS
PARK

125TH ST

116TH ST

110TH ST

CENTRAL PARK

RIVERSIDE-WEST 105TH

RIVERSIDE-WEST END

96TH ST

CARNEGIE HILL

RIVERSIDE DRIVE–WEST 80TH–
WEST 81ST STREET

86TH ST

HENDERSON PLACE

FDR DRIVE

METROPOLITAN MUSEUM

WEST END-COLLEGIATE

72ND ST

UPPER EAST SIDE

CENTRAL PARK WEST–
WEST 76TH STREET

TREADWELL FARM

WEST 71ST STREET

59TH ST

TUDOR CITY

CENTRAL PARK WEST–
WEST 73RD-74TH

TURTLE BAY GARDENS

BROADWAY

FIFTH AVE

UPPER WEST SIDE

42ND ST

SNIFFEN COURT

34TH ST

LADIES' MILE

23RD ST

GRAMERCY PARK

CHELSEA

STUYVESANT SQUARE

14TH ST

GREENWICH VILLAGE

ST. MARK'S

HOUSTON ST

CHARLTON-KING-VANDAM

MACDOUGAL-
SULLIVAN GARDENS

TRIBECA WEST

CANAL ST

SOHO-CAST IRON

CHAMBERS ST

FULTON ST

SOUTH STREET SEAPORT

WALL ST

FRAUNCES TAVERN BLOCK

**MANHATTAN
HISTORIC
DISTRICTS**

Hickson W. Field Stores, also known as the Baker, Carver & Morrell Building, 170–176 John Street (1840; addition, Buttrick, White & Burtis, 1981–82). Erected for a commission merchant, this building is a rare surviving example of a Greek Revival warehouse with an all-granite front. This building type, characterized by an austere facade and a ground floor articulated by post-and-lintel construction, represents a form first perfected in Boston and introduced to New York in 1826 by Ithiel Town at his Tappan Store (demolished) on Pearl Street. For much of the 20th century the building housed the Baker, Carver & Morrell ship's chandlery. The top story was added in 1981–82 during conversion into a restaurant and apartments.

First Precinct Police Station, South Street at Old Slip (Hunt & Hunt, 1909–11). Hunt & Hunt, the firm established by the sons of the famed Richard Morris Hunt, designed this limestone police station in the form of an Italian Renaissance palazzo. The arched openings, rustication, and imposing cornice have been compared to those of the 15th-century Palazzo Riccardi in Florence. The building is currently vacant.

Fraunces Tavern, 54 Pearl Street (1719; reconstruction, William H. Mersereau, 1904–07). The original building on this site was erected in 1719 by Stephen DeLancey. In 1763 the house was converted into a tavern by Samuel Fraunces, and it was here that George Washington gave his famous farewell address to his officers. The building suffered several additions and fires in the 19th century. In 1904 the heavily altered and deteriorated building was purchased by the Sons of the Revolution, which sponsored a somewhat speculative reconstruction that is an important example of Colonial Revival design. Fraunces Tavern is now a museum and restaurant.

🍎 **Fraunces Tavern Block Historic District.** The low-rise buildings of this square block provide an unusual illustration of the early building history of Lower Manhattan. Dating primarily from the early 19th century, these buildings stand in marked contrast to the surrounding 20th-century skyscrapers. The block escaped the fire of December 1835 that devastated most of Lower Manhattan. Thus, the district retains 11 buildings erected between 1827 and 1833, including a rare example of a warehouse in the Federal style (62 Pearl

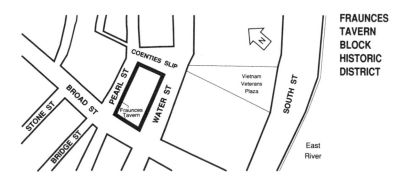

FRAUNCES
TAVERN
BLOCK
HISTORIC
DISTRICT

Street) and several Greek Revival counting houses. Also in the district is
Fraunces Tavern (see p. 17). Much of the block was saved from demolition in
1974.

Hanover Bank, now India House, 1 Hanover Square (1852–53). The former
Hanover Bank is the only survivor of the many Italianate banks erected in
Manhattan's financial district in the 1850s. The brownstone-fronted building
was based on Italian Renaissance palazzo prototypes, appropriate since many
of the Renaissance families made their fortunes in banking. The building served
as the Cotton Exchange and as the headquarters of W. R. Grace & Co. before
being converted into India House, a private club whose founders were involved
in foreign trade. The name was chosen because *India* and *the Indies* allude to
exotic (and profitable) trading centers.

Interborough Rapid Transit System: Control Houses, Battery Park and West
72nd Street (Heins & LaFarge, 1904–05); **Manhattan Valley Viaduct**,
Broadway from West 122nd to West 135th streets (William B. Parsons, engineer,
1900–04); **Underground Stations**, Wall Street, Fulton Street, City Hall,
Bleecker Street, Astor Place, and 33rd Street, Manhattan, and Borough Hall,
Brooklyn, on the Lexington Avenue IRT Line; 59th Street–Columbus Circle,
72nd Street, 79th Street, 110th Street, and 116th Street–Columbia University on
the Seventh Avenue IRT Line (Heins & LaFarge, architect, and William B.
Parsons, engineer, Contract 1, 1899–1904; Contract 2, 1902–08). Following a
succession of aborted attempts to build a subway system in Manhattan, a contract
was signed in 1899 for the construction of the Interborough Rapid Transit
Company's first subway. The original IRT line ran from City Hall to Grand
Central and then turned west to Times Square and north along Broadway to the
Bronx. In 1902 the system was continued south from City Hall through Lower
Manhattan and into Brooklyn. Chief Engineer Parsons and his staff were responsible for the construction of the system. One of the most spectacular engineering
features planned by Parsons is the Manhattan Valley Viaduct, which carries the
Broadway line over a valley at 125th Street and which consists of approaches
faced with rock-fronted granite blocks, steel viaducts, and a central span with
three parabolic arches. Although the engineers sited and planned each subway
station, the architecture firm of Heins & LaFarge designed the ornamentation.
The architects were required to use white tile and light-colored brick except
where color was "introduced for architectural effect." Color was used for the
mosaic sign panels and for the terra-cotta and faience plaques (provided by the
Rookwood Pottery of Cincinnati and the Grueby Faience Company of Boston)
that embellish each station. At many stations the plaques were designed with an
attribute unique to that stop. These include the beavers at Astor Place (John Jacob
Astor made his initial fortune in beaver pelts), a caravel at Columbus Circle, and
the seal of Columbia University at 116th Street. In addition to the subterranean
stations, Heins & LaFarge designed the above-ground entrance structures.
Although all of the original cast-iron entrance canopies have been removed (a
canopy has been reconstructed at Astor Place), two of the Flemish-inspired brick
and terra-cotta control houses still stand in Manhattan—at Battery Park just south
of Bowling Green and at Broadway and West 72nd Street.

John Street Methodist Church, 44 John Street (1841). John Street is the oldest Methodist congregation in North America. Founded in 1766 as the Wesleyan Society in America, the congregation erected its first church in 1768. The well-proportioned Georgian-inspired building with a brownstone facade is the third church on the site.

Liberty Tower, 55 Liberty Street (Henry Ives Cobb, 1909–10). This handsome neo-Gothic skyscraper—clad entirely in white terra cotta and enlivened with fanciful ornament, including birds and alligators—is an important antecedent to the Woolworth Building (see p. 41). The freestanding building, which at the time of its construction was known as "the tallest building in the world on so small an area of ground," was also one of the earliest residential conversion projects in Lower Manhattan.

90–94 Maiden Lane Building (attributed to Charles Wright, 1870–71). One of the few mid-19th-century commercial structures still standing in Lower Manhattan, this small French Second Empire building has an iron front, cast at Daniel D. Badger's Architectural Iron Works, that united three early 19th-century warehouses. The facade was commissioned by Roosevelt & Son, the nation's leading importer of plate glass and mirrors, among whose principals was Theodore Roosevelt, the father of the country's 26th president.

J. P. Morgan & Company, now the Morgan Guaranty Trust Company, 23 Wall Street (Trowbridge & Livingston, 1913). At a time when skyscrapers were being erected throughout Lower Manhattan, the Morgan Bank erected this small headquarters building on one of the most valuable pieces of land in New York City, the juncture of Wall and Broad streets. The low-scaled, austere classical building, clad in white marble, symbolized the wealth and power of this banking institution. The importance of the bank was further underscored by the absence of a name on the exterior; for those wealthy enough to bank at Morgan, no introduction was needed.

National City Bank (incorporating the Merchants' Exchange), now Citibank, 55 Wall Street (Isaiah Rogers, 1836–41; additions, McKim, Mead & White, 1904–10). The National City Bank Building appears to be a single unified structure but is actually the result of two building campaigns begun 68 years apart. The Boston architect Isaiah Rogers designed the original building for the Merchants' Exchange. The three-story Greek Revival structure of Quincy granite with a dome and a colonnade of 12 Ionic columns, each a single block of stone, was one of the most impressive early 19th-century buildings in America. In 1862 the U.S. Custom Service moved from its home at 28 Wall Street (see p. 23) into this building, where it remained until a new custom house (see p. 23) was erected on Bowling Green. In 1907 James Stillman, president of the National City Bank, recognized that this freestanding Wall Street landmark would be a fitting home for his growing bank, and he arranged for its purchase from the government. Charles McKim was commissioned to enlarge the building. The dome was removed, the interior gutted, and four floors added; a second granite colonnade was carefully proportioned to align with the original.

New York Stock Exchange, 8–18 Broad Street (George B. Post, 1901–03). This marble-fronted building has been the home of America's principal securities market since 1903. The exchange—which dates back to 1792, when stock dealers met under a buttonwood tree on Wall Street—had been housed at a number of different sites before it moved into a building at 12 Broad Street (John Kellum, architect), just south of Wall Street, in 1865. That building was enlarged in 1880–81 (James Renwick, Jr., architect) and eventually replaced by the present structure, whose six monumental Corinthian columns and pediment contain an allegorical sculptural ensemble entitled *Integrity Protecting the Works of Man,* designed by John Quincy Adams Ward and executed by Paul Wayland Bartlett.

Pier A, Battery Park (George Sears Greene, Jr., engineer, 1884–86; addition, 1900). Jutting into New York Bay at the southern end of Manhattan, Pier A was built for the city's Department of Docks and Harbor Police and was designed by the department's chief engineer. It is the last surviving historic pier in Manhattan. Additions include the three-story pier head (1900) and the clock located in the tower at the west end of the pier, which was installed in 1919 as a memorial to servicemen who died in World War I; the clock peals the time on ship's bells.

Schermerhorn Row Block, 2–18 Fulton Street, 189–195 Front Street, 159–171 John Street, and 91–92 South Street (1811–49). Historically and architecturally, this block is the most important in the South Street Seaport area. All of the buildings were erected as warehouses or counting houses for New York's

Pier A, Battery Park (George Sears Greene, Jr., engineer, 1884–86; addition, 1900).
Photo: Caroline Kane

rapidly expanding mercantile sector. The oldest buildings on the block are 191 and 193 Front Street, both probably erected c. 1793 but redesigned in the 19th century. The principal developer on the block was Peter Schermerhorn, a leading merchant and a member of a prominent New York family. He was responsible for the famous Schermerhorn Row (1811–12), the four-story brick warehouses on Fulton and intersecting streets that were built in the Georgian-Federal style and were originally linked by distinctive sloping roofs with tall chimneys (the mansard on the building at the corner of Fulton and South streets was added in 1868 when the building was a hotel). Contemporaneous with Schermerhorn Row was a group of six counting houses on John Street, only one of which (No. 165) survives. In the 1830s Greek Revival buildings began to appear throughout New York's business district. Among the finest of these is A. A. Low & Brothers' stone warehouse at 167–171 John Street (1850), built for one of the most important firms involved in the China trade. Simpler Greek Revival brick warehouses are located at the corner of Front and John streets (1835–36). In the early 1980s all of these buildings were restored (Jan Hird Pokorny, architect) for the South Street Seaport Museum and Marketplace.

❦ **South Street Seaport Historic District**. Within this district is the largest concentration of early commercial buildings surviving in New York City. The district's noteworthy structures include the Schermerhorn Row Block (see above), the Hickson W. Field Stores (see p. 17), and the restored buildings and piers of the South Street Seaport Museum and Marketplace, as well as the late 18th- and early 19th-century warehouses and counting houses to the north. These Georgian-Federal and Greek Revival brick and granite buildings evoke the period when New York was rapidly developing as the leading port in North America and mercantile buildings were erected to serve the needs of expanding shipping interests. After years of neglect and deterioration, many of the buildings in this district have been rehabilitated for use as shops, galleries, offices, and housing. Notable new construction includes the building faced with steel panels emulating cast iron at 15–19 Fulton Street (Beyer Blinder Belle, 1977–83) and the Seamen's Church Institute (James Stewart Polshek & Partners, 1989–91) at 241 Water Street.

Street Plan of New Amsterdam and Colonial New York, including all or part of Beaver, Bridge, Broad, Hanover, Marketfield, New, Pearl, South William, Stone, Wall, Whitehall, and William streets; Exchange Place; Hanover Square; Mill Lane; and Broadway. The present street plan of Lower Manhattan, south of Wall Street, was laid out by the Dutch in the 17th century; minor additions and alterations were subsequently made by the British. These narrow streets are the only visible above-ground evidence in Manhattan of the colonial settlement. Streets developed in an organic manner from the original waterfront at Pearl Street. Broadway was the major colonial street, running north from the original fort at the Battery. Broad Street ran from the waterfront and contained a canal, thus accounting for its exceptional width.

Trinity Building and United States Realty Building, 111 and 115 Broadway (Francis H. Kimball, 1904–07). These two skyscrapers were designed with

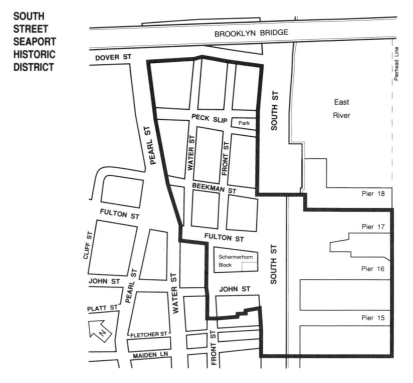

SOUTH STREET SEAPORT HISTORIC DISTRICT

Gothic detail to harmonize with neighboring Trinity Church (see below) and were dubbed by the *New York Times* as "twin examples of Gothic splendor." The construction of these enormous slabs was a major undertaking, entailing the relocation of Thames Street and the construction of caissons 80 feet into the marshy subsoil. The limestone-faced buildings are carefully detailed with towers, gables, and fanciful carved ornament.

Trinity Church (Episcopal) and Graveyard, Broadway at Wall Street (Richard Upjohn, 1839–46; sacristy, Frederick Clarke Withers, 1876–77; All Saints' Chapel, Thomas Nash, 1911–13; Manning Wing, Adams & Woodbridge, 1966). One of the first Gothic Revival buildings in New York and one of Upjohn's earliest works, Trinity Church was for many years the tallest structure in the city, its spire towering over New York's business district. The present church is the third built on this site for New York's oldest Episcopal congregation. The building was constructed of New Jersey brownstone whose original light and varied hues were revealed when the exterior was cleaned in 1990–91. The church has had several important additions, including the sacristy, chapel, and Manning Wing at the west end, and the bronze entrance doors (1890–96) donated as a memorial to John Jacob Astor III, which were designed by Richard Morris Hunt in collaboration with the sculptors Karl Bitter, J. Massey Rhind, and Charles Niehaus. The surrounding graveyard contains the tombs of such famous Americans as Alexander Hamilton, Albert Gallatin, Francis Lewis, William Bradford, and Robert Fulton.

United States Custom House, later the U.S. Sub-Treasury, now Federal Hall National Memorial, 28 Wall Street (Town & Davis, Samuel Thompson, William Ross, and John Frazee, 1833–42). This building at the juncture of Wall and Broad streets in the heart of New York's financial district occupies one of the most historic locations in New York—the site of the original Federal Hall, where Washington took the oath of office as the nation's first president (commemorated by John Quincy Adams Ward's 1883 sculpture of Washington on the building's steps). Town & Davis designed the imposing marble Custom House, adapting the form of the Parthenon to the needs of a great 19th-century civic monument. Although Davis had hoped to supervise construction, the job went to the builder Samuel Thompson. Thompson and his successors, Ross and Frazee, were responsible for design changes that distressed Davis. **Interior**: The rotunda is among the finest Greek Revival rooms in New York, especially notable for its Corinthian columns, saucer dome, and elegant iron railings cast in the form of classical maidens and twining vines. In 1862, when the Custom Service moved to the old Merchants' Exchange (see National City Bank, p. 19), this building became a branch of the sub-treasury. The building was designated a National Historic Site in 1939 and a National Memorial in 1955.

United States Custom House, Bowling Green (Cass Gilbert, 1899–1907). In 1899 the Minnesota architect Cass Gilbert won the competition for New York's new Custom House with a masterful essay in Beaux-Arts design. The building has bold three-dimensional massing and an extensive sculptural program on themes related to commerce and trade; the most notable sculptures are Daniel

United States Custom House, later the U.S. Sub-Treasury, now Federal Hall National Memorial, 28 Wall Street (Town & Davis, Samuel Thompson, William Ross, and John Frazee, 1833–42). Photo: Caroline Kane

Chester French's *Four Continents*, which flank the grand entrance stairway. The **interiors** on the main floor are as ornate as the exterior. The richly detailed marble entrance hall leads to an oval rotunda embellished with a mural cycle by Reginald Marsh installed in 1936–37 as part of the Treasury Department's Depression-era arts project. Magnificently decorated offices are arranged along the front of the building. After standing empty for many years, the Custom House has been reopened for use by the Federal Bankruptcy Court; plans call for the conversion of part of the space into a branch of the Museum of the American Indian.

United States Realty Building. See Trinity Building and United States Realty Building, p. 21.

James Watson House, now the Rectory of the Shrine of St. Elizabeth Ann Seton, 7 State Street (attributed to John McComb, Jr., 1793; extension, 1806). In 1793–1806, when this house was erected, Lower Manhattan was still a fashionable residential area. The original Georgian structure has an elegant addition in the Federal style with an Ionic portico conforming to the curve of the street. The building is now a shrine to the first native-born American (and New Yorker) granted sainthood by the Catholic Church.

Whitehall Ferry Terminal, now the Battery Maritime Building, 11 South Street (Walker & Morris, 1906–09). The ferry terminal, designed with seven slips, only three of which were built, is a Beaux-Arts steel building reminiscent of French exposition architecture. The only survivor of the many historic ferry terminals that once lined New York's waterfront, it now serves ferries running to Governors Island.

FULTON STREET TO HOUSTON STREET

All Saints' Free Church (Episcopal), later St. Augustine's Chapel, now St. Augustine's Episcopal Church, 290 Henry Street (1827–29; enlargement, 1849). This "free" church (i.e., rent was not charged for pews) is the most imposing of the four Georgian-Gothic landmark churches built of Manhattan schist on the Lower East Side. The design incorporates a double pediment and a projecting tower. In 1945 Trinity Church took over the operation of All Saints'. Four years later Trinity's St. Augustine's Chapel moved into the building. St. Augustine's became an independent parish in 1976.

Anshe Chesed Synagogue, later Anshe Slonim Synagogue, 172–176 Norfolk Street (Alexander Saeltzer, 1849–50). Built for the city's third Jewish congregation, this is the oldest surviving building in New York City erected specifically for use as a synagogue and is the earliest synagogue on the Lower East Side. Curiously, the building was designed in a Gothic Revival style and, at the time of construction, was even compared with Cologne Cathedral. The structure is now vacant and badly deteriorated.

Barclay-Vesey Building, 140 West Street (Ralph Walker, architect in charge, McKenzie, Voorhees & Gmelin, 1923–27). The first major design of Ralph

Walker, this brick-clad building, whose name derives from its location between Barclay and Vesey streets, was commissioned by the New York Telephone Company for its headquarters. It is one of the most significant structures in the annals of skyscraper design, since it was the first building in New York City to exploit the requirements of the 1916 zoning code, leading to the tower's dramatic massing. Walker also pioneered in the use of complex, nontraditional, naturalistic, carved ornament. **Interior:** Exterior ornamental motifs are repeated in the lobby, which contains veined marble walls, travertine floors with bronze medallions, and a vaulted ceiling embellished with murals depicting the stages in the evolution of human communication.

Bowery Savings Bank, 130 Bowery (McKim, Mead & White, 1893–95). The present bank building is the third erected at this location since the Bowery Savings Bank opened its doors in 1834. For this especially challenging L-shaped site, Stanford White designed two limestone street fronts, each in a Roman classical style with Corinthian columns supporting pediments sculpted by Frederic MacMonnies. White was the first to popularize the Roman classical style for bank design, and his choice established a trend; the Bowery became a prototype for other banks in New York and throughout the United States.

287 Broadway Building (John B. Snook, 1871–72). This cast-iron commercial building in the French Second Empire style was erected as a speculative venture. In order to increase its allure for potential tenants, the building was crowned with an impressive mansard roof featuring lacy iron cresting and was equipped with a very early Otis passenger elevator. The iron elements were cast by Jackson, Burnet & Co., which maintained foundries on Centre and East 13th streets.

319 Broadway Building (D. & J. Jardine, 1869–70). The lone survivor of a pair of buildings known as the "Thomas Twins" that once occupied the two western corners of Broadway at Thomas Street, this Italianate structure has facades of iron cast at Daniel D. Badger's Architectural Iron Works.

359 Broadway Building (1852). This unusual Italianate commercial building reflects the rapid shift from residential to commercial tenancy that occurred on Broadway south of Canal Street following the construction of the A. T. Stewart Store (see p. 39) in 1845. The stone building is of special historic importance because the upper three floors were occupied by the photographer Mathew Brady's portrait studio between 1853 and 1859. Brady, one of the most important photographers in American history, is renowned for his portraits and Civil War images.

361 Broadway Building, also known as the James S. White Building, (W. Wheeler Smith, 1881–82). While most early examples of cast-iron construction appear to be attempts to simulate stone, cast-iron buildings of the late 1870s and 1880s were designed to exploit the properties of the material itself and are often extremely flamboyant. Commissioned by James S. White, this late example of a building with cast-iron facades contains very large windows set in a framework of elaborately decorated iron columns and piers.

Brooklyn Bridge. See p. 156. See p. 156.

David S. Brown Store, also known as the 8 Thomas Street Building (J. Morgan Slade, 1875–76). A manufacturer of laundry and toilet soaps commissioned this rare New York City example of Victorian Gothic masonry design from J. Morgan Slade, who, before his untimely death at age 30 in 1882, distinguished himself as an exceedingly accomplished architect of commercial buildings. The use of banded stone arches and other Venetian Gothic motifs reflects the influence of the English theoretician John Ruskin, while the honest use of cast iron on the ground floor indicates Slade's interest in French architectural theory.

254–260 Canal Street Building (1856–57). Resembling an Italian Renaissance palazzo, this building is an important early example of cast-iron architecture in New York City. There is strong evidence to suggest that this commercial palace, with its seemingly endless array of arched windows, contains iron elements cast by James Bogardus, a pioneer in the construction of cast-iron buildings, little of whose work survives.

Cary Building, 105–107 Chambers Street (King & Kellum, 1856–57). A masterpiece of cast-iron design, the Cary Building extends through the entire block between Chambers and Reade streets. Its Italian Renaissance facades, with their arched windows supported by Corinthian columns, were cast in the form of rusticated stone blocks at Daniel D. Badger's Architectural Iron Works on East 14th Street. Erected by the dry goods firm of Cary, Howard & Sanger, the building reflects the mid-19th-century transformation of the area west and north of City Hall into an important commercial district.

🍎 Charlton-King-Vandam Historic District. Now located at the edge of an industrial area, this historic district is an extraordinary remnant of early 19th-century residential New York, containing the city's largest concentration of row houses in the Federal style, as well as a significant concentration of Greek Revival houses. The district was once the site of Richmond Hill, a Georgian mansion that served variously as Washington's headquarters, the official vice presidential residence, and the home of Aaron Burr. Burr had the land surveyed and mapped out the present block and street system in 1797, but he lost the property to John Jacob Astor, who was responsible for the area's development into a residential neighborhood beginning in the 1820s. Later additions to the district include Public School 8, a lively Queen Anne–style building now converted into apartments.

City Hall, City Hall Park (Joseph-François Mangin and John McComb, Jr., 1802–11). City Hall is one of the most beautiful early 19th-century public buildings in the United States. Mangin and McComb's design was the winning entry in a competition held in 1802. It is generally believed that the French-trained Mangin was responsible for the exterior, since it closely resembles 18th-century French civic structures. The exterior stonework, originally Massachusetts marble with a brownstone rear elevation, deteriorated so extensively that in 1954–56 it was replaced with Alabama limestone above a

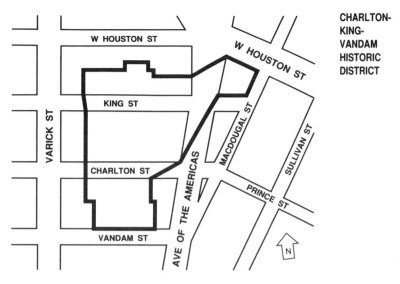

Missouri granite base. The **interior** is especially notable. The main entrance hall leads to a central rotunda in which a pair of spectacular cantilevered stairs curve upward to the second floor, where a series of marble Corinthian columns support a coffered dome. The lobby, stairs, and columns are original features; the dome is part of a restoration undertaken by Grosvenor Atterbury in 1912.

William and Rosamond Clark House, also known as the 51 Market Street House (1824–25). This row house in the late Federal style, apparently erected for the grocer William Clark and his wife, was built when the Lower East Side was an affluent residential neighborhood. The house retains a beautiful fanlit entrance, as well as original ironwork and window lintels. The two upper floors were added later in the 19th century.

Condict Store, also known as the 55 White Street Building (John Kellum & Son, 1861). Commissioned by John and Samuel Condict to house their saddlery business, this structure is one of New York City's most significant commercial buildings of the mid-19th century. It is also the largest surviving example of a cast-iron "sperm candle" design, identifiable by the thin two-story columns resembling the expensive candles made of sperm whale oil. The facade, whose iron components were cast at Daniel D. Badger's Architectural Iron Works, was restored in 1988–89 as part of a residential conversion (Liebman Melting Partnership, architects).

Eldridge Street Synagogue (Congregation Khal Adath Jeshurun), 12–16 Eldridge Street (Herter Brothers, 1886–87). In the late 19th century large numbers of Eastern European Jews settled on Manhattan's Lower East Side. The Eldridge Street Synagogue, the first Orthodox synagogue erected by these immigrants, is the most lavish synagogue ever built in the neighborhood. The brick and terra-cotta facade combines Moorish, Gothic, and Romanesque features

Eldridge Street Synagogue (Congregation Khal Adath Jeshurun), 12–16 Eldridge Street (Herter Brothers, 1886–87). Photo: Janet O'Hare

in a fanciful and imposing manner. Currently undergoing a major restoration (Giorgio Cavaglieri, architect), the building will continue to serve as a synagogue and as a center for education, celebrating American Jewish and immigrant history.

Emigrant Industrial Savings Bank,

51 Chambers Street (Raymond F. Almirall, 1908–12). The Emigrant Savings Bank was organized in 1850, under the auspices of Roman Catholic bishop John Hughes and the Irish Emigrant Society, to protect the savings of newly arrived Irish immigrants. In 1908 the bank commissioned designs for a new building that would front both Chambers and Reade streets. This limestone-faced skyscraper in the Beaux-Arts style was the first to be laid out on an H-plan, providing light and air to almost all office spaces. The building is now owned by New York City and used for municipal offices. **Interior:** The Department of Motor Vehicles occupies the banking hall. This richly decorated space has marble walls and floors, bronze grilles, original tellers' cages, and a series of stained-glass skylights with allegorical figures representing mining, manufacturing, agriculture, and other modes of employment.

Fire Engine Company No. 31, now the Chinese-American Planning Council and Downtown Community Television Center, 87 Lafayette Street (Napoleon Le Brun & Sons, 1895). The firm of Napoleon Le Brun & Sons was responsible for the design of many of the city's late 19th-century firehouses. Engine Company No. 31, modeled on early 16th-century Loire Valley châteaux in the style of François I, is the firm's most impressive civic design.

Forward Building, 173–175 East Broadway (George A. Boehm, 1912). This prominent 11-story Classical Revival building, erected on the Lower East Side as the home of the *Jewish Daily Forward*, the most significant Yiddish-language newspaper published in America, symbolizes the importance of the publication to the local Eastern European Jewish community. The *Forward* was a socialist paper that fought for the Jewish masses and was closely allied with Jewish labor and social improvement organizations, notably the Amalgamated Clothing Workers Union and the Workmen's Circle (which had offices in the building). The political leanings of the *Forward* are evident in the building's ornamentation, which includes a series of flaming torches (symbols of the socialist vanguard) as well as low-relief portraits of such socialist leaders as Marx and Engels on the frieze (now covered by signage) above the entrance. The Chinese characters currently found on the facade are a reflection of the building's new ownership and the change in the ethnic makeup of the neighborhood.

Fourteenth Ward Industrial School, 256–258 Mott Street (Vaux & Radford, 1888–89). In the late 1880s and 1890s the Children's Aid Society erected a series of schools to serve the city's poor, the earliest of which was this superb Victorian Gothic building. The school, founded to teach skills to immigrant children, was built with funds provided by John Jacob Astor II as a memorial to his wife, a longtime supporter of the society. The building has been converted into housing.

Hall of Records, now Surrogate's Court—Hall of Records, 31 Chambers Street (John R. Thomas and Horgan & Slattery, 1899–1907). This boldly detailed Beaux-Arts structure was erected by New York City as a representation of the importance of civic government. Designed by Thomas, the building was completed, following his death, by a firm closely allied with New York's Tammany politicians. Built of Maine granite, the building supports a profusion of sculptural detail that depicts New York's history. The decoration is at its most lavish in the magnificent **interior**, particularly the foyer, with its Siena marble walls and vaulted mosaic ceiling by the artist William de Leftwich Dodge; the double-height marble lobby with a skylight and a divided stair; the encircling corridors; and the two fifth-floor courtrooms, one paneled in Santo Domingo mahogany and the other in quartersawn English oak.

Harrison Street Houses, 25–41 Harrison Street (1796–1828). Around 1800 the Lower West Side area now known as Tribeca developed into a residential neighborhood of modest brick and frame houses in the Federal style. The houses near the waterfront were gradually engulfed by the expansion of Washington Market, and many of the older buildings in the area were altered for commercial use. As part of an urban renewal project begun in the late 1960s, the nine houses in this L-shaped enclave were incorporated into the Independence Plaza housing complex; three of the houses were moved from Washington Street, including two designed by John McComb, Jr.—No. 25 (1819) and the architect's own home, now at No. 27 (1796–97). All of the houses were extensively rehabilitated by Oppenheimer & Brady.

Haughwout Building, 488–492 Broadway (John P. Gaynor, 1856–57). A masterpiece of early cast-iron construction, the Haughwout Building was commissioned by E. V. Haughwout for his fashionable china, silver, and glassware

Haughwout Building, 488–492 Broadway (John P. Gaynor, 1856–57). Detail of clock
and cast-iron arcades made of components manufactured at Daniel D. Badger's
Architectural Iron Works. Photo: Caroline Kane

emporium. The iron components were manufactured at Daniel D. Badger's
Architectural Iron Works and were originally painted a color referred to in
1859 as "Turkish drab." The attempt to create a beautiful building using only a
limited number of mass-produced parts is evident in this structure's insistent
repetition of round arches and Corinthian columns, motifs adapted from the
facade of the Sansovino Library in Venice.

Henry Street Settlement, 263 and 265 Henry Street (1827; later alterations)
and 267 Henry Street (Buchman & Fox, 1900). In 1893 Lillian Wald, a middle-
class woman of German-Jewish descent, founded the Nurses' Settlement, later
renamed the Henry Street Settlement, to assist the Lower East Side populace
and to help educate and Americanize the Eastern European Jewish immigrant
population settling in the area. Two years later the German-Jewish philanthropist Jacob Schiff purchased 265 Henry Street for use by the organization. A
single story was added to this well-preserved Federal-style row house, a survivor from a once affluent residential neighborhood; Schiff donated the building to the settlement in 1903. Three years later another German-Jewish
philanthropist, Morris Loeb, purchased No. 267 from the Hebrew Technical
School for Girls and gave it to the settlement. This Greek Revival house had
received a Colonial Revival facade in 1900 when Buchman & Fox donated
their services for the redesign of the technical school. The settlement's third
building on Henry Street, No. 263, a Federal-style house with an extensively
altered facade, was leased for use as classrooms and apartments in 1938 and
was acquired by the settlement in 1949.

Henry Street Settlement, 263 and 265 Henry Street (1827; later alterations) and 267 Henry Street (Buchman & Fox, 1900). Photo: Carl Forster

Home Life Insurance Company Building (incorporating the Postal Telegraph Building), 256–257 and 253 Broadway (Pierre Le Brun, architect in charge, Napoleon Le Brun & Sons, 1892–94; Harding & Gooch, 1892–94). Home Life, founded in Brooklyn in 1860, has had a branch office on this site since 1866. The company held a competition for the design of a new Manhattan office in 1892. The result was Pierre Le Brun's Renaissance-style marble-clad building, an early example of a steel-skeleton-framed skyscraper. The building is a fine example of the tripartite expression of high-rise design, with its ornate arcaded base, simple shaft, and impressive pyramidal crown. Adjacent to the former Home Life Building is the Postal Telegraph Building, erected for a major competitor of Western Union. In 1947 Home Life purchased the neighboring structure and connected the two buildings internally.

Hopkins Store, also known as the 75 Murray Street Building (1857). The Venetian Renaissance–inspired cast-iron facade of this five-story commercial structure, built to house the glassware business of Francis and John Hopkins, was probably cast in the foundry of James Bogardus. It is among a handful of surviving buildings with iron elements attributed to Bogardus, the self-proclaimed inventor of cast-iron architecture.

Interborough Rapid Transit System Underground Station, City Hall. See p. 18.

Kitchen, Montross & Wilcox Store, also known as the 85 Leonard Street Building (1861). Commissioned by a firm of dry goods merchants, this cast-iron-fronted structure is one of the few surviving buildings in New York known to have been fabricated at the iron works of the pioneer cast-iron founder James Bogardus. It is also one of a small group of mid-19th-century commercial buildings in the "sperm candle" style, identifiable by its two-story columns resembling candles made from sperm whale oil.

Long Distance Building of the American Telephone & Telegraph Company, 32 Sixth Avenue (Ralph Walker, partner in charge, Voorhees, Gmelin & Walker, 1930–32). This massive Art Deco office building and communications center, conceived as a major enlargement and redesign of an earlier structure, was the world's largest long-distance communications center at the time of its completion. The rough-textured brick facade, with its bold sculptural massing and linear ornament, reflects a technology-inspired aesthetic in keeping with the building's function. **Interior:** The lobby, clad in fine materials with artistic detail reflecting the building's original purpose, has ceramic tile walls with marble trim, terrazzo floors, and bronze doors and highlighting. One wall is decorated with a vast tile map of the world; the ceiling features stucco and glass mosaic allegories of long-distance communication to Africa, Asia, Australia, and Europe.

Manhattan Bridge Arch and Colonnade, Manhattan Bridge Plaza at Canal Street (Carrère & Hastings, 1910–15). Carrère & Hastings's monumental gateway to the Manhattan Bridge was designed in the form of a triumphal arch flanked by curved colonnades. This "City Beautiful" project placed a grand entry at one of the key links between Manhattan and Brooklyn. Preliminary designs for the Manhattan approach were drawn in 1910, the year after the bridge opened. In 1912 Carrère & Hastings prepared final designs that included pylons carved by Carl A. Heber and a frieze by Charles Rumsey entitled *Buffalo Hunt*—a rather odd theme for a New York project.

Edward Mooney House, 18 Bowery (1785–89). Built at some point between 1785 and 1789, this house in the Georgian style is thought to be the oldest surviving row house in Manhattan. The building retains many original features above its carefully reconstructed ground story.

149 Mulberry Street House, also known as the Stephen Van Rensselaer House (c. 1816). This brick-faced, wood-frame house exemplifies the small row houses in the Federal style that were once common in Manhattan south of 14th Street. The Flemish bond brickwork, paneled stone lintels, gambrel roof, and dormer windows are characteristic of the style. The house was one of many in the area erected by Stephen Van Rensselaer; it was originally located on the northwest corner of Mulberry and Grand streets, and was moved in 1841.

Municipal Building, 1 Centre Street (McKim, Mead & White, 1907–14). In 1907 New York City announced a competition for the design of a skyscraper office building to be erected on a site straddling Chambers Street; the building was to house administrative agencies and to incorporate a large subway station. McKim, Mead & White partner William M. Kendall's brilliant functional solution won the competition and was constructed between 1909 and 1914. The base of the limestone building is articulated by a screen of Corinthian columns flanking a central triumphal arch that bridges Chambers Street. The intricate terra-cotta vault above the street is modeled on the entrance treatment of the Palazzo Farnese in Rome. At the south end of the building is the subway entrance, an arcaded plaza covered by dramatic Guastavino vaults. The simple office shaft rises 25 stories to a templed cupola crowned by Adolph Weinman's gold statue *Civic Fame;* Weinman also created the allegorical relief panels at the base. A major rehabilitation project was completed in 1992 (Wank Adams Slavin, architects).

New York City Police Headquarters, now the Police Building Apartments, 240 Centre Street (Hoppin & Koen, 1905–09). Following the creation of Greater New York in 1898, the city's police department expanded rapidly and a large new headquarters building was planned. In 1905 Mayor George McClellan laid the cornerstone of this monumental limestone-faced, steel-framed, Edwardian Baroque structure whose tall dome is visible from the City Hall area to the south. The Police Department relocated in 1973 and, after standing empty for over a decade, the building was converted into luxury housing (Ehrenkrantz Group & Eckstut, architects).

New York County Courthouse, also known as the Tweed Courthouse, 52 Chambers Street (John Kellum and Leopold Eidlitz, 1861–81). This marble building just north of City Hall is intimately associated with New York's corrupt political boss William M. Tweed. The New York County Courthouse was the first permanent government building erected by New York City after the completion of City Hall (see p. 26) in 1811. As conceived by John Kellum, the courthouse was a grand Italianate monument with a Corinthian portico and a long staircase (later removed) facing Chambers Street. Kellum died before the building's completion, and Leopold Eidlitz designed the south wing in a medieval-inspired style. The building contains some of the finest mid-19th-century **interiors** in New York, including Kellum's cast-iron staircases; an octagonal rotunda (largely the work of Eidlitz) with brick arcades; and Eidlitz's courtroom, which is distinguished by its encaustic tile floors, foliate columns, fireplace, and Gothic detail.

New York County Courthouse, now the New York State Supreme Court, Foley Square (Guy Lowell, 1913–27). In 1927 the New York County Court moved from the old "Tweed Courthouse" (see above) to this spacious granite-faced building. The Boston architect Guy Lowell won a competition in 1913 with a design for a round building. Construction was delayed and the design altered to a hexagonal form; work finally began in 1919. The Roman classical style chosen was popular for courthouse architecture in the first decades of the 20th century. The monumental character of the exterior continues on the **interior,** with its central rotunda and radial corridors. In the 1930s, under the sponsorship of the federal government's artists' relief programs, Attilio Pusterla painted a series of murals on the vestibule ceiling and on the rotunda dome; these were restored in 1992.

New York County Lawyers' Association, 14 Vesey Street (Cass Gilbert, 1929–30). This building, designed in the 18th-century English Georgian style, is a late work by Gilbert. Commissioned by an organization that had been founded in 1908 to serve the public interest and the legal profession, the building handsomely complements the 18th-century St. Paul's Chapel (see p. 37) across the street.

New York Evening Post Building, 20 Vesey Street (Robert D. Kohn, 1906–07). Built as the offices and printing plant of the *New York Evening Post*, this 13-story limestone-faced structure is a rare example of a New York City building inspired by the early 20th-century Central European artistic reform movement known as the Vienna Secession. Kohn designed several buildings in the style, notably this structure and the meetinghouse of the New York Society for Ethical Culture (see p. 127). The building's refined classicism, rational expression of structure, and stylized ornament are evocative of Viennese precedents. Of special note are the four statues on the 10th floor known as the *Four Periods of Publicity*; two are by Gutzon Borglum, the sculptor of Mount Rushmore, and two are by Estelle Rumbold Kohn, the architect's wife.

New York Life Insurance Company Building, 346 Broadway (Stephen Decatur Hatch and McKim, Mead & White, 1894–99). The New York Life Insurance Company, one of America's oldest life insurance firms, erected its headquarters building on Broadway between Thomas and Leonard streets in 1868–70. In 1894 Hatch was commissioned to extend the building eastward. Shortly thereafter he died, and the commission was taken over by McKim, Mead & White. Hatch's rear extension was built, but the company then decided to replace its earlier building. The elevations facing the narrow side streets continue Hatch's design, while McKim, Mead & White's Broadway frontage is a flamboyant palazzolike pavilion crowned by a clock tower. Although now housing municipal offices, the building retains many of New York Life's original **interior** spaces, including a marble lobby, a 13-story stair hall, a banking hall, executive offices, and the clock tower machinery room.

Norfolk Street Baptist Church, now Beth Hamedrash Hagodol Synagogue, 60–64 Norfolk Street (1850). America's oldest congregation of Orthodox Russian Jews, established in 1852, converted this Gothic Revival church into a synagogue in 1885. Among the notable original features are the Gothic woodwork and the iron fence.

Northern Reformed Church, also known as the Market Street Reformed Church, later the Sea and Land Church, now the First Chinese Presbyterian Church, 61 Henry Street (1817–19). This is the most elegant of the four surviving Georgian Gothic–style churches of the Lower East Side. Built of local Manhattan schist, the church retains its beautifully proportioned one- and two-story clear-glass windows. The Reformed Church became known as the Sea and Land Church in 1866 when it began ministering to local sailors. The present Chinese congregation reflects the ethnic character of the surrounding neighborhood.

Odd Fellows Hall, 165–171 Grand Street (Trench & Snook, 1847–48; roof addition, John Buckingham, 1881–82). The former Odd Fellows Hall is one of the city's earliest Italianate buildings, designed only a few years after Trench & Snook had introduced the style to New York in the A. T. Stewart Store (see p. 39). The Independent Order of Odd Fellows, which was incorporated in New York in 1844, occupied the building from 1848 until the early 1880s, when the northward movement of the city's affluent residents led to a relocation uptown. The building was subsequently converted for commercial and industrial use.

Oliver Street Baptist Church, now Mariners' Temple (Baptist), 12 Oliver Street (attributed to Isaac Lucas, 1844–45). This building is one of several brownstone-fronted Greek Revival churches erected in Manhattan's newly developing residential neighborhoods in the 1830s and 1840s. The facade of the Mariners' Temple features a pair of slender Ionic columns. The little-known architect Isaac Lucas is mentioned in the 1844 church minutes, but it is not clear whether he was the architect or simply the building superintendent.

203 Prince Street House (1834). This handsomely restored house in the late Federal style was built on land that was once part of Aaron Burr's estate. Originally two-and-a-half stories tall, the house received a full third floor in 1888. The reconstructed, elliptically arched entranceway above a high stoop is a fine example of Federal-style design.

Puck Building, 295–309 Lafayette Street (Albert Wagner, 1885–86 and 1892–93; Herman Wagner, 1899). With its seemingly endless round-arched arcades and complex brickwork, the Puck is a masterpiece of late 19th-century New York commercial architecture. The Romanesque Revival building was erected to house the offices and printing plant of *Puck,* a prominent humor magazine, and the J. Ottman Lithographing Co., which printed the magazine's famous chromolithographic cartoons. The two original wings, designed by Albert Wagner, fronted only on Houston and Mulberry streets. In the late 1890s Lafayette Street was extended through the block, and two bays of the Puck Building's Houston Street facade and the building's entire west wall were demolished. Herman Wagner, who was related to Albert, designed the new Lafayette Street elevation to conform to the original design. The main entrance was moved from the corner of Houston and Mulberry to Lafayette Street. Each entrance is marked by a statue of Shakespeare's Puck; the statue at the original entrance is by Casper Buberl and the one on Lafayette Street is the work of Henry Baerer. The building was handsomely rehabilitated and converted into offices in 1983–84.

St. James R. C. Church, 32 St. James Street (1835–37). St. James, the second oldest Roman Catholic church building in New York, is constructed of field-stone and has an imposing pedimented Greek Revival brownstone facade that features a pair of Doric columns. The detailing of the facade is modeled on designs published by the architect Minard Lafever, and while the building has frequently been attributed to Lafever, there is no supporting documentary evidence.

**St. Patrick's Old Cathedral,
Mott Street at Prince Street
(Joseph-François Mangin,
1809–15; restoration, 1868).
View of the Mulberry Street
facade as restored in 1868.
Photo: Janet O'Hare**

**St. Patrick's Old
Cathedral Complex**.
New York City's Roman
Catholic cathedral was dedi-
cated to the patron saint of
Ireland. The original cathedral complex was on Prince Street, in what was a
rapidly developing residential neighborhood in the early 19th
century.

St. Patrick's Old Cathedral, Mott Street at Prince Street (Joseph-François
Mangin, 1809–15; restoration, 1868). Mangin, the architect of City Hall,
designed the original St. Patrick's Cathedral in a rather fanciful Gothic-
inspired style. The church was built of local stone, with facades facing Mott
and Mulberry streets. The building was extensively restored following a disastrous fire in 1866.

Roman Catholic Orphan Asylum, now St. Patrick's Convent and Girls'
School, 32 Prince Street (1825–26). The Roman Catholic Orphan Asylum,
founded in 1817, was operated by the Sisters of Charity. This large brick
building with an elegant doorway is the most significant institutional building in the Federal style surviving in New York City. Originally housing
both boys and girls, the asylum became a girls' institution in 1851. In 1886
the asylum was converted into a school.

St. Patrick's Chancery Office, later St. Michael's Chapel, now St.
Michael's Russian Catholic Church, 266 Mulberry Street (James Renwick,
Jr., with William Rodrigue, 1858–59). This small Gothic Revival building

was designed to harmonize with the nearby cathedral. The architects were James Renwick, Jr., the designer of the new St. Patrick's Cathedral (see p. 91), which was under construction at the time, and William Rodrigue, a relative of Archbishop John Hughes. Rodrigue, who also assisted Renwick at St. Patrick's, had previously designed buildings for Fordham University (see p. 204).

St. Paul's Chapel (Episcopal) and Graveyard, Broadway at Fulton Street (1764–66; porch, 1767–68; tower, James C. Lawrence, 1794). Manhattan's oldest surviving church is also one of the finest Georgian buildings in the United States. St. Paul's, the "uptown" chapel for Trinity Church, is a simplified version of James Gibbs's London masterpiece, St. Martin-in-the-Fields on Trafalgar Square. Built of local stone with brownstone trim, the church has a modest portico on its towered front facade, which faces the 18th-century graveyard. The rear elevation on Broadway features an imposing brownstone Ionic porch—part of the original plan, but not built until 1767–68—sheltering a large Palladian window. The design of the church is often ascribed to Thomas McBean, but no evidence supports this attribution. George Washington worshiped at St. Paul's during the brief period when New York was the nation's capital.

St. Peter's R. C. Church, 22 Barclay Street (John R. Haggerty and Thomas Thomas, 1936–40). St. Peter's is the oldest Roman Catholic parish in New York City. This imposing Greek Revival granite church, with its six Ionic columns, replaced an earlier building of 1785.

Shearith Israel Graveyard, 55–57 St. James Place (1683–). This tiny graveyard is all that remains of the earliest surviving burial ground of Congregation Shearith Israel, the oldest Jewish congregation in North America. The graveyard is one of three small Manhattan cemeteries once used by the congregation. The others are on West 11th Street (in the Greenwich Village Historic District, see p. 45) and West 21st Street (in the Ladies' Mile Historic District, see p. 58).

Fleming Smith Warehouse, 451–453 Washington Street (Stephen Decatur Hatch, 1891–92). Crowned by eccentric gables and dormers, Hatch's brick warehouse is a skillful combination of Romanesque Revival and Flemish Renaissance design. The central gable contains the date of design and the owner's initials, all wrought in metal. The building was one of the earliest in Tribeca converted for residential use.

SoHo–Cast Iron Historic District. SoHo (standing for South of Houston) is a commercial district, developed in the mid- to late 19th century, containing the world's largest collection of buildings with cast-iron fronts. Such buildings were popular between the 1850s and the early 1880s because of the speed with which they could be erected and cast iron's facility in imitating the more expensive stone traditionally used in the construction of commercial palaces. The iron parts were mass-produced at local foundries and assembled at the building sites. The SoHo district includes a large number of Italianate and French Second Empire cast-iron buildings from the 1850s and 1860s, including the masterful Haughwout Building (see p. 29), as well as many examples of the

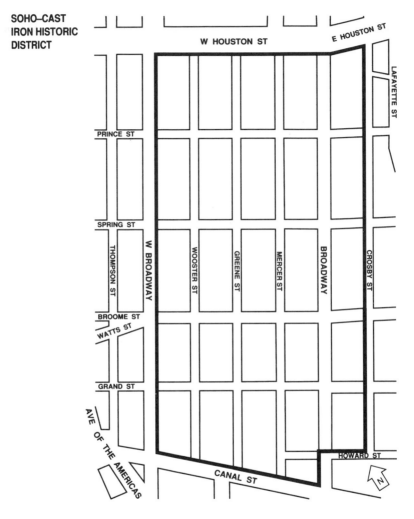

SOHO–CAST IRON HISTORIC DISTRICT

W HOUSTON ST

E HOUSTON ST

LAFAYETTE ST

PRINCE ST

SPRING ST

THOMPSON ST

W BROADWAY

WOOSTER ST

GREENE ST

MERCER ST

BROADWAY

CROSBY ST

BROOME ST

WATTS ST

GRAND ST

AVE OF THE AMERICAS

HOWARD ST

CANAL ST

N

masonry structures that the cast-iron buildings sought to emulate. Also within the district are notable late examples of cast-iron design by such prominent architects as Richard Morris Hunt (478–482 Broadway, 1873–74), Vaux & Withers (448 Broome Street, 1871–72), Renwick & Sands (34 Howard Street, 1868), and William Potter (435 Broome Street, 1873), and a sizable number of turn-of-the-century loft buildings. In the 1960s artists began moving into the district's underutilized loft spaces, which led to the growth of SoHo as a major arts center.

326 Spring Street House, also known as the James Brown House (c. 1817). A rare survivor from the period when the Lower West Side was a residential area, this gambrel-roofed house in the Federal style was probably erected in 1817 for the tobacconist James Brown. Original features include a facade of brick laid in Flemish bond, splayed window lintels, and a pair of dormers.

A. T. Stewart Store, later the New York Sun Building, 280 Broadway (Joseph Trench & Co., 1845–46; additions, Trench & Snook, 1850–51 and 1852–53; Frederick Schmidt, 1872; Edward D. Harris, 1884; 1921). The A. T. Stewart Store was one of the most influential buildings ever erected in New York City, as its style, materials, use, and location helped determine the course of architecture and commerce in the city. In 1846 Alexander Turney Stewart opened New York's first department store. Located on the corner of Broadway and Reade Street, the store inaugurated the commercial development of Broadway north of City Hall. As the first Italianate commercial building in New York, it established what would become the style of choice for hundreds of stores and warehouses erected through the succeeding decades. In addition, the store was the first major commercial structure faced with Tuckahoe marble, a material that would later become common on such buildings; it was innovative also in its use of imported French plate glass for the ground-floor windows. The store expanded along Broadway, Reade Street, and Chambers Street, with three-bay modules echoing those of the original design (the final bays were built in 1884). By the early 1850s cast iron was employed on the ground floor to support the upper walls. The building served as Stewart's retail store until 1862, when it became a warehouse. The sixth and seventh floors are 1884 additions (the seventh-floor corners were added in 1921) built when the store was converted into offices. The *New York Sun* occupied the building between 1919 and 1952. The Stewart Store now houses municipal offices.

83 and 85 Sullivan Street Houses (1819). This pair of modest houses retains original Federal-style doorways with leaded transoms (among the earliest surviving in the city), low stoops with wrought-iron railings, Flemish bond brickwork, and multipaned wooden sash windows. Each house was originally two-and-a-half stories tall but now has a full third floor.

116 Sullivan Street House (1832; upper two floors, 1872). This house in the Federal style retains an extremely unusual doorway. In the manner of many local doorways, the six-paneled door is flanked by Ionic colonnettes and crowned by a fanlight. However, the sidelights—each of which is broken into three ovals with wooden frames carved to simulate a cloth curtain drawn through a series of rings—are unique survivors.

🍎 **Tribeca West Historic District.** The western part of Tribeca (standing for Triangle Below Canal), focused around Duane Park, was once the heart of New York's most important wholesaling district for commodities, produce, and dairy products. The presence of the nearby Washington Market spurred merchants in food-related businesses to construct substantial "store and loft" buildings and warehouses in the area beginning in the mid-19th century. Warehouse construction, which reached its peak in the late 1880s, continued through the first decade of the 20th century. The Queen Anne–style New York Mercantile Exchange Building (Thomas R. Jackson, 1885), at 2–6 Harrison

TRIBECA WEST
HISTORIC
DISTRICT

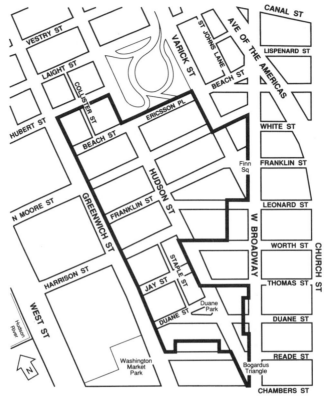

Street, with its dramatic entrance tower and hipped roof, survives as a reminder of the importance of the food industry in the history of Tribeca. Tribeca West contains an exceptional concentration of Romanesque Revival buildings clad in varied shades of brick fashioned into complex and dynamic patterns. Contemporary architecture critics saw the architectural expression of warehouses such as these as a discrete, particularly American building type. Many of the buildings that determine the architectural character of this historic district have been successfully adapted to a diverse mix of residential, commercial, office, and retail uses.

United States Courthouse, 26 Foley Square (Cass Gilbert, 1933–36). Cass Gilbert's last building is a Classical Revival skyscraper that rises from a base of monumental Corinthian columns to a golden pyramidal crown. The building is carefully aligned with the New York County Courthouse (see p. 33) to the north and the Municipal Building (see p. 32) to the south, and its tower balances that of Gilbert's earlier Woolworth Building (see p. 41), located on the opposite side of City Hall Park.

175 West Broadway Building (Scott & Umbach, 1877). A Newark, New Jersey, architecture firm designed this exceptional late 19th-century example of a commercial building with a polychromatic brick facade. The design was inspired by European, particularly German, sources. The corbeled window arches and the corbeled brick cornice are without parallel in New York City architecture.

Western Union Building, 60 Hudson Street (Ralph Walker, partner in charge, Voorhees, Gmelin & Walker, 1928–30). This massive brick-clad building, which occupies an entire block, shows the influence of Dutch and German Expressionist design on American architecture. The influence is especially evident in Walker's exploitation of brick—both on the exterior, where the color of the brick cladding lightens as the building rises in bold setbacks, and in the **interior** vestibules and lobby, with their complexly patterned orange brick walls and matching barrel-vaulted Guastavino tile ceiling. Erected as the headquarters of Western Union, the building contained the corporation's offices, equipment rooms, an auditorium, a cafeteria, shops, and classrooms for company messengers. The building now houses a variety of firms, many of them in the communications industry.

2 White Street House (1808–09). A brick-fronted frame house with a gambrel roof and dormers, this corner building is one of the few survivors from the period when the Lower West Side area now known as Tribeca was developing as a residential area. The house, built for Gideon Tucker, owner of the nearby Tucker & Ludlum plaster factory, has probably always had a ground-floor store.

Willett Street Methodist Episcopal Church, now Bialystoker Synagogue, 7–13 Bialystoker Place (1826). The simplest of the four early 19th-century landmark stone churches on the Lower East Side, this building has housed the Bialystoker Synagogue since 1905. The history of the building reflects the changes that occurred in this neighborhood at the turn of the century as tens of thousands of Eastern European Jews arrived in New York. The present congregation was founded in 1878 by Jews from Bialystok, then a part of the Russian Empire and now located in Poland.

Woods Mercantile Buildings, 46–50 White Street (1865). The Woods Mercantile Buildings are handsome examples of the Italianate commercial palaces faced in Tuckahoe marble that transformed the streets adjacent to Broadway just north of City Hall into a prime business district in the 1850s and 1860s. The two buildings, designed as a single unit, have cast-iron shopfronts and are crowned by an unusual pedimented cornice emblazoned with the name and date of the buildings.

Woolworth Building, 233 Broadway (Cass Gilbert, 1910–13). The Woolworth Building was commissioned by F. W. Woolworth, who instructed his architect to design the world's tallest building. Cass Gilbert's neo-Gothic masterpiece, clad almost entirely in terra cotta, rapidly became one of the symbols of New York City. The building's prominence on the skyline was a constant advertisement for Woolworth's stores. The F. W. Woolworth Company, which still owns and occupies the building, has undertaken a major rehabilitation of the facade (Ehrenkrantz & Associates, architects) that has included the replacement of much of the terra cotta with cast stone. **Interior:** The symmetrically planned lobby is among the most spectacular of the early 20th century. Its rich decorative treatment includes an Early Christian–inspired mosaic barrel vault; a stained-glass skylight; marble walls; bronze furnishings; murals entitled *Labor* and *Commerce* on the mezzanine balconies; and plaster grotesques depicting some of the men involved with the building's construction, among them Woolworth (counting his nickels and dimes) and Gilbert (cradling a model of the building).

Zion English Lutheran Church, now the Church of the Transfiguration (R. C.), 25 Mott Street (1801; additions, Henry Engelbert, 1868). This former Lutheran Church, one of four Georgian-Gothic landmark churches built of locally quarried Manhattan schist on the Lower East Side, became a Roman Catholic church in 1853. In 1868 the tower was added; the heavy Gothic window frames probably also date from this remodeling.

HOUSTON STREET TO 14TH STREET

Astor Library, now the Joseph Papp Public Theater, 425 Lafayette Street (south wing, Alexander Saeltzer, 1849–53; center section, Griffith Thomas, 1856–69; north wing, Thomas Stent, 1879–81). New York's first public library was built with a bequest from John Jacob Astor. The building, which appears to be a single unified structure, was actually erected in three campaigns, each with a different architect of record. The German-born Alexander Saeltzer established the building's form with his use of the German round-arched style, based on Northern Italian precedents. The building served for many years as the headquarters of the Hebrew Immigrant Aid Society (HIAS), but was vacant and endangered in 1965 when the theatrical producer Joseph Papp persuaded the city to acquire it. In 1966 Giorgio Cavaglieri converted the building for use by one of America's most innovative theatrical institutions.

Bayard-Condict Building, 65–69 Bleecker Street (Louis Sullivan; Lyndon P. Smith, associate architect, 1897–99). New York City's only work by Louis Sullivan, the Bayard-Condict is a superb illustration of Sullivan's ideas on skyscraper design. The structure of this 12-story steel-frame loft building, clad entirely in white terra cotta, is clearly manifested in the six emphatic vertical bays of the facade. The building is divided horizontally into three sections, demonstrating Sullivan's conviction that a skyscraper should have an ornate base to attract people's attention, a shaft of identical stories stacked atop one another, and a decorated crown to cap the building's upward thrust. The design is enhanced by Sullivan's distinctive organic ornament.

Bond Street Savings Bank, now the Bouwerie Lane Theater, 330 Bowery (Henry Engelbert, 1873–74). The Atlantic Savings Bank commissioned this Italianate cast-iron building in 1873; by the time the bank was completed, it was known as the Bond Street Savings Bank. This institution soon failed, and in 1879 the property was conveyed to the German Exchange Bank, which

Bayard-Condict Building, 65–69 Bleecker Street (Louis Sullivan; Lyndon P. Smith, associate architect, 1897–99). Detail of sculptured terra cotta at the building's crown. Photo: Caroline Kane

catered to the area's large German immigrant population. The former bank has housed a theater since 1963.

131 Charles Street House (1834). This well-preserved two-and-a-half-story brick house in the Federal style provides a contrast to the later lofts and warehouses of its West Village neighborhood.

Cooper Union, Cooper Square (Frederick A. Peterson, 1853–59; later rooftop additions). Dedicated to "the advancement of science and art," Cooper Union was established as a school offering free education to working-class men and women. The Italianate building, faced in brownstone, is among the first structures to employ rolled iron beams (fabricated at Peter Cooper's Trenton, New Jersey, foundry) and was also among the earliest buildings designed to accommodate an elevator. The original structure rose only five stories with income-producing stores on the first floor. Several rooftop additions have led to significant structural alterations, including the replacement in 1886 of the original rectangular second-floor windows with segmental arched openings (Leopold Eidlitz, architect). In 1975–76 the cast-iron storefronts were restored (new pieces were cast in aluminum by the school's art students) and the street level converted into a library; these changes were part of an extensive renovation designed by John Hejduk, the dean of Cooper Union's architecture school.

De Vinne Press Building, 393–399 Lafayette Street (Babb, Cook & Willard, 1885–86; addition, 1890–92). Theodore De Vinne, who was in the forefront of the revival of printing as an art form, was responsible for the printing of many major magazines, including *The Century* and *Scribner's Monthly*. De Vinne's

Romanesque Revival printing house is a masterpiece of 19th-century commercial architecture with a sophisticated fenestration pattern and subtle terra-cotta detail. The focus of the front elevation is a trio of three-story arches with deeply recessed window frames that accent the massive quality of the walls.

Fire Engine Company No. 33, 44 Great Jones Street (Flagg & Chambers, 1898–99). This Beaux-Arts firehouse is one of the grandest small-scale civic buildings erected in New York City at the turn of the century. The design is dominated by a monumental arch capped by a flamboyant cartouche. The metal infill of the arch and the metal brackets of the cornice are evidence of the influence that contemporaneous French design had on Ernest Flagg, one of the most sophisticated French-trained architects active in New York.

First Houses, 29–41 Avenue A and 112–138 East 3rd Street (Frederick L. Ackerman, 1935–36). First Houses was the nation's earliest public-sponsored, low-income housing project and the first effort of the city's newly established Housing Authority. The L-shaped complex was planned as a renovation of older tenements; every third building was to be removed, creating a series of courtyards. As work proceeded, however, the remaining buildings had to be substantially reconstructed. The open space to the rear of the buildings was landscaped with trees, benches, fanciful sculpture, and playgrounds.

Hamilton Fish Park Play Center, 130 Pitt Street (Carrère & Hastings, 1898–1900). The monumental Beaux-Arts Petit Palais in Paris was the model for this small pavilion. The play center and adjacent park were constructed as part of a movement to create parks in New York City's most densely crowded neighborhoods. Rather than a simple utilitarian structure, the building was intended as a sophisticated work that, it was hoped, would exert a positive influence on the area's poor immigrant population. Although the park has been redesigned several times, the pavilion has survived relatively unchanged and was restored in 1989–91.

Nicholas and Elizabeth Stuyvesant Fish House, also known as the Stuyvesant-Fish House, 21 Stuyvesant Street (1803–04). The Fish House was built by Peter Stuyvesant, great-grandson of the last director general of New Amsterdam, on land owned by the Stuyvesant family since the 17th century. The brick dwelling in the Federal style was a wedding gift to Stuyvesant's daughter Elizabeth and her husband, Nicholas Fish, a veteran of Valley Forge.

German Dispensary, now Stuyvesant Polyclinic, 137 Second Avenue (William Schickel, 1883–84). The German Dispensary and the neighboring Ottendorfer Library (see p. 49) were commissioned by Anna and Oswald Ottendorfer, philanthropists concerned with the welfare of New York's German immigrant community. This exuberant Italian Renaissance–inspired structure, designed by the German-born architect William Schickel, is among the first buildings in New York to display extensive ornamental terra cotta, including busts of important figures in the history of medicine.

Grace Chapel (Episcopal) and Hospital, now Immaculate Conception R. C. Church and Clergy House, 406–412 East 14th Street (Barney & Chapman,

1894–96). Barney & Chapman designed two distinguished and distinctive Episcopal church complexes in the French Gothic style—Grace Chapel and the Church of the Holy Trinity (see p. 108). This chapel of brick and terra cotta was built by Grace Church (see below) as a free church that would minister to all, regardless of income—i.e., no pew rents were charged. Adjoining the church is an austere complementary structure erected as a hospital. In 1943 the Episcopal chapel was converted into a Roman Catholic church and the hospital became a clergy house.

Grace Church (Episcopal) Complex, 800 and 804 Broadway and 92, 94–96, and 98 Fourth Avenue (church, James Renwick, Jr., 1843–46; with additions, James Renwick, Jr., Edward T. Potter, Heins & LaFarge, and William W. Renwick; rectory, James Renwick, Jr., 1846–47; Grace House, James Renwick, Jr., 1880–81; Grace Church Houses, now Grace Church School: Memorial House, James Renwick, Jr., 1881–83; Clergy House, Heins & LaFarge, 1902–03; Neighborhood House, Renwick, Aspinwall & Tucker, 1906–07). Grace Church is one of the most significant early examples of Gothic Revival architecture in America. Designed in a French Gothic mode, the marble church and its picturesque rectory were among the first works of James Renwick, Jr. The church is strategically sited at a point where Broadway curves, so that the vista up Broadway from the Battery terminates with the church tower. This location underscores the Episcopal parish's standing as one of the most prestigious religious organizations in New York City. Over the years the church has had many additions and alterations, all of them in keeping with Renwick's original scheme. Among these are Renwick's Grace House (1880–81), which connects the church and rectory; his 1883 replacement of the original wood spire with the present marble spire; Edward T. Potter's Chantry (1879; alterations by William W. Renwick, 1910); and a chancel extension (Heins & LaFarge, 1903). As the nature and needs of the congregation changed in response to population changes in the surrounding area, new buildings were added to the complex, including a series of structures on Fourth Avenue that display great stylistic coherence. In 1881 Renwick designed Grace Memorial House in a Gothic style that echoes his earlier church design. This building is thought to have housed New York's first day-care center. Twenty-one years later the building was expanded to the south with the addition of the Clergy House, an exact copy of the original building. The complex was further expanded in 1907 with the more austere Neighborhood House. An addition to the Grace Church School was built behind the facades of the Memorial House, Clergy House and part of Neighborhood House in 1974–75.

🍎 **Greenwich Village Historic District.** The architecture of this district reflects the physical growth and continuing change that have occurred in Greenwich Village since what was a small rural community began to be urbanized in the 1820s as people moved into the area to escape from the overcrowded city and especially from its frequent cholera epidemics. Many modest two-and-a-half-story row houses in the Federal style survive from this early period, especially west of Seventh Avenue South. The creation of Washington Square Park in 1826 spurred construction in the eastern part of the district. In

**Greenwich Village Historic District. The south side of Grove Street between
Bedford and Hudson streets. Federal houses built between 1825 and 1834. Photo:
Carl Forster**

the 1830s Greek Revival houses were built, including the large row houses on
Washington Square North and the somewhat smaller, simpler houses on nearby
streets. Many prominent institutional buildings were also erected during the
period of initial residential development. Notable among these are the Northern
Dispensary (1831), New York's oldest medical clinic, and such churches as the
modest Federal-style St. Luke's Episcopal (1821–22) on Hudson Street and the
grander Gothic Revival–style Episcopal Church of the Ascension (Richard
Upjohn, 1840–41) and First Presbyterian (Joseph C. Wells, 1844–46), both on
Fifth Avenue. Later in the 19th century, with an influx of poor immigrants,
most of them Irish or Italian, many of the row houses were converted into multiple dwellings, and others were replaced by tenements. During this period one
of the neighborhood's most important landmarks was built—Frederick Clarke
Withers's Victorian Gothic–style Jefferson Market Courthouse (1874–77), now
a branch of the New York Public Library. In the early 20th century artists and
bohemians were attracted to the Village, leading to the conversion of many of
the old houses into studios. Since the 1960s increasing interest in history and
preservation has led to restoration of both individual homes and major public
monuments in this heterogeneous historic district.

Irad Hawley House, now the Salmagundi Club, 47 Fifth Avenue (1853). This
Italianate mansion was built for Irad Hawley, president of the Pennsylvania
Coal Company, which had its yards along the Greenwich Village waterfront.
The house is the last survivor of the mansions that once lined fashionable lower
Fifth Avenue. The Salmagundi Club, established in 1871 for "the promotion of

social intercourse among artists and the advancement of art," has occupied the house since 1917.

Interborough Rapid Transit System Underground Stations, Bleecker Street and Astor Place. See p. 18.

26, 28, and 30 Jones Street Houses (1844). These virtually intact Greek Revival row houses typify vernacular residential design of the 1840s. Of special note are the original stoops, wrought-iron railings, modest templelike entrances (at Nos. 26 and 28), and dentiled cornices.

Judson Memorial Church, Tower, and Hall, 51–55 Washington Square South (church, 1888–93; tower and hall, 1895–96—all McKim, Mead & White). Built as a memorial to Adoniram Judson, the first American Baptist missionary in Asia, by his son, the Rev. Dr. Edward Judson, and funded in part by John D. Rockefeller, Judson Memorial is one of Stanford White's most elegant works. White combined Italian Early Christian and Renaissance features into a rich composition that remains one of the key elements of the Washington Square skyline. The architect's choice of mottled yellow Roman brick with extensive white terra-cotta trim introduced light coloration into American church architecture. The activist congregation continues to occupy the church, but the hall and tower are now residences for New York University. Adjacent to the hall is an 1877 building designed by John G. Prague as a young men's boarding house.

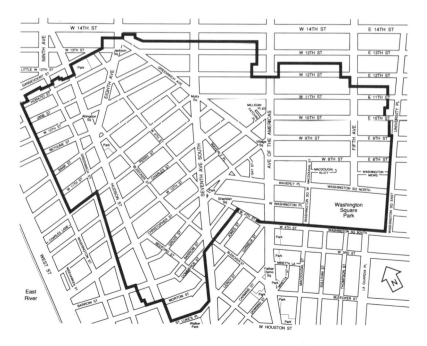

GREENWICH VILLAGE HISTORIC DISTRICT

376–380 Lafayette Street Building (Henry J. Hardenbergh, 1888–89). With its varied materials and colors and its use of wide, segmentally arched openings, this corner warehouse is among New York's most monumental commercial buildings of the 1880s. Although the solidity of the masonry walls is mitigated by wide window openings, enormous squat stone columns resting on granite bases accentuate the weight of the building's structure.

La Grange Terrace, also known as Colonnade Row, 428, 430, 432, and 434 Lafayette Street (attributed to Seth Geer, 1832–33). These four houses survive from a row of nine Greek Revival marble-fronted residences that, at the time of their completion, were among the grandest dwellings in New York and were occupied by members of New York's leading families. Erected, and possibly designed, by the developer Seth Geer and named for Lafayette's estate in France, the row is unified by the use of a Corinthian colonnade that was once crowned by a continuous band of anthemia (now visible only at No. 434). The buildings began to deteriorate in the post–Civil War era as the wealthy moved out of this neighborhood, and the houses were subdivided into apartments and commercial spaces. The row now contains apartments, restaurants, and theaters.

🕯 **MacDougal-Sullivan Gardens Historic District.** MacDougal-Sullivan Gardens, a small enclave planned around a central garden, became a prototype for related New York developments of the 1920s. In 1920 William Sloane Coffin, president of the Hearth and Home Corporation, purchased 22 deteriorated Greek Revival row houses, built between 1844 and 1850, and commissioned a rehabilitation from the architects Francis Y. Joannes and Maxwell Hyde. All of the stoops were removed, the two street facades were given a homey Colonial Revival appearance, and, most important, the rear yards were combined to create a private community garden. Each row house was divided into spacious, airy, and well-lit apartments affordable to middle-income people.

Metropolitan Savings Bank, now the First Ukrainian Evangelical Pentecostal Church, 9 East 7th Street (Carl Pfeiffer, 1867). Built to serve the largely German inhabitants of this East Village neighborhood, the Metropolitan Savings Bank is a significant example of French Second Empire design.

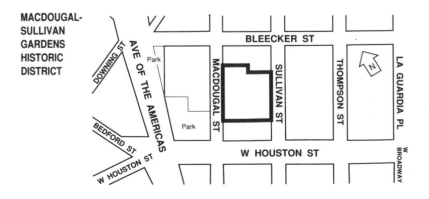

MACDOUGAL-SULLIVAN GARDENS HISTORIC DISTRICT

Pfeiffer handled the Second Empire idiom in a sophisticated manner, creating a dynamically massed structure on a relatively small site. In 1937 the marble building was purchased by the First Ukrainian Assembly of God, and it has since served as a church.

New York City Marble Cemetery, 52–74 East 2nd Street (1831–). Opened one year after the nearby New York Marble Cemetery (see below), this cemetery was the second nonsectarian burial ground in the city. Among the distinguished citizens buried beneath the stone markers and monuments are members of the Fish, Kip, Lenox, and Roosevelt families.

New York County National Bank, now Manufacturers Hanover Trust Co. Bank, 77–79 Eighth Avenue (DeLemos & Cordes with Rudolph L. Daus, 1906–07). The New York County National Bank, founded in 1855, erected this small but imposing neoclassical limestone-faced bank with Beaux-Arts motifs on a prominent intersection at the northern edge of Greenwich Village. The French influence is especially evident in the arched windows, with their visible iron framing, and in the exuberant quality of the carving.

New York Free Circulating Library, Ottendorfer Branch, now the New York Public Library, Ottendorfer Branch, 135 Second Avenue (William Schickel, 1883–84). The German-American philanthropists Oswald Ottendorfer, publisher of the *Staats-Zeitung*, and his wife Anna, built this library and the adjacent German Dispensary (see p. 44) as part of their efforts to improve the minds and bodies of their fellow German immigrants. The library is an ornate red brick Queen Anne– and Renaissance-inspired building with extensive terra-cotta detail that incorporates such symbols of wisdom and knowledge as globes, owls, books, and torches. Even before it was completed the Ottendorfers donated their library to the New York Free Circulating Library, a privately funded library system (see p. 127). The Ottendorfer is now the oldest operating branch of the New York Public Library system, and its **interior** retains its original character, with reading rooms on the first and second floors and cast-iron book stacks at the rear of the first floor and on the glass-floored mezzanine.

New York Marble Cemetery, interior of the block bounded by East 2nd and 3rd streets, Second Avenue, and the Bowery (1830–). Entered through an alley off Second Avenue, Manhattan's first nonsectarian cemetery was founded in 1830 as a commercial venture in a then fashionable section of the city. The cemetery consists of 156 underground vaults of Tuckahoe marble. There are no monuments, only plaques set into the north and south walls bearing the names of the original vault owners.

Old Merchant's House, also known as the Seabury Tredwell House, 29 East 4th Street (1831–32). The Old Merchant's House was built on speculation by Joseph Brewster as part of a row of six identical dwellings. Brewster lived here for two years, then sold the house to the prosperous hardware merchant Seabury Tredwell. Gertrude, Tredwell's eighth child, was born in a second-floor bedroom in 1840 and lived in the house until her death in 1933, maintain-

Old Merchant's House, also known as the Seabury Tredwell House, 29 East 4th Street (1831–32). View of the rear parlor. Photo: Carl Forster

ing the house "as Papa wanted it." At Gertrude's death, a relative saved the house and its contents, converting the building into a museum that illustrates the life of an affluent 19th-century family. The three-and-a-half-story row house is in a transitional late Federal–Greek Revival style. The exterior is basically Federal in design, distinguished by its Flemish bond brickwork, marble entrance enframement with a Gibbs surround, sloping roof punctuated by dormers, and delicate railings (restored). The **interior,** on the other hand, contains stylish Greek forms, notably the Ionic column screen that separates the front and rear parlors on the main floor. In 1971 a major restoration of the house was undertaken by the architect Joseph Roberto and the designer Carolyn Roberto.

Robbins & Appleton Building, 1–5 Bond Street (Stephen Decatur Hatch, 1879–80). The Robbins & Appleton Building is an impressive French Second Empire cast-iron commercial structure erected as a factory for a firm that manufactured watch cases. Three of the floors were leased to D. Appleton & Co., a notable publishing firm of the era. The facade, with its rows of large windows and its massive mansard roof, was restored in 1986.

🍎 **St. Mark's Historic District.** The land within this district was once part of Peter Stuyvesant's "bouwerie," or farm. The transformation of the area into an urban neighborhood began in the late 18th century when Petrus Stuyvesant, the great-grandson of the Dutch governor, began to subdivide the land into building lots. Stuyvesant Street, running due east-west (at an angle to the later grid), dates from this era, as do two houses—the Nicholas and Elizabeth Stuyvesant

Fish House (see p. 44) and the Nicholas William Stuyvesant House (1795) at 44 Stuyvesant Street—and St. Mark's-in-the-Bowery Church (see below). The Fish House had a large garden that was developed in 1861 with "the Triangle," the magnificent complex of Anglo-Italianate houses facing onto Stuyvesant and East 10th streets.

St. Mark's-in-the-Bowery Church (Episcopal), East 10th Street at Second Avenue (1799; tower, Town & Thompson, 1826–28; portico, 1854). The second oldest church building in Manhattan, St. Mark's is a survivor from the period when the East Village was sparsely populated. The land on which the church is built, the former site of the Dutch governor Peter Stuyvesant's private chapel (Stuyvesant is buried in the churchyard), was sold to the Episcopal Church for one dollar by Stuyvesant's great-grandson. The original fieldstone church was a simple pedimented structure with beautifully proportioned window openings. In 1828, by which time the area around the church was developing into the city's most affluent residential neighborhood, a stylish Greek Revival tower was constructed, turning the church into one of the most prominent buildings in the vicinity. An Italianate cast-iron portico was added in 1854. As the community changed over the years, the church building deteriorated significantly; at the same time the St. Mark's congregation developed into one of the most politically and socially committed in the city. A restoration project that was begun in 1975 included training local residents in construction; this project, which continued even after a fire severely damaged the church in 1978, was completed in 1983.

20 St. Mark's Place House, also known as the Daniel Leroy House (1832). In the 1830s the south side of St. Mark's Place between Second and Third avenues was developed with an elegant row of three-and-a-half-story brick houses erected on speculation by Thomas E. Davis. The sole intact survivor is No. 20, whose exceptional marble entrance surround is ornamented with vermiculated blocks. The original residents appear to have been the South Street merchant Daniel Leroy and his wife, Elizabeth Fish.

Samuel Tredwell Skidmore House, 37 East 4th Street (1845). This three-and-a-half-story Greek Revival row house with a freestanding Ionic portico is one

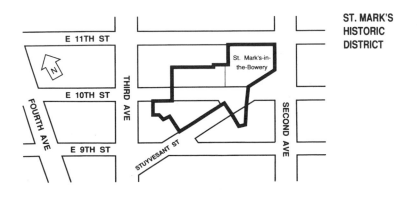

ST. MARK'S
HISTORIC
DISTRICT

E 11TH ST

E 10TH ST

E 9TH ST

FOURTH AVE

THIRD AVE

SECOND AVE

STUYVESANT ST

St. Mark's-in-
the-Bowery

of the few surviving houses from the period in the mid-19th century when the East Village was an affluent residential neighborhood. The house was built for the businessman Samuel Tredwell Skidmore, a cousin of Seabury Tredwell, whose house still stands to the west at 29 East 4th Street (see Old Merchant's House, p. 49).

United States Appraisers' Store, later the U.S. Federal Building, now the Archives Apartments, 641 Washington Street (Willoughby J. Edbrooke and others, 1892–99). The U.S. Department of the Treasury built this Romanesque Revival brick building, occupying an entire square block, as a warehouse for imported goods awaiting customs appraisal. The two lowest floors were built to the designs of Supervising Architect of the Treasury Edbrooke. While Edbrooke designed an additional eight stories, as did one of his successors, William M. Aiken, the upper floors, as constructed, differ from the published designs of both architects. The massive building was used as archival storage for many years and has now been converted into 479 apartments.

14TH STREET TO 34TH STREET

Appellate Division Courthouse, Appellate Division, New York State Supreme Court, 27 Madison Avenue (James Brown Lord, 1896–99). This small Beaux-Arts limestone courthouse is especially notable for the manner in which art is incorporated into the design to create a structure that is unified architecturally and symbolically. The three-dimensional exterior, with its projecting Corinthian porticos, supports an extensive display of sculpture by 16 artists on themes relating to the law. **Interior:** The main hall, courtroom, and anteroom are richly decorated with furniture designed specifically for the courthouse by Herter Brothers and with an elaborate series of allegorical murals painted by various American muralists.

Bank of the Metropolis, 31 Union Square West (Bruce Price, 1902–03). Price was an important early skyscraper designer with a particular interest in adapting the tripartite form of the column to tall buildings. This neo-Renaissance limestone-faced example is clearly massed in Price's preferred base-shaft-capital manner. The Bank of the Metropolis, founded in 1871 to serve the needs of businesses in the Union Square area, maintained its offices on the square until 1918, when it was absorbed by the Bank of Manhattan (now Chase Manhattan).

Century Building, 33 East 17th Street (William Schickel, 1880–81). The red brick Century Building is a rare New York example of a Queen Anne commercial structure. Erected to house the prestigious Century Publishing Company, publishers of *The Century* and *St. Nicholas* magazines, the building is characteristic of the finest Queen Anne design in its free use of classical motifs in stone and terra cotta and its employment of the style's trademark sunflowers.

Chelsea Apartments, now the Chelsea Hotel, 222 West 23rd Street (Hubert, Pirsson & Co., 1883–85). The famous Chelsea Hotel was built as one of the city's earliest cooperative apartment houses. The facade of the picturesque

Queen Anne building, executed in a variety of materials, is enhanced by tiers of remarkable iron balconies ornamented with flowers. Since its conversion into a hotel in 1905, the Chelsea has attracted hundreds of famous writers, artists, and musicians.

♨ Chelsea Historic District. In 1750 Capt. Thomas Clarke purchased a large plot of land along the Hudson and laid out a country estate that he called Chelsea. A portion of the property was deeded to Clarke's grandson Clement Clarke Moore in 1813. Moore, a wealthy, well-educated scholar, poet, and country gentleman, is remembered today as the author of "A Visit from St. Nicholas." As the city moved northward, Moore realized that his land would soon be ripe for development. He had the area divided into building lots with restrictions placed on the design and quality of new housing. Between 1825 and 1860 almost the entire area was built up. The district is especially rich in Greek Revival row houses, notably Cushman Row on West 20th Street between Ninth and Tenth avenues, and also contains New York City's largest concentration of Anglo-Italianate row houses, identifiable by their low stoops and sunken basements. Moore donated land on West 20th Street for St. Peter's Episcopal Church (1836–38), an early example of the Gothic Revival in America, and also gave the land on which the General Theological Seminary was constructed. The oldest surviving building on the Episcopal seminary's block is a small Gothic Revival stone structure of 1836; most of the campus was the work of Charles C. Haight, who prepared a master plan in 1883 and designed a series of Collegiate Gothic buildings.

Church Missions House, now the Protestant Welfare Agencies Building, 281 Park Avenue South (Robert W. Gibson and Edward J. N. Stent, 1892–94). Beginning in the late 19th century the area immediately south of East 23rd Street became a center for the offices of charitable organizations. The Church Missions House, a steel-frame structure whose facade was modeled on a

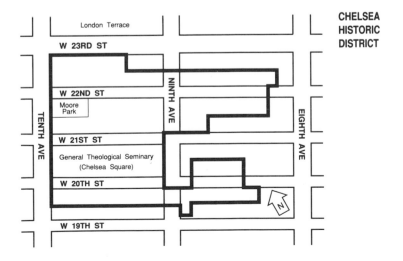

medieval Flemish guild hall, was the headquarters for the missionary activities of the Episcopal Church.

Colony Club, now the American Academy of Dramatic Arts, 120 Madison Avenue (McKim, Mead & White, 1904–08). Founded in 1903, the Colony Club was the first private women's club in New York City to erect its own clubhouse. Stanford White's building was modeled on 17th-century houses in Annapolis (he even escorted building committee members on a trip to view the original houses), with header-bond brickwork laid in a diaper pattern. By 1914 the club had outgrown this building and a new clubhouse was erected on Park Avenue. Since 1963 the building has housed the American Academy of Dramatic Arts, the oldest professional acting school in the English-speaking world.

Decker Building, now the Union Building, 33 Union Square West (John Edelmann in the employ of Alfred Zucker, 1892–93). A rare example of a Moorish-inspired skyscraper, the headquarters of the Decker Piano Company was designed by John Edelmann, mentor and friend of Louis Sullivan. Many features of the Decker Building, most notably the naturalistic ornament, reflect Sullivan's influence.

326, 328, and 330 East 18th Street Houses (1853). These three Italianate brick row houses form a pleasant enclave in the middle of the blockfront of East 18th Street between First and Second avenues. The houses have deep front yards, a rarity in Manhattan, and superb cast-iron verandas.

Empire State Building, 350 Fifth Avenue (Shreve, Lamb & Harmon, 1929–31). Among the best-known symbols of New York City, the Empire State Building was designed to be the world's tallest building and is a product of the frenzy of skyscraper construction that produced the great Art Deco towers of the late 1920s and early 1930s. The building was conceived by General Motors vice president John Raskob and was promoted by former New York governor Al Smith, who served as president of the Empire State Corporation. Unfortunately, the Depression left much of the office space vacant; the building was saved from bankruptcy by the popularity of its observation deck. The brick-clad edifice with a stone base was massed in accordance with zoning laws, while accommodating the constraints of elevator placement, a restricted budget, and an effort to have no office space more than 28 feet from a window. **Interior:** The lobby is laid out in a functional manner with all corridors leading to the elevators. The walls are clad with two varieties of German marble highlighted by aluminum detailing. Major ornamental features include aluminum bridges, bronze medallions depicting the crafts and industries involved with the building's construction, and a marble panel with an aluminum relief of the building superimposed on a map of New York State.

Everett Building, 200 Park Avenue South (Goldwin Starrett & Van Vleck, 1908). Located on the north side of Union Square, the Everett Building exemplifies an important development in the design of commercial high-rise buildings—the construction of functional, fireproof structures with large windows, open floor space, and simple classical detail. This emphasis on functionalism reflects the influence of Chicago skyscraper designs; in fact, the architect, Goldwin Starrett, had worked for four years in the Chicago office of Daniel Burnham.

Flatiron Building, Broadway and Fifth Avenue at 23rd Street (D. H. Burnham & Co., 1901–03). The Chicago architect Daniel Burnham designed this triangular-shaped steel-framed skyscraper on what was, at the turn of the century, among the most prominent sites in New York City—Madison Square at the juncture of Fifth Avenue and Broadway—anchoring the north end of the prestigious Ladies' Mile shopping district. Built as offices for the Fuller Construction Company (see p. 75), the skyscraper was dubbed the Flatiron because its shape resembles that of a clothing iron. Many early 20th-century painters and photographers were inspired by the building's singular form and it became a world-famous symbol of the romantic New York skyline. The slender 22-story building is clad in traditional Italian Renaissance ornament, most of it white terra cotta; the light coloration was again revealed in 1991 when the building was cleaned. The small metal and glass extension (known as the "cow-catcher") at the apex of the building was designed by the Burnham firm in 1902.

Friends Meeting House, now Brotherhood Synagogue, 144 East 20th Street (King & Kellum, 1857–59). A doctrinal split in the Quaker community led to the construction of two Manhattan meetinghouses in the mid-19th century (see below). New York's Orthodox Quaker community, the more worldly of the city's two Quaker congregations, commissioned the prominent firm of King & Kellum to design a meetinghouse for this site on Gramercy Park. The chaste but beautifully detailed Italianate building was constructed of extremely fine yellow sandstone from Ohio. The meetinghouse was carefully restored (James Stewart Polshek, architect) in the 1970s as part of its conversion into a synagogue.

Friends Meeting House and Seminary, 15 Rutherford Place and 226 East 16th Street (attributed to Charles T. Bunting, 1861). This austere brick meetinghouse and the adjoining seminary, with its finely proportioned massing and original multipaned windows, were erected by a group of Quakers known as the Hicksites, who were more traditional in their mode of worship than the Orthodox Quakers (see above). The two groups reconciled in 1958, retaining this building as their meetinghouse.

Germania Life Insurance Company Building, now the Guardian Life Building, 50 Union Square East (D'Oench & Yost, 1910–11). Prominently located on a corner site overlooking Union Square, the headquarters of the Germania Life Insurance Company (renamed Guardian Life in 1918 in response to anti-German sentiment during World War I) is a 20-story tower with a tripartite massing. The building is crowned by an enormous mansard roof atop which stands an early example of electric signage.

Gilsey House, 1200 Broadway (Stephen Decatur Hatch, 1869–71). The exuberant French Second Empire cast-iron building that dominates the intersection of Broadway and West 29th Street was a premier 19th-century New York hostelry.

With its projecting frontispieces and extraordinary mansard roof, the baroque structure was erected when this section of Broadway was being transformed into New York's entertainment district. In 1979 the building was converted into housing.

Gorham Manufacturing Company Building, 889–891 Broadway (Edward Hale Kendall, 1883–84; alteration, John H. Duncan, 1912). This uncommon example of a commercial building in the Queen Anne style was erected for the Gorham Manufacturing Company, a leading American silver firm, as its retail outlet in the exclusive Ladies' Mile shopping district. The Gorham is an early example of a mixed-use building: only the lower two floors were occupied by the store; the upper floors were rented as bachelor apartments. By 1893, however, the building was entirely in commercial use. The architect John H. Duncan is responsible for a remodeling of the building in 1912 that entailed the removal of a corner tower and the addition of roof dormers. The building now contains shops at street level and apartments above.

🍎 **Gramercy Park Historic District.** The special character of Gramercy Park is largely the result of a plan established by the developer Samuel B. Ruggles, who purchased a large tract of land in 1831 with the intention of creating a prime residential neighborhood around a small private park open only to the owners of adjacent lots. In order to attract builders, Ruggles not only planned the park and enclosed it with a tall iron fence (still extant), but also laid out Irving Place and Lexington Avenue. It was not, however, until the 1840s that fine row houses, many still surviving on the west and south sides of the park, were erected and sold to prominent citizens. Somewhat smaller row houses were erected on the blocks to the south of the park; several fine examples from the 1850s can be found on East 18th Street. In conjunction with this residential

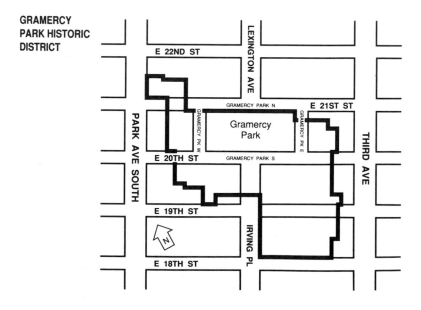

GRAMERCY
PARK HISTORIC
DISTRICT

development, impressive buildings such as Calvary (Episcopal) Church (Park Avenue South at East 21st Street; James Renwick, Jr., 1846) and the Friends Meeting House (see p. 55) were constructed, helping to establish Gramercy Park as a neighborhood of great prestige. Later in the century, as the area's pre-eminence waned, several early apartment houses were built; the Queen Anne–style Gramercy (34 Gramercy Park East; George Da Cunha, 1883) and the neo-Gothic 36 Gramercy Park East (George Reily Gordon, 1908–10) are notable examples. Clubs were also attracted to the neighborhood—both the Players (see p. 61) and the National Arts Club (see p. 64) are housed in converted residences. By the early 20th century the Gramercy Park area was home to an affluent, artistic group of people living in older buildings, in new duplex cooperatives (e.g., 24 Gramercy Park South; Herbert Lucas, 1908), and in renovated row houses. On several blocks the old-fashioned row houses were rediscovered and redesigned with stucco facades embellished with simple artistic details. This is especially evident on East 19th Street between Irving Place and Third Avenue, known as the "Block Beautiful," where, beginning in 1909, the architect Frederick H. Sterner renovated many houses.

Grand Hotel, 1232–1238 Broadway (Henry Engelbert, 1868). The Grand Hotel is a handsome marble-fronted building erected at a time when Broadway between Madison and Herald squares was being transformed into a glittering entertainment district. French Second Empire in style, the hotel is distinguished by its pavilion massing, its chamfered corner, and its imposing mansard roof with large pedimented dormers and ocular windows.

Grolier Club, 29 East 32nd Street (Charles W. Romeyn, 1889). Founded in 1884 for "the literary study and promotion of the arts pertaining to the production of books," the Grolier Club occupied this building from 1890 until 1917, when it moved to larger quarters on East 60th Street. The highly original late Romanesque Revival design has been executed in Roman brick and stone.

Church of the Holy Apostles (Episcopal), 300 Ninth Avenue (Minard Lafever, 1845–48; additions, Minard Lafever, 1853–54; transepts, Richard Upjohn & Son, 1858). Lafever's only surviving building in Manhattan is a rare New York example of an Italianate church. The brick building, which has a prominent spire, has been enlarged several times. In 1853–54 it was extended 25 feet with the construction of a new chancel, and in 1858 transepts were constructed to the designs of Charles Babcock of the firm of Richard Upjohn & Son. The building contains several stained-glass windows designed by William Jay Bolton, which survived a devastating fire in 1990.

Church of the Holy Communion Complex (Episcopal), now Limelight Discotheque, Sixth Avenue at West 20th Street (church, 1844–46; rectory and parish house, c. 1850; Sisters' House, 1854—all Richard Upjohn). Although a small building, the former Church of the Holy Communion was one of the most influential churches of the 19th century in its design. Holy Communion was the first asymmetrical, Gothic Revival church edifice in the United States and was the prototype for hundreds of similar buildings erected all across the country. Upjohn designed the building to resemble a small medieval English parish church; the rectory and other additions complement the church in style and massing. The church's founder, the Rev. William Muhlenberg, a leader of the evangelical Catholic movement within the Episcopal Church, was closely involved with the design; it was apparently he who suggested the use of transepts and other features that were more common in Roman Catholic churches of the era. As part of his work at Holy Communion, Muhlenberg organized St. Luke's Hospital, established a library that became the Muhlenberg Branch of the New York Public Library, and founded the first boys' choir and the first Episcopal sisterhood in America. (The small three-story building on Sixth Avenue was the Sisters' House.)

Interborough Rapid Transit System Underground Station, 33rd Street. See p. 18.

Ladies' Mile Historic District. The Ladies' Mile Historic District was developed largely in the decades following the Civil War, when commerce intruded on the residential neighborhoods between Union and Madison squares. In the late 1860s businesses such as Arnold Constable (881–887 Broadway; Griffith Thomas, 1868–76) and Lord & Taylor (see p. 59) erected imposing Italianate and French Second Empire marble or cast-iron department stores along Broadway. They were soon joined by Gorham Silver (see p. 56), W. & J. Sloane (880–886 Broadway; W. Wheeler Smith, 1881–82), and other prestigious emporia. Sixth Avenue also became a center for department stores, with B. Altman & Co. opening on the southwest corner of West 19th Street in 1877

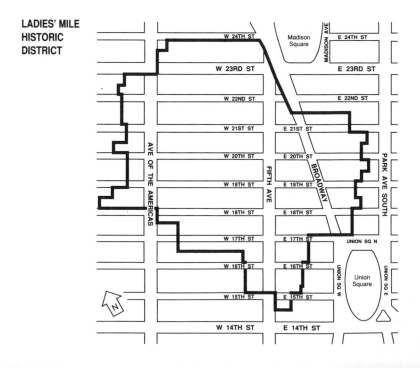

LADIES' MILE HISTORIC DISTRICT

(D. & J. Jardine, architect). Altman's was followed by a succession of other stores, culminating in the 1895–97 construction of the monumental Siegel-Cooper Department Store (DeLemos & Cordes, architect) between 18th and 19th streets. Fifth Avenue attracted smaller shops, publishing houses (see Scribner's, p. 61), the offices of charitable institutions, and skyscrapers (see Flatiron Building, p. 55). With the exception of 23rd Street, with its large department stores (notably Stern Brothers, 32–46 West 23rd Street; Henry Fernbach, 1878, with later additions), the side streets in the district were redeveloped at the turn of the century with loft buildings in which many of the goods sold in the nearby stores were manufactured. A wave of restoration and rehabilitation began in the 1980s as the area was rediscovered by architects, publishing houses, advertising firms, and other businesses. These businesses have in turn attracted restaurants, boutiques, and other fashionable shops to Broadway, Fifth Avenue, and the adjacent side streets.

Lincoln Building, 1–3 Union Square West (R. H. Robertson, 1889–90). The Lincoln Building is representative of the early skyscraper form as it evolved in New York, where architects chose to adapt already popular styles to this new building type. Robertson designed the Lincoln Building in the same Romanesque Revival style that he used for churches, houses, and other structures. The building, faced in limestone, granite, brick, and terra cotta, marks an important transitional phase in skyscraper engineering; it was constructed with a metal skeleton frame in combination with traditional masonry bearing walls.

Lord & Taylor Store, 901 Broadway (James H. Giles, 1869–70). Two English immigrants, Samuel Lord and George Taylor, founded the dry goods firm Lord & Taylor around 1830. The business joined the northward migration of Manhattan's commercial establishments when it opened this impressive French Second Empire store in the fashionable Ladies' Mile shopping district. James Giles's original cast-iron building was considerably larger than the present structure; much of the Broadway frontage was rebuilt after Lord & Taylor moved in 1914 to its present home on Fifth Avenue at 39th Street. The building is notable for its bold three-dimensional massing, its large windows, and the chamfered corner topped with a mansard roof that was designed to attract the attention of shoppers traveling south on Broadway from uptown residential neighborhoods.

Marble Collegiate Church, 275 Fifth Avenue (Samuel A. Warner, 1851–54). Like West End Collegiate (see p. 137) on the Upper West Side, Marble Collegiate traces its history back to the city's first church, a Reformed congregation established by Dutch colonists in 1628. This Early Romanesque Revival building, with its Gothic trim and Wren-like steeple, is clad entirely in the Tuckahoe marble from which the church derives its name.

Metropolitan Life Insurance Company Tower, 1 Madison Avenue (Pierre Le Brun, architect in charge, Napoleon Le Brun & Sons, 1907–09). The 54-story tower that rises along the east side of Madison Square was planned by the Metropolitan Life Insurance Company as the world's tallest building and was intended as a corporate symbol. Designed by Pierre Le Brun, the tower evokes the form of the famous campanile in the Piazza San Marco in Venice. Despite the fact that much of the tower's ornament was removed in a renovation of 1960–64, the tower's form is intact, as are the most prominent features of the design, the ornate four-faced clock and the crowning cupola and lantern.

New York House and School of Industry, now the Young Adults Institute, 120 West 16th Street (Sidney V. Stratton, 1878). Founded in 1850, the New York House and School of Industry was organized by members of several of New York's wealthiest families to assist destitute women by providing them with employment in the form of needlework, ranging from mundane sewing to the production of fancy embroidery. The charity's 1878 headquarters is thought to be the earliest building in the Queen Anne style in the city. The stone, terra-cotta, and slate trim, the projecting paneled oriel with multipaned windows, and the free use of classical motifs are characteristic of highly sophisticated Queen Anne design.

New York Savings Bank, later the New York Bank for Savings, 81 Eighth Avenue (R. H. Robertson, 1896–97). This corner building, designed to be a visual landmark at the intersection of West 14th Street and Eighth Avenue, is an early example of Classical Revival bank design, begun only a year after the completion of McKim, Mead & White's pioneering Bowery Savings Bank (see p. 25). Faced entirely in Vermont marble, the bank has a temple front supported by a pair of Corinthian columns and is crowned by a commanding copper dome with a clerestory of 20 stained-glass windows. The **interior** of the L-shaped building consists of a grand banking hall with a shallow coffered vault supported by columns and pilasters of Siena marble. The building is now vacant and awaiting conversion to a new use.

New York School of Applied Design for Women, later Pratt–New York Phoenix School of Design, now the Vocational Rehabilitation Agency, 160 Lexington Avenue (Harvey Wiley Corbett, 1908–09). In the late 19th century women began to enter the art world in increasing numbers and became especially active in the decorative arts. The New York School of Applied Design for Women was established in 1892 to offer "women instruction which may enable them to earn a livelihood . . . in the application of ornamental design to manufacture and the arts." The school, which specialized in such fields as book illustration, textile and wallpaper design, and interior decoration, was unusual in that its programs were geared specifically to the education of poor women. The architect of the school's facility, Harvey Wiley Corbett, was also an instructor there. He designed an idiosyncratic version of a classical temple, complete with casts from the Parthenon frieze.

Andrew Norwood House, 241 West 14th Street (1845–47). This beautifully restored house is a survivor from a row of three transitional Greek Revival/ Italianate residences erected by the stockbroker Andrew Norwood, who was an active developer in the 14th Street area. Norwood built this house, the central unit of the trio, for himself. As the first masonry buildings on the block, these houses marked the beginning of the transformation of 14th Street into a fashionable residential thoroughfare.

The Players, 16 Gramercy Park South (1845; redesign, McKim, Mead & White, 1888–89). The house occupied by the Players since 1888 was originally part of a row of Gothic Revival brownstone dwellings; Gothic drip lintels are extant on the upper floors. Edwin Booth, who established the Players as a club for men in the theatrical profession, commissioned his friend Stanford White to redesign the building. White removed the stoop and added the elegant, Italian Renaissance–inspired, two-tiered porch with its magnificent ironwork, as well as the cornice that incorporates theatrical masks.

Public Baths, Asser Levy Place at East 23rd Street (Brunner & Aiken, 1904–06). In the late 19th century progressive social reformers lobbied for the creation of public baths that would help alleviate sanitary problems in New York City's slum neighborhoods, where few residents had access to a bath or shower. Appropriately, the design precedent for the Asser Levy Place baths was the public baths of ancient Rome, as evidenced by the paired columns and semicircular thermal windows. Now a swimming pool and recreation center, the building was restored by the Parks Department in 1989–90.

Theodore Roosevelt Birthplace, now the Theodore Roosevelt Birthplace National Historic Site, 28 East 20th Street (Theodate Pope Riddle, 1923) At his death in 1919 Theodore Roosevelt was revered as a great American hero. Three years earlier his boyhood home, a modest Gothic Revival row house on East 20th Street (much altered after the Roosevelt family moved uptown in 1872), had been demolished. The Woman's Roosevelt Memorial Association, founded with the intention of honoring Roosevelt's memory, purchased the birthplace site, along with the adjacent home (also significantly altered) of Theodore's uncle, Robert Roosevelt. The association proceeded to demolish the uncle's house and to commission Theodate Pope Riddle, one of the first female architects in America, to reconstruct Theodore Roosevelt's childhood home as it had existed in 1865, when a mansard roof had been added and the interiors redesigned. A modest museum wing was built on the adjoining site. In 1963 the house was donated to the National Park Service.

St. George's Church (Episcopal), Rutherford Place at East 16th Street (Blesch & Eidlitz, 1846–56). This Episcopal church, a massive round-arched stone building that dominates Stuyvesant Square, is one of the first and most significant examples of Early Romanesque Revival church architecture in America. The exterior, probably the work of the Bavarian-born architect Otto Blesch, reflects the influence that the German round-arched style known as *Rundbogenstil* had on American design in the 1840s. The interiors were the work of Leopold Eidlitz, who also restored the church after it was damaged by fire in 1865. The design was ideally suited to the requirements of its rector, Stephen Higginson Tyng, an ardent leader of the evangelical wing of the Episcopal Church and one of the greatest preachers of his time. The original stone spires were removed in 1889; the church's facade was restored in the 1980s.

Scribner Building, now the United Synagogue of America, 153–157 Fifth Avenue (Ernest Flagg, 1893–94). The publishing firm of Charles Scribner's

Sons commissioned this building for use as a bookstore and corporate head-quarters. The limestone-fronted building, Flagg's first commercial work, indicates the architect's sophisticated understanding of contemporary French design, especially evident in the use of heavy load-bearing corner piers that flank a more open central area with large windows, attenuated iron colonnettes, and a wide shopfront. The Scribner company was founded in 1846 by Charles Scribner and flourished, under various names, until Scribner's death in 1871. By the late 1870s Scribner's sons had taken over the firm, which grew into one of America's most prestigious publishing houses, introducing works by Henry James, Edith Wharton, F. Scott Fitzgerald, and Ernest Hemingway, among others. The Fifth Avenue building, designed by Charles Scribner II's brother-in-law, was the first built specifically for the company (see p. 92).

Sidewalk Clocks. Clocks were once an important part of the street fabric of American cities. Large cast-iron sidewalk clocks, many of which served as advertisements for jewelers and other businesses, proliferated in the early 20th century. In Manhattan four such clocks are landmarks (see pp. 93 and 116). There are, in addition, two landmark clocks in Queens (see p. 198) and one in Brooklyn (see p. 183).

200 Fifth Avenue at West 23rd Street (Hecla Iron Works, 1909). This clock, as the words on its faces announce, was installed by the Fifth Avenue Building (now the Toy Center), which opened in 1909. It is the most ornate sidewalk clock in New York City, with its fluted Ionic column supporting a clock framed by wreaths of oak leaves and crowned by a cartouche.

574 Sixth Avenue Building (Simeon B. Eisendrath, 1903–04). Erected as a retail store for the Knickerbocker Jewelry Company, this building has a simple, rationally massed facade crowned by an exuberant cornice that was designed to attract the attention of riders on the Sixth Avenue Elevated, which ran in front of the building.

Sixty-ninth Regiment Armory, 68 Lexington Avenue (Hunt & Hunt, 1904–06). The 69th Regiment Armory was the first New York City armory built after the Seventh Regiment Armory (see p. 115) that was not designed in the form of a medieval fortress. Hunt & Hunt rejected the medieval form in favor of a French Beaux-Arts mode with a severe military aspect. The armory is famous as the home of "the Fighting 69th," New York's only official Irish regiment, and as the site of the legendary 1913 Armory Show, which introduced modern art to the American public.

Starrett-Lehigh Building, 601–625 West 26th Street (Cory & Cory; Yasuo Matsui, associate; consulting engineers, Purdy & Henderson, 1930–31). The striking Starrett-Lehigh Building is an enormous freight terminal, warehouse, and factory occupying an entire block. It was built as a joint venture of the Starrett Investing Corporation and the Lehigh Valley Railroad. The building—with its setback massing, curved corners, and horizontal bands of steel ribbon windows alternating with brick and concrete spandrels—was in the forefront of modern design when it was erected in 1930–31. This was one of only a handful

Starrett-Lehigh Building, 601–625 West 26th Street (Cory & Cory; Yasuo Matsui, associate; consulting engineers, Purdy & Henderson, 1930–31). Photo: Carl Forster

of American designs included in the Museum of Modern Art's pioneering 1932 "International Style" exhibition.

🍎 **Stuyvesant Square Historic District.** Stuyvesant Square was laid out in 1846 on land donated to the city by Peter Gerard Stuyvesant. The square is divided by Second Avenue, and each of its two parts is surrounded by an original cast-iron fence. Stuyvesant Square provides a fine setting for two of New York's most distinguished landmarks, the Friends Meeting House and Seminary (see p. 55) and St. George's (Episcopal) Church (see p. 61). (see p. 55) (see p. 61) The ear-

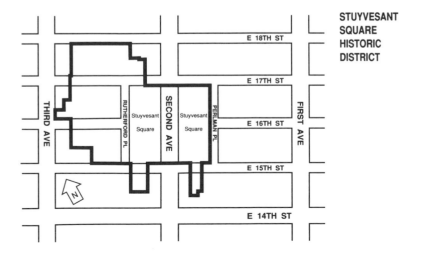

liest Greek Revival houses in the district were erected in the 1840s, when residential development reached north of 14th Street. Most of the district's houses, however, were built in the 1850s, when late Greek Revival, Italianate, and Anglo-Italianate rows were constructed. One of the latest single-family dwellings in the district is the Sidney Webster House (1883) at 245 East 17th Street, the only surviving residence in New York City designed by the architect Richard Morris Hunt.

Samuel Tilden House, now the National Arts Club, 15 Gramercy Park South (Vaux & Radford, 1881–84). Calvert Vaux's masterful Victorian Gothic facade results from a remodeling of two earlier row houses. This work was undertaken for Samuel J. Tilden, a lawyer who resigned as governor of New York to run for the presidency in 1876, losing in the electoral college to Rutherford B. Hayes. Reflecting the influence of John Ruskin's architectural theories, the house's polychromatic facade is enlivened with sculptural ornament depicting various plants, animals, and birds native to the New York area, as well as with busts of notable writers and thinkers, chosen to reflect Tilden's literary interests. At his death, Tilden's private library, and a considerable fortune, helped to establish the New York Public Library (see p. 86). In 1906 the National Arts Club, an organization dedicated to support of the arts, purchased the building.

Church of the Transfiguration (Episcopal), also known as the Little Church Around the Corner, 1 East 29th Street (church and rectory, 1849–50; church addition, 1852; lych-gate, Frederick Clarke Withers, 1896; lady chapel, 1906; mortuary chapel, 1908). The Church of the Transfiguration consists of a series of Gothic Revival structures built around a quiet garden. The original one-story church and adjoining rectory were designed by an unidentified architect in 1849, and the guild hall, transepts, and tower were added a few years later. Frederick Clarke Withers's English-inspired lych-gate was described by a contemporary critic as "the one touch necessary to make the surroundings of the church . . . the most picturesque and charming of any in New York." The church acquired its sobriquet in 1870, when the minister of a fashionable church nearby, declining to conduct a funeral service for an actor, referred the mourners to "the little church around the corner." The church has welcomed actors ever since.

Trinity Chapel (Episcopal) Complex, now the Serbian Orthodox Cathedral of St. Sava and Parish House, 15 West 25th Street (chapel, Richard Upjohn, 1850–55; clergy house, R. & R. M. Upjohn, 1866; parish school, Jacob Wrey Mould, 1860). This symmetrically massed, Early English Gothic–inspired building was erected to serve the congregants of Trinity Church (see p. 22) who in the mid-19th century were moving to the newly developing neighborhoods around Madison Square. To the east of the church and the adjoining clergy house is the parish school (now the parish house), a small polychromatic building that is an early and notable example of the Victorian Gothic style in the United States as well as Mould's only surviving building in New York City. In 1943 the complex was sold to the Serbian Orthodox Church.

United States General Post Office, now the James A. Farley Building, Eighth Avenue at West 31st Street (McKim, Mead & White, 1908–13). William M. Kendall, a partner in the McKim, Mead & White firm, designed this enormous granite structure as a companion to Pennsylvania Station, which once stood across the street. The building features a colonnade of 20 Corinthian columns, each 53 feet high, and stretches along two full city blocks.

5, 7, 9, 17, 19, 21, and 23 West 16th Street Houses (c. 1845–46). In the 1840s the streets adjacent to Fifth Avenue just north of 14th Street were developed with row houses. Most of these structures were demolished as commerce invaded the area in the late 19th century, but West 16th Street retains a significant number of Greek Revival houses. The most impressive are the four survivors of a row of nine wide houses—Nos. 5, 7, 9 and 17—each of which has a full-height curving bay on its front facade, an extremely rare feature in New York. In 1930 the family planning pioneer Margaret Sanger moved her Birth Control Clinical Research Bureau into No. 17. Nos. 19 and 21 are simpler houses displaying fine ironwork, while No. 23 has a magnificent cast-iron balcony and stoop railing. All of the houses have wide stone entrance enframements with battered sides and eared corners; this is a classic Greek form copied from the Parthenon and other ancient Greek monuments.

126, 128, 130–132, 136, and 140 West 18th Street Stables (1864–65). These five landmark buildings are rare survivors of a row of 13 private carriage houses designed in a utilitarian round-arched style. Erected on a street devoted exclusively to stables, they served the large residences built north of 14th Street in the mid-19th century.

437–459 West 24th Street Houses (1849–50). This long row of 12 paired houses was erected by the builder Philo V. Beebe to provide housing for the merchants and professionals who moved into the Chelsea neighborhood in the 1840s. Most of these transitional Greek Revival/Italianate dwellings have deep landscaped yards and retain their original stoops, iron railings, and other details.

34TH STREET TO 59TH STREET

Actors Studio, originally the Seventh Associate Presbyterian Church, 432 West 44th Street (c. 1858). The Actors Studio, founded in 1947, is best known for its association with Lee Strasberg, who became director of the studio in 1949. Strasberg was the leading American advocate of the "Method" acting technique pioneered by Stanislavsky at the Moscow Art Theater. In 1955 the Actors Studio purchased this late Greek Revival church structure and converted it for use as a drama school.

Algonquin Hotel, 59–61 West 44th Street (Goldwin Starrett, 1902). The Algonquin Hotel is famous for playing host to literary and theatrical visitors, most prominently the legendary Round Table, a group of critics and humorists who convened on the premises almost daily in the 1920s.

B. Altman & Co. Department Store, 355–371 Fifth Avenue (Trowbridge & Livingston, 1905–13). The imposing B. Altman & Co. store was among the first of the great department stores on Fifth Avenue. Designed to complement the nearby mansions, the store was a major catalyst for the transformation of Fifth Avenue into a boulevard lined with magnificent stores. Although the building appears to be a single unified structure, it was erected in several stages, with the first Fifth Avenue wing opening in 1906. The Italian Renaissance–inspired structure is now vacant; the eastern portion is to be converted into the New York Public Library's Science, Industry, and Business Division, while the west section awaits a new commercial use.

Alvin Theater, now the Neil Simon Theater, 244–254 West 52nd Street (Herbert J. Krapp, 1926–27). Built to house the musical comedies of the producers Alex Aarons and Vinton Freedley (whose names were merged in the theater's original name), the Alvin is one of the prolific theater architect Herbert Krapp's most impressive Adamesque designs. **Interior:** The lobbies and auditorium continue the use of the Adamesque detail seen on the exterior. The theater has housed an extraordinary number of hit productions since its debut with George and Ira Gershwin's *Funny Face*, including the Gershwins'

Alwyn Court Apartments, 182 West 58th Street (Harde & Short, 1907–09). Detail of corner bay, 1938. Photo: Berenice Abbott, Museum of the City of New York

Girl Crazy and *Porgy and Bess*, Ethel Merman in *Anything Goes*, Henry Fonda in *Mister Roberts*, Judy Holliday in *Bells Are Ringing*, and James Earl Jones in *The Great White Hope*.

Alwyn Court Apartments, 182 West 58th Street (Harde & Short, 1907–09). Almost every inch of this apartment house is covered with terra-cotta ornament in the François I style. Located just south of Central Park, in an area that attracted a significant number of Manhattan's early apartment houses, Alwyn Court originally boasted expansive 14-room apartments (later subdivided during the Depression), each with five baths. The facade was cleaned and restored in 1980–81 (Beyer Blinder Belle, architects).

Ambassador Theater (interior), 215–223 West 49th Street (Herbert J. Krapp, 1919–21). Krapp made lavish use of paint and plaster in the Adamesque style to create the illusion of opulence on the interior of this theater. The Ambassador is one of numerous Broadway houses commissioned by the Shuberts in the 1920s; it has since housed more than 120 different productions.

American Fine Arts Society, now the Art Students League, 215 West 57th Street (Henry J. Hardenbergh, 1891–92). With its design adapted from a hunting lodge erected by François I in the forest of Fontainebleau in the early 16th century, this building is one of several New York City landmarks that reflect Hardenbergh's interest in Northern European architecture. The American Fine Arts Society was incorporated in 1889 by the New York Architectural League, the Society of American Artists, and the Art Students League to raise funds for a building that would contain offices, galleries, and studios for the three organizations. Each originally had space in the building; it is now used solely by the Art Students League.

American Radiator Building, 40 West 40th Street (Raymond Hood with Godley & Fouilhoux, 1923–24). Raymond Hood's first New York City skyscraper is highlighted by conservative Gothic-inspired detail but was, at the time of its construction, quite daring in its dramatic exploitation of the setback massing required by the 1916 zoning law. The building's most unusual feature is the use of black brick, chosen by Hood in an attempt to devise a unified facade (the facades of most earlier skyscrapers were light-colored masonry punctuated by dark window openings). The gold crown of the building was originally brightly lit at night to simulate the glow of a hot radiator.

Amster Yard, 211–215 East 49th Street (1869–70; renovation, Harold Sterner, 1945). In 1945 James Amster commissioned Sterner to convert a group of run-down buildings of the late 1860s into shops, offices, and apartments grouped around a landscaped courtyard.

Association of the Bar of the City of New York, 42 West 44th Street (Cyrus L. W. Eidlitz, 1895–96). This imposing limestone building, with street facades on both 43rd and 44th streets, illustrates Eidlitz's individualistic approach to the handling of classical architectural forms. Eidlitz designed the building for the Association of the Bar, New York's leading legal organization, which was founded in 1870 "for the purpose of maintaining the honor and dignity of the profession of the law, of cultivating social relations among its members, and increasing its usefulness in promoting the due administration of justice."

Barrymore Theater, 243–251 West 47th Street (Herbert J. Krapp, 1928). Built by the Shuberts to honor their star performer, Ethel Barrymore, this theater is among Krapp's most interesting designs—its facade takes the form of a giant classical Roman window with a terra-cotta grid. The **interior** is unusual for its mock-Elizabethan decoration. Ethel Barrymore appeared in the first production at the theater as well as in three other plays performed there between 1929 and 1931. Among the theater's many successful productions were *Gay Divorce* (with Fred Astaire), *The Women*, *Key Largo*, *A Streetcar Named Desire*, and *Raisin in the Sun*.

Beaux-Arts Apartments, 307 and 310 East 44th Street (Kenneth M. Murchison and Raymond Hood of the firm Raymond Hood, Godley & Fouilhoux, 1929–30). This pair of apartment houses was among the first in New York City to reflect the trend toward modernism, as evidenced in the horizontal massing, the use of steel casement windows, and the lack of applied ornament. The buildings contain studio and one-bedroom apartments planned for artists and others who wished to live in the artistic community that grew up around the nearby Beaux-Arts Institute of Design (see below).

Beaux-Arts Institute of Design, 304 East 44th Street (Frederic C. Hirons of the firm Dennison & Hirons, 1928). The Society of Beaux-Arts Architects, dedicated to furthering the architectural ideas promulgated at the Ecole des Beaux-Arts in Paris, held a competition for the design of a new school in 1927. The winning entry combines traditional Beaux-Arts ideas of symmetry, solidity, monumentality, and the use of symbolic art work (by René Chambellan) with ornament reflecting the contemporary Art Deco design aesthetic. The building was rehabilitated in 1989–92 (Milo Kleinberg Design Associates, architects) as offices for the American Federation of Musicians and Employers Pension Welfare Fund.

Martin Beck Theater, 302–314 West 45th Street (C. Albert Lansburgh, 1923–24). Among the most spectacular theaters in the Broadway theater district, this Moorish-inspired structure was built by the producer Martin Beck, who operated the theater until his death in 1940. The **interiors** reflect Beck's desire to build the most lavish legitimate theater in the Broadway area. The fantastical Moorish-Byzantine–style spaces were designed by Lansburgh in collaboration with the painter Albert Herter. Since the 1960s the Martin Beck Theater has been a popular venue for musicals and has housed such hits as *Bye Bye Birdie*, *Man of La Mancha*, and *Into the Woods*.

Belasco's Stuyvesant Theater, now the Belasco Theater, 111–121 West 44th Street (George Keister, 1906–07). The actor, director, and manager David Belasco, one of the most important figures in the history of the American stage, conceived this theater as a "living room" in which actors and audience would come in close contact. The use of the homey neo-Georgian style for the exterior heightens the domestic theme. The **interior** is especially notable for its Tiffany glass lamps, column capitals, and ceiling panels and for the 18 murals by the Ash Can artist Everett Shinn. In 1991 the Belasco became the home of the National Actors Theater, founded by Tony Randall.

Biltmore Theater (interior), 261–265 West 47th Street (Herbert J. Krapp, 1925–26). One of six Broadway theaters built by Irwin Chanin, the Biltmore has a handsome Adamesque interior laid out in an unusual horseshoe-shaped plan. The relatively small house, which has been home to such long-running hits as Neil Simon's *Barefoot in the Park* and the classic rock musical *Hair,* has been vacant for many years.

Booth Theater, 222–232 West 45th Street (Henry Herts, 1912–13). The Booth and the neighboring Shubert Theater (see p. 93) were designed as a pair by the prominent theater architect Henry Herts. The **interior** of the Booth was planned as an intimate setting for drama. The theater has been enormously successful, housing such notable American plays as *You Can't Take it With You*; *The Time of Your Life*; *Come Back, Little Sheba*; *That Championship Season*; *For Colored Girls. . .* ; and *Sunday in the Park with George.*

Broadhurst Theater, 235–243 West 44th Street (Herbert J. Krapp, 1917–18). One of many Broadway theaters built by the Shuberts, the Broadhurst opened under the personal management of the playwright George Broadhurst. Built as a companion to the Plymouth Theater (see p. 88), the building has a handsome neoclassical facade of patterned brick and terra cotta. The plan of the Adamesque **interior** is characteristic of the many theaters designed by Krapp: the space is wider than it is deep and has a single curving balcony. Among the celebrated actors to have appeared in plays at the Broadhurst are Eva Le Gallienne, Lionel and Ethel Barrymore, Leslie Howard, Barbara Stanwyck, Humphrey Bogart, Karl Malden, Rosalind Russell, Joel Grey, Katharine Hepburn, George C. Scott, and Dustin Hoffman.

Bryant Park Scenic Landmark, Sixth Avenue at West 42nd Street (east end, Carrère & Hastings, 1898–1911; main park, Lusby Simpson, 1933–34; redesign, Hanna/Olin, 1988–91). Bryant Park was built on the site of two of New York's most famous 19th-century structures, the Crystal Palace and the Croton Reservoir. Established in 1884, the park was not actually laid out until the 20th century. The terraces and kiosks at the east end were designed by Carrère & Hastings as part of the New York Public Library (see p. 86) commission and include the sculptor Herbert Adams's Bryant Memorial. The main park, planned in the tradition of formal French gardens, was laid out as a Depression-era public works project. The park was restored, and sections of it redesigned, in 1988–91.

Bryant Park Studios, 80 West 40th Street (Charles A. Rich, 1900–01). The Bryant Park Studios, like a handful of other buildings erected in New York City around 1900, were designed as combined living and studio spaces for artists. The large windows with unobstructed north light (Bryant Park is across the street) illuminate the double-height studios. Among the building's tenants were the artists Edward Steichen and Fernand Leger.

Bush Tower, 130–132 West 42nd Street and 133–137 West 41st Street (Helmle & Corbett, 1916–18, 1921). The setback massing of Bush Tower, built by the Bush Terminal Company as an international merchandise market, became a prototype for the skyscrapers erected in New York City in the following decade. According to Corbett, the setbacks were a purely aesthetic solution, planned prior to the passage of the 1916 zoning law. The narrow neo-Gothic midblock building is unusual for its decorated brick side elevations.

Carnegie Hall, West 57th Street at Seventh Avenue (William B. Tuthill, 1889–91; office wing, William B. Tuthill, 1892–95; studio wing, Henry Hardenbergh, 1896–97). Carnegie Hall, one of America's greatest concert halls, was built by steel magnate Andrew Carnegie as part of his efforts toward "the improvement of mankind." Known originally as the Music Hall, Carnegie Hall opened in 1891 with the American conducting debut of Tchaikovsky and since then has hosted many of the world's leading musicians. The building, faced in Roman brick and designed in an Italian Renaissance–inspired style, was originally crowned by a mansard roof; this roof was replaced by a full top floor early in the 1890s. The hall has two major additions: Tuthill's office tower on 56th Street and Hardenbergh's studio tower on 57th Street. Carnegie Hall was saved from demolition in 1960 when it was purchased by the city; it was handsomely refurbished in 1981–90 by James Stewart Polshek & Partners. An office tower, designed by Cesar Pelli & Associates and containing improved backstage facilities, was erected immediately to the east of the studio tower in 1986–90.

Central Synagogue (Congregation Ahavath Chesed), 652 Lexington Avenue (Henry Fernbach, 1871–72). Central Synagogue is the oldest building in New York State in continuous use by a single Jewish congregation. The congregation was founded in 1846 on the Lower East Side by Jews from Bohemia. Following the city's population northward, the congregation purchased a corner site on Lexington Avenue at East 55th Street and commissioned the design of a new sanctuary from the Prussian-born Jewish architect Henry Fernbach. The masterful Moorish-inspired form reflects the heritage of Jews in Moorish Spain and was a response to the 19th-century debate on the appropriate style for synagogues. The earliest Moorish-inspired synagogues were in Germany, but beginning with the 1866 design for America's oldest Reformed congregation, Congregation B'nai Jeshurun in Cincinnati, Moorish temples were erected throughout the United States. The brownstone-faced Central Synagogue, with its banded arches and onion domes, is a masterpiece of the style.

Century Association Clubhouse, 7 West 43rd Street (McKim, Mead & White, 1889–91). McKim, Mead & White's design for the Century Association, a club organized in 1847 "to promote the advancement of art and literature," established the Italian Renaissance palazzo mode as the favored style for the many private clubhouses built in American cities in the late 19th and early 20th centuries. In New York City this influence is evident in such later buildings as the Metropolitan Club (see p. 109) and the University Club (see p. 95). The facade of the Century combines light-colored stone, Roman brick, and terra cotta, and is highlighted by magnificent ironwork.

Chanin Building, 122 East 42nd Street (Irwin S. Chanin with Sloan & Robertson, 1927–29). This Art Deco structure, designed in part by its builder, Irwin Chanin, is one of the most significant New York skyscrapers of the 1920s, as it is one of the earliest with a solid base, setback massing, and a buttressed crown inspired by the form of Eliel Saarinen's influential entry in the 1922 Chicago Tribune building competition. The base is ornamented with decoration by René Chambellan, including a terra-cotta frieze with stylized curvilinear and angular naturalistic forms set in a complex pattern that is the quintessence of Art Deco design. Below this frieze is a bronze band illustrating the theory of evolution—beginning with primitive marine life and extending as far as birds.

Chrysler Building, 405 Lexington Avenue (William Van Alen, 1928–30). The Chrysler's stunning Art Deco design is the embodiment of the romantic New York skyscraper. The 77-story building, distinguished by its abundant automotive imagery (e.g., silver hood ornaments embellish the setbacks and stylized racing cars appear at the 31st floor) and a striking crown, was a personal symbol of Walter P. Chrysler and an advertisement for his corporation. **Interior:** The spectacular lobby contains red Moroccan marble walls and yellow Siena marble floors; a ceiling mural by Edward Trumbull, which, according to a contemporary source, depicts "the vision, human energy, and engineering ability which made possible the structure"; steel, aluminum, and onyx ornament; and elevator cabs that are among the most glorious ever created.

Civic Club, now Estonian House, 243 East 34th Street (Thomas A. Gray, 1898–99). The Civic Club was founded by Frederick Goddard, a wealthy New Yorker involved in turn-of-the-century social reform efforts who sought specifically to improve the lives of people residing between 23rd and 42nd streets east of Fourth Avenue. Goddard not only founded the Civic Club but also erected its Beaux-Arts clubhouse. The building remained in the Goddard family until 1946, when it was sold to the Estonian Educational Society, an organization that sponsors activities for Estonian-Americans.

Thomas Benedict and Fanny Clarke House, now the Collectors Club, 22 East 35th Street (McKim, Mead & White, 1901–02). For his friend the art collector and dealer Thomas B. Clarke, Stanford White designed one of his most delightful town houses. The street facade combines what is basically a Colonial Revival brick front with an unusual medieval-inspired multipaned bowed window reminiscent of those favored by the British architect Richard Norman Shaw in the 1870s. In 1937 the house was purchased by the Collectors Club, a leading organization devoted to philately.

Cort Theater, 138–146 West 48th Street (Thomas Lamb, 1912–13). Among the oldest and most beautiful of Broadway theaters, the Cort is an adaptation of the Petit Trianon (1762) at Versailles. The theater was designed for the producer John Cort by one of America's most prominent theater architects. The elegant

interior is decorated with French neoclassical detail and a mural depicting a dance in the gardens of Versailles. The theater has housed a large number of dramas, including many revivals. Among the long-running shows that have played the Cort are *The Diary of Anne Frank*, *Sunrise at Campobello*, *The Magic Show*, and *Sarafina*.

Coty Building, now part of the Henri Bendel Store, 714 Fifth Avenue (Woodruff Leeming, 1907–08; glass front, René Lalique, 1910). The former Coty Building, originally a row house erected in 1871, received a new commercial front in 1907–08. The building was leased in 1910 by the French perfumer François Coty, who commissioned what is now the only extant architectural glass work in New York City designed by the great French glass maker René Lalique. Lalique's composition of intertwining vines initially rose from the second through the fifth floors (the narrow second-floor level has been lost) and was designed to fit within the preexisting commercial frame. The glass was restored in 1989–90.

Daily News Building, 220 East 42nd Street (Raymond Hood, 1929–30). Joseph Patterson, founder of the *Daily News*, commissioned this building as the home and symbol of America's first tabloid and the country's largest newspaper. As designed by Hood, the building combines Art Deco and modernist forms in a striking manner. The flat roof and freestanding slablike massing are significant modern innovations, but Hood's use of striped brickwork and an entrance adorned with a large relief panel of light rays shining on a diverse urban populace are characteristic decorative forms of Art Deco design.

Joseph Raphael De Lamar House, now the Consulate General of the Republic of Poland, 233 Madison Avenue (C. P. H. Gilbert, 1902–05). This Beaux-Arts mansion, the largest in Murray Hill and one of the grandest in all of New York, was designed for a Dutch-born entrepreneur who made his fortune in the California Gold Rush. The subtly asymmetrical house, with an entrance that is flanked by marble columns and crowned by a pair of putti, is surmounted by an exceptionally imposing mansard.

Adelaide L. T. Douglas House, now the Guatemalan Permanent Mission to the United Nations, 57 Park Avenue (Horace Trumbauer, 1909–11). New York socialite Adelaide L. Townsend Douglas commissioned this house from the fashionable Philadelphia architect Horace Trumbauer a year after her divorce from William Douglas, the developer of Douglaston, Queens. Trumbauer designed the house in the Louis XVI style that he favored for urban residences. The facade contains especially interesting sculpted friezes.

152 East 38th Street House (1858; redesign, Robertson Ward, 1934–35). This house is an example of the extensive redesign that many of New York's older houses underwent in the 1920s and 1930s. Set far back from the lot line, the house appears originally to have been an outbuilding on an estate belonging to a member of President Martin Van Buren's family. In 1934 the developer Russell A. Pettengill commissioned Robertson Ward to convert the building and its neighbor into a residence and office for his own use. The old facade was stuccoed and a low wall with thin colonnettes and other Regency-inspired detail was constructed near the front of the lot. In 1944 the house was sold to the publisher Cass Canfield.

312 East 53rd Street House (1865–66). One of a pair, this small frame mansard-roofed house in the French Second Empire style is an intact example of a type of modest dwelling that was once common in New York City but is now exceptionally rare.

311 and 313 East 58th Street Houses (1856–57). These two vernacular houses with Italianate details are reminders of the simple dwellings that once dotted midtown Manhattan. Both houses are below sidewalk level as a result of the construction of a new approach to the Queensboro Bridge in 1930.

Eleventh District Municipal Court/Seventh District Magistrates' Court, now the American Theater of Actors, 314 West 54th Street (John H. Duncan, 1894–96). This former courthouse is an example of the imposing small-scale civic buildings erected throughout New York City in the late 19th century. For the limestone and brick structure Duncan employed Renaissance forms ornamented with terra-cotta detail incorporating symbols of justice.

Embassy Theater (interior), now the Embassy I Theater, 1556–1560 Broadway (Thomas Lamb, 1925). The Embassy Theater, planned as an experiment to determine whether an elegant, intimate movie house would attract an exclusive high-society audience, has an ornate French-inspired interior designed by architect Thomas Lamb and the decorating firm of Rambush Studio that features elaborate plasterwork and murals by Arthur Crisp. As part of the effort to create a salonlike atmosphere, a woman (the heiress Gloria Gould) was appointed manager of the theater. The exclusivity lasted only a few years; in 1929 the Embassy became the first newsreel theater in the country.

Erlanger Theater, now the St. James Theater, 246–256 West 44th Street (Warren & Wetmore, 1926–27). The restrained Beaux-Arts facade of this theater is the work of an important New York architecture firm. Commissioned by the producer Abraham Erlanger, the theater was renamed the St. James by new owners following Erlanger's death in 1930. The **interior,** which contains a large auditorium, is unusual in its reliance on spatial organization rather than on ornament for effect. The St. James has housed such great American musicals as *Oklahoma!*; *The King and I*; and *Hello, Dolly!*

647 Fifth Avenue House, also known as the George W. Vanderbilt House, now Olympic Airlines (Hunt & Hunt, 1902–05; addition, Charles L. Fraser, 1917). This town house in the Louis XV style and its neighbor, the Morton and Nellie Plant House (see p. 87), are reminders of the residential character of Fifth Avenue early in the 20th century. The house, one of a pair known as the "Marble Twins," was commissioned by George W. Vanderbilt and sold to his brother William K. Vanderbilt prior to completion. It is the last survivor of a group of Vanderbilt residences built on this section of Fifth Avenue. The house was designed by the sons of Richard Morris Hunt, the architect of George Vanderbilt's famous Biltmore estate in North Carolina. Robert Goelet and his wife, Elsie, were the only residents, prior to the 1917 sale of the house to the art dealers Gimpel & Wildenstein.

712 Fifth Avenue Building, later the Rizzoli Building, now part of the Henri Bendel Store, 712 Fifth Avenue (Albert S. Gottlieb, 1907–08). When the Fifth Avenue Presbyterian Church commissioned this commercial building for a site adjacent to the church, Fifth Avenue was primarily residential. Thus, the building was designed in accordance with 18th-century French prototypes as a five-story, limestone-fronted structure that would blend with the nearby houses and maintain the elegant character of the street. The first tenant was the fashionable decorating establishment of L. Alavoine & Co. From 1964 to 1985 the Rizzoli bookstore and publishing company occupied the premises.

Film Center Building (interior), 630 Ninth Avenue (Ely Jacques Kahn, 1928–29). The ground-floor vestibule, lobby, and hallway of the Film Center, comprising one of the most beautiful Art Deco interiors in New York, were designed by Kahn in his idiosyncratic manner. Much of the interior reflects a pre-Columbian influence. Of special interest are the geometrically patterned terrazzo floors, the ziggurat shape of the plaster ceilings, the superb metalwork, and—the lobby's most striking feature—a polychromatic mosaic on the wall between the elevator banks.

Fire Engine Company No. 23, 215 West 58th Street (Alexander H. Stevens, 1905–06). Engine Company No. 23 is a straightforward Beaux-Arts limestone and brick building that served as a model for other early 20th-century firehouses. The building is one of the first to have been designed by the fire department's superintendent of buildings rather than by an outside architect.

Fire Engine Company No. 65, 33 West 43rd Street (Hoppin & Koen, 1897–98). Erected at a time when West 43rd Street between Fifth and Sixth avenues was being developed as the location of some of the city's most prestigious clubs and hotels, this four-story Italian Renaissance–inspired firehouse was designed to resemble the nearby Century Association Clubhouse (see p.70).

Forrest Theater (interior), later the Coronet Theater, now the Eugene O'Neill Theater, 230–238 West 49th Street (Herbert J. Krapp, 1925–26). Built by the Shuberts, the Forrest was named for the celebrated American actor Edwin Forrest (see Fonthill, p. 204), and renamed in honor of the great American playwright Eugene O'Neill in 1953. The auditorium is an elegant example of the Adamesque design favored by Krapp. The most famous production staged in this theater was *Tobacco Road*, which moved to the Forrest in 1934, several months after opening at the Theater Masque (see p. 83), and which ran for 3,182 performances, a Broadway record.

Forty-sixth Street Theater, now the Richard Rodgers Theater, 226–236 West 46th Street (Herbert J. Krapp, 1924). The first Broadway theater built by the Chanin Organization, the 46th Street is an elaborate Renaissance-inspired work that features several innovations in theater design, notably a single entrance and, on the **interior**, stadium-type seating with a steeply raked orchestra and a single balcony (Irwin Chanin thought such seating would democratize theater-going). Many hit musicals have played the 46th Street, including *Good News*, *Finian's Rainbow*, *Guys and Dolls*, *Damn Yankees*, and *1776*.

Four Seasons Restaurant (interior), 99 East 52nd Street (Philip Johnson, 1958–59). An integral part of Mies van der Rohe's Seagram Building (see p. 92), the Four Seasons Restaurant is one of the most notable International Style interiors in the United States. Planned as a first-class restaurant, the beautifully proportioned interior spaces are clad in travertine, bronze, aluminum, wood, rawhide, and other materials, all of which have been installed with expert craftsmanship that accentuates their natural beauty. For this design Johnson collaborated with an interior designer, a lighting consultant, horticulturists, artists, and furniture and industrial designers to create a unified series of environments, including the long narrow lobby, the Grill Room, and the Pool Room.

Fred F. French Building, 551 Fifth Avenue (H. Douglas Ives and Sloan & Robertson, 1926–27). The prominent Fred F. French real estate firm erected this skyscraper with massed setbacks for its corporate headquarters and for rental income. The use of detail inspired by ancient Mesopotamian art is an indication of the exotic historicism that was prevalent during the 1920s. The exotic influence is especially evident at the base, where the bronze entrances and storefronts are embellished with mythological figures and Near Eastern ornament. **Interior:** The ornamental motifs pick up exterior design elements in the magnificent lobby, which has a vaulted ceiling, bronze doors, and other elaborate Near Eastern features.

Fuller Building, 41 East 57th Street (Walker & Gillette, 1928–29). Erected as the headquarters of the Fuller Construction Company, this prominently sited corner building was planned to house retail stores and art galleries on the first six floors and offices above. The design, with its modernist interpretation of classical architectural forms, reflects the conservative aspects of the Art Deco style. The building has a black Swedish granite base; the upper floors are clad in a light-colored limestone. A pair of figures by the noted sculptor Elie Nadelman crowns the imposing three-story entrance. The stylized modern classicism of the exterior continues on the **interior,** where the vestibules and lobby are richly decorated with marble walls, mosaic floors, and bronze detail. Of special note are the round mosaic floor panels representing the company's three successive headquarters buildings—the Tacoma Building in Chicago, the Flatiron Building (see p. 55), and the Fuller Building—and the bronze elevator doors depicting scenes of building construction.

Gainsborough Studios, 222 Central Park South (Charles W. Buckham, 1907–08). The Gainsborough was planned as combined living and studio space for artists. The double-height windows facing Central Park provide north light to the studios; duplex apartments are located at the rear. The facade (restored in 1988) acknowledges the building's artist residents with its bust of Thomas Gainsborough, a frieze by Isidore Konti entitled *A Festival Procession of the Arts*, and an art tile mural produced at Henry Mercer's Moravian Tile Works.

General Electric Building, 570 Lexington Avenue (Cross & Cross, 1929–31). The Radio Victor Corporation of America (RCA) was a subsidiary of General Electric when it commissioned this Art Deco building as its headquarters. But when, in 1931, as part of an effort to gain corporate independence, the firm moved to Rockefeller Center, it deeded this building to General Electric. The octagonal brick tower, rising from a base with rounded corner, is one of the most expressive skyscrapers of its era. Especially noteworthy features are the complex brickwork and terra cotta in colors chosen to blend with the neighboring St. Bartholomew's Church (see p. 91) and the use of details symbolic of the building's tenant: the corner clock whose projecting arms grasp electric bolts; the spectral figures with boltlike bodies above the shopfronts; and the stylized figures at the building's crown, each with a halo of electric rays. The building was restored in 1984–87.

The Gerard, 123 West 44th Street (George Keister, 1893–94). The Gerard exhibits an unusual combination of Romanesque, Gothic, and Northern European Renaissance forms. This apartment hotel was in the vanguard of the movement that was to transform the low-rise residential area north of Times Square into a district of theaters, hotels, and related facilities.

Globe Theater, now the Lunt-Fontanne Theater, 203–217 West 46th Street (Carrère & Hastings, 1909–10). Built as the headquarters of the influential Broadway producer Charles Dillingham, the Beaux-Arts Globe is the only surviving theater designed by Carrère & Hastings. After serving as a movie house for many years, the Globe was returned to legitimate use in 1958; at the same time, however, its interior was gutted and its name was changed. Dillingham was able to attract many major stars to play the Globe, including Sarah Bernhardt, Lynn Fontanne, Fred and Adele Astaire, and Fanny Brice. In more recent years the theater has been favored for musicals, most notably *The Sound of Music* and *Sophisticated Ladies.*

James J. and Josephine Goodwin Residence, also known as the 9–11 West 54th Street House, now the U.S. Trust Company (McKim, Mead & White, 1896–98). The wealthy businessman James Junius Goodwin, a cousin and business partner of J. P. Morgan, was responsible for commissioning one of McKim, Mead & White's finest Colonial Revival residences. Modeled on Charles Bulfinch's Third Harrison Gray Otis House (1806) in Boston, this elegant brick structure was planned as a double house; the Goodwins resided in the larger unit at No. 11. The building underwent an award-winning restoration and conversion into a bank between 1980 and 1981 (Haines, Lundberg, Wachler, architects).

Gotham Hotel, now the Peninsula Hotel, 696–700 Fifth Avenue (Hiss & Weekes, 1902–05). The Italian Renaissance–inspired Gotham Hotel is among the handsomest surviving early 20th-century luxury hotels in New York City. The 20-story limestone building was designed to harmonize with the adjoining University Club (see p. 95) and to complement the St. Regis Hotel (see p. 92), begun one year earlier on a site across Fifth Avenue.

Helen Miller Gould Carriage House, now the Unity Center of Practical Christianity, 213 West 58th Street (York & Sawyer, 1902–03). Although planned for a utilitarian function, this structure is a sophisticated example of early French Renaissance-inspired design. Built for the eldest daughter of the "robber baron" Jay Gould, the carriage house is an early work of York & Sawyer, an architecture firm best known for its banks.

Grand Army Plaza Scenic Landmark. See p. 105.

Grand Central Terminal, East 42nd Street at Park Avenue (Reed & Stem and Warren & Wetmore, 1903–13). One of the world's great railway terminals, often referred to as the "gateway to the nation," Grand Central is a masterpiece of Beaux-Arts design. The engineer William Wilgus and the architects Reed & Stem were responsible for the terminal's innovative plan, with its extensive tunnels, ramp system, and upper and lower concourses. The monumental facades and the sumptuous interior spaces were the work of Whitney Warren. Grand Central was designed on axis with Park Avenue; Jules-Félix Coutan's clock and *Transportation* statue at the apex of the building terminate the avenue's northward vista. The **interiors** are laid out in a formal, axial Beaux-Arts manner with a grand waiting room and an even grander concourse, famous

Grand Central Terminal, East 42nd Street at Park Avenue (Reed & Stem and Warren & Wetmore, 1903–13). Detail of *Transportation* (Jules-Félix Coutan, sculptor). Photo: Caroline Kane

for its windowed east and west elevations—through which shafts of light penetrate the space—and its high vaulted ceiling appropriately decorated with constellations highlighted by electric stars. Ramps lead down to the more modest lower concourse, planned for suburban trains, and to the famous Oyster Bar, whose vaulted ceiling is clad in Guastavino tiles. The designation of Grand Central Terminal sustained a series of legal challenges that culminated in a 1978 United States Supreme Court decision affirming the validity of New York City's landmarks law.

Guild Theater, later the ANTA Theater, now the Virginia Theater, 243–259 West 52nd Street (Crane & Franzheim, 1924–25). The Theater Guild, an organization founded by members of the theater community for the express purpose of presenting high-quality plays, commissioned this building as a theater and a theatrical resource center. The facade design was inspired by 15th-century Tuscan villas. The Guild produced a series of classical and modern plays (premiering Eugene O'Neill's *Mourning Becomes Electra* and *Ah, Wilderness!*) with all-star casts before it was forced to give up the theater in 1943. From 1950 to 1981 the American National Theater and Academy (ANTA) owned the theater; among its productions was the American premiere of *A Man for All Seasons.*

Hammerstein's Theater (interior), now the Ed Sullivan Theater, 1697–1699 Broadway (Herbert J. Krapp, 1927). The neo-Gothic style chosen for the vestibule, lobbies, and auditorium of the former Hammerstein's Theater is unique on Broadway. The theater was built by Arthur Hammerstein (see Arthur and Dorothy Dalton Hammerstein House, p. 194) as a memorial to his father, Oscar Hammerstein I, and no expense was spared in making the interiors as imposing as possible. Unfortunately, the theater was never successful as a legitimate playhouse. It served for many years as a dance hall and then became a radio theater. In 1945 it was converted for use by television and housed the Ed Sullivan Show, the longest-running program in television history.

Harvard Club of New York City, 27 West 44th Street (McKim, Mead & White, 1893–94; rear addition, 1900–05; west wing, 1913–16). Appropriately, the Harvard Club was designed in a Colonial-inspired style reminiscent of the early buildings on the university's Cambridge, Massachusetts, campus. Charles McKim, who had unsuccessfully studied engineering at Harvard and later designed several buildings and memorial gates on the Harvard campus, was responsible for the original building of dark red "Harvard brick" with limestone trim. The same style and materials were used by McKim, Mead & White for the two additions.

Hearst Magazine Building, 951–969 Eighth Avenue (Joseph Urban and George B. Post & Sons, 1927–28). Built as the headquarters of William Randolph Hearst's publishing empire, this building was designed by the Viennese-born and -educated architect Joseph Urban, a leading theater designer of the 20th century. The six-story building, faced in cast limestone, was planned as a base for a skyscraper that was never built. It combines Art Deco ornament, Viennese Secessionist forms, and a baroque theatricality that exemplify Urban's architectural vision. Of special note are the paired sculptural figures representing comedy and tragedy, art and music, sport and industry, and printing and science.

Edward and Frances Holbrook House. See p. 88

Harry B. and Evelina Hollins Residence, now the Consulate General of Argentina, 12–14 West 56th Street (McKim, Mead & White, 1899–1901; alteration, J. E. R. Carpenter, 1924). The banker and broker Harry B. Hollins commissioned this handsome Colonial Revival brick house in 1899, at a time when many town houses were being built in north Midtown. Commerce soon overwhelmed the neighborhood, and in 1914 the house was converted into the Calumet Club. Ten years later the club removed the original central entrance and constructed the porch and wing to the east. Since 1947 the house has been occupied by the Argentine consulate.

Hollywood Theater, later the Mark Hellinger Theater, now Times Square Church, 217–239 West 51st Street (Thomas Lamb, 1929). The Hollywood, built as a movie palace with its entrance on Broadway (now demolished), is the sole survivor of the great Broadway movie palaces. The exterior, with its combination of modernist elements (a massing derived from Frank Lloyd Wright's Unity Temple and a series of figures inspired by those on Eliel Saarinen's Helsinki Railroad Station), hides a lavish Baroque-inspired **interior** with rich gilded plaster surfaces, large mirrors, murals of nymphs and clouds, and ornate chandeliers. Run as a movie theater for only five years, the theater was convert-ed into a legitimate house and renamed for a noted columnist and producer. The building was sold to the Times Square Church in 1991.

Hudson Theater, now Hudson Theater of the Macklowe Hotel, 139–141 West 44th Street (J. B. McElfatrick & Son and Israels & Harder, 1902–04). The Hudson, one of the oldest Broadway theaters, was built by the producer Henry B. Harris as a showcase for his stars. The theater has a restrained Beaux-Arts facade and an exuberant **interior** with elegant plasterwork and stained glass. It was restored in 1990 as part of the construction of the adjacent Macklowe Hotel.

Imperial Theater (interior), 249 West 45th Street (Herbert J. Krapp, 1923). Built by the Shuberts, the Imperial has long been one of the most successful Broadway theaters. Planned as a showcase for musicals and revues, the theater has premiered such hits as *Rose-Marie*; *Oh, Kay!*; *Annie Get Your Gun*; *Gypsy*; *Oliver!*; *Fiddler on the Roof*; *Cabaret*; and *Dreamgirls*. The Imperial has an elegant Adamesque interior with fine plasterwork.

Church of the Incarnation (Episcopal) and Rectory, 205 and 209 Madison Avenue (church, Emlen T. Littell, 1864; restoration and additions, D. & J. Jardine, 1882; rectory, Edward P. Casey, 1905–06). The Church of the Incarnation was erected at the time Murray Hill was being developed as a pres-tigious residential neighborhood. Built of brownstone with light-colored sand-stone trim, the Gothic Revival structure's most prominent feature is its tall broached spire. D. & J. Jardine restored and enlarged the building following a fire in 1882. The church contains some of the finest ecclesiastical art work in America, including stained-glass windows designed by William Morris, Edward Burne-Jones, Louis Comfort Tiffany, and John LaFarge; sculpture by the American masters Daniel Chester French and Augustus Saint-Gaudens; and a monument designed by Henry Hobson Richardson. A rectory built adjacent to the church in 1868–69 was largely rebuilt and given a new facade in a neo-Jacobean style in 1905–06 and is currently used as a parish house. A major restoration project was begun in 1991 (Jan Hird Pokorny, architect).

Knickerbocker Hotel, 1462–1470 Broadway (Marvin & Davis with Bruce Price, 1901–06; annex at 143 West 41st Street, Trowbridge & Livingston, 1906). At the turn of the century several grand hotels were erected in the Times Square area; the only survivor is the Knickerbocker. Financed by John Jacob Astor IV, this Beaux-Arts red brick building with terra-cotta detail and a prominent mansard roof was among the city's most lavish hostelries and was a popular dining and dancing spot in New York's new theater district. The hotel closed during the Depression, and the building was converted for office use.

Knox Building, now part of the Republic National Bank Building, 452 Fifth Avenue (John H. Duncan, 1901–02). With its limestone and white brick facades, the Knox Building is a fine example of Beaux-Arts commercial archi-tecture. Erected for a prominent hat company at a time when business development was sweeping north along Fifth Avenue, the building is conspicuously sited on the corner immediately south of the New York Public Library's plaza.

Lambs Club, now the Manhattan Church of the Nazarene, 128 West 44th Street (McKim, Mead & White, 1903–05; addition, George A. Freeman, 1915). Founded in 1874, the Lambs was a club for actors and theater enthusiasts. In 1903 the commission for the Lambs' new clubhouse went to the firm of McKim, Mead & White—all three principals were members. Stanford White was responsible for the Colonial Revival design ornamented with lambs' and rams' heads. The size of the building was doubled in 1915 when an addition to the west, a virtual copy of White's original, was constructed.

James F. D. and Harriet Lanier House, 123 East 35th Street (Hoppin & Koen, 1901–03). At the turn of the century many of the old residences in Murray Hill were replaced by imposing new town houses. The banker James Franklin Doughty Lanier and his wife demolished two modest houses of 1854 and erected this richly detailed Beaux-Arts dwelling.

Philip and Carrie Lehman House, also known as the 7 West 54th Street House (John H. Duncan, 1899–1900). Philip Lehman, son of a founder of the banking firm of Lehman Brothers and himself a partner in the firm, commissioned this limestone-fronted Beaux-Arts town house, one of five adjacent landmark residences on the north side of West 54th Street. After Philip's death in 1947 the house was occupied by his son Robert, who amassed an extraordinary art collection; this collection was later given to the Metropolitan Museum of Art, where it is now installed along with interiors removed from the house.

William Lescaze House and Office, 211 East 48th Street (William Lescaze, 1933–34). The pioneer modern architect William Lescaze designed this house for his own family and incorporated an office into the basement level. The building, actually a redesign of an old row house, is generally considered to be the first truly "modern" structure in New York. It has a complex, rationally designed street front with precisely balanced solids and voids. The stuccoed facade is pierced by casement ribbon windows and expanses of glass block; this is the first use of glass block in New York City.

Lever House, 390 Park Avenue (Gordon Bunshaft, partner in charge, Skidmore, Owings & Merrill, 1950–52). The construction of the 24-story glass and stainless steel Lever House heralded the beginning of a new wave in American skyscraper design and a turning point in the history of modern architecture. Lever House established the suitability of the International Style for office building design and signaled the transformation of the style from one associated with an idealistic European social movement into one symbolizing corporate America. Lever House also signaled the beginning of the transformation of Park Avenue south of 59th Street from a street of masonry apartments and institutions into an avenue of glass towers. Lever House was the first skyscraper in the form of a vertical slab erected in New York City after the passage of the 1916 zoning resolution; the setbacks required by the 1916 law were not necessary if a building occupied only 25 percent of its lot. Bunshaft's design is especially dramatic because the slab is set perpendicular to Park Avenue and appears to float above the street and above the one-story base and open plaza.

Little Theater, now the Helen Hayes Theater, 238 West 44th Street (Ingalls & Hoffman, 1912; interior remodeling, Herbert J. Krapp, 1917–20). The construction of the Little Theater marked a new direction in Broadway theater design. The theater was commissioned by the producer Winthrop Ames to house the type of drama known as "intimate theater." The small size (the theater sat only 299 people) and the use of the primarily domestic Colonial Revival style on both the exterior and **interior** contribute to the feeling of intimacy. The balcony was added in 1917 in an effort to make the theater more profitable.

Longacre Theater, 220–228 West 48th Street (Henry B. Herts, 1912–13). The Longacre was designed in the French neoclassical style for the Broadway producer and baseball magnate Harry Frazee (who owned the Boston Red Sox). The **interior,** with its simple French-inspired decor (now somewhat altered), incorporated many innovations in design, planning, and ventilation. Although the theater has had a checkered history, it has housed a number of long-running hits, notably *Ain't Misbehavin'* and *Children of a Lesser God.*

Lyceum Theater, 149–157 West 45th Street (Herts & Tallant, 1902–03). The Beaux-Arts facade of the Lyceum is the most imposing in the Broadway theater district. Built for the early 20th-century theater impresario Daniel Frohman, the playhouse was designed by New York's most talented theater architects. Although a two-balcony house, the **interior** is relatively small and was planned for intimate plays. Lush plaster detail embellishes walls and ceilings and is adorned with the monogram *L.* The theater is further enhanced by marble paneling and lobby murals by James Wall Finn. The Lyceum has housed many of Broadway's most famous comedies and dramas, including a run of classic plays produced in the late 1960s by the APA-Phoenix Theater. The list of great stars who performed at the Lyceum is unparalleled and includes William Gillette, Ethel Barrymore, Billie Burke, Walter Huston, Bette Davis, Miriam Hopkins, Cornel Wilde, Joseph Cotton, Maurice Evans, John Garfield, Montgomery Clift, Ruth Gordon, Melvyn Douglas, Alan Bates, Lauren Bacall, Angela Lansbury, Billy Dee Williams, Helen Hayes, Rosemary Harris, and Nancy Marchand.

McGraw-Hill Building, 330 West 42nd Street (Raymond Hood, Godley & Fouilhoux, 1930–31). The 35-story McGraw-Hill Building is a major work of the great skyscraper architect Raymond Hood. The massing, with horizontal setbacks that allow the building to be read as a modern slab, and the simple detailing illustrate the transition between the decorative Art Deco style and the austere slab forms of International Style design. With the McGraw-Hill Building, Hood also introduced to New York the idea of horizontal ribbon windows, a feature that would become common on modern skyscrapers. Color was an important element of the design. Almost the entire building is clad in blue-green terra cotta; the metal windows were originally apple green with a band of vermillion across the top; the entranceway is clad in alternating bands of blue and green metal; and the building is crowned by a sign with the corporate name spelled out in 11-foot-tall letters originally painted white with an orange stripe. The building was erected west of Eighth Avenue in an area zoned for industrial use because it housed not only McGraw-Hill's corporate offices but also its printing plant.

Majestic Theater, 245–257 West 44th Street (Herbert J. Krapp, 1926–27). The Majestic, a large musical house (seating 1,800), was built by Irwin Chanin as one of a trio of theaters that included the Royale (see p. 91) and the Theater Masque (see below). The eclectic exterior is in a style that Chanin and his architect referred to as "modern Spanish." The **interior** is decorated in a neo-classical manner and is laid out in the so-called "stadium plan" that Chanin and Krapp first introduced at their 46th Street Theater (see p. 74). Among the hit musicals that have played the Majestic are *Carousel*, *South Pacific*, *The Music Man*, *Camelot*, *The Wiz*, and *The Phantom of the Opera.*

Mansfield Theater, now the Brooks Atkinson Theater, 256–262 West 47th Street (Herbert J. Krapp, 1925–26). Named originally for the 19th-century American actor Richard Mansfield, and renamed in 1960 for the theater critic Brooks Atkinson, this theater is one of six erected in the 1920s by the Chanin Organization. The theater was designed in the "modern Spanish" style favored by Irwin Chanin. The exceptional **interior** reflects the expertise of Chanin, Krapp, and Roman Meltzer, former architect to Czar Nicholas II, who supervised the ornamental scheme, which includes fine plasterwork and murals. The theater has housed a number of successful dramas and comedies, among them *Green Pastures*, *Come Blow Your Horn*, *Talley's Folly*, and *Noises Off.*

Theater Masque, now the Golden Theater, 252–256 West 45th Street (Herbert J. Krapp, 1926–27). Built by Irwin Chanin in conjunction with the Majestic (see above) and the Royale (see p. 91), the Theater Masque, which was renamed for the producer John Golden in 1937, is a small house planned for intimate dramas. Both the exterior and **interior** of the theater were designed in the "modern Spanish" style used by Krapp for several of his Chanin commissions. *Tobacco Road* premiered at the Masque and was followed by many other successful productions, including, in recent years, *The Gin Game*, *Crimes of the Heart*, *'Night Mother*, and *Glengarry Glen Ross.*

Mecca Temple, now the City Center 55th Street Theater, 131 West 55th Street (H. P. Knowles, 1922–24). Famed since 1943 as the home of several of New York's major performing arts organizations, the City Center Theater was originally a temple for the Ancient Order of Nobles of the Mystic Shrine, better known as the Shriners. A Moorish-inspired design, the building is clad in sandstone blocks and is crowned by a huge tiled dome. The facade is enlivened by entrances featuring brightly colored terra cotta and glazed tile in an Islamic design. The temple consists of a huge auditorium above a basement banquet room (now the Manhattan Theater Club) and a 12-story wing to the rear that originally housed lodge and club rooms (now offices). Mecca Temple was never a financial success, and in 1942 New York City foreclosed on the property. Mayor LaGuardia conceived of the idea of converting the hall into a cultural center that offered tickets at affordable prices. The City Center of Music and Drama was officially organized in 1943. City Center's constituents have included the New York City Ballet, the New York City Opera, the Joffrey Ballet, and the Alvin Ailey Dance Theater. Since 1976 the building has been managed by the 55th Street Dance Theater Foundation.

Mechanics' and Tradesmen's Institute, 20 West 44th Street (Lamb & Rich, 1890; additions, Ralph S. Townsend, 1903–05). The Mechanics' and Tradesmen's Institute was built in two separate campaigns that created a single unified design. The original building was erected by the Berkeley School, a private boys' school that emphasized military drill exercise. In 1899 the property was acquired by the General Society of Mechanics and Tradesmen, an organization founded in 1785 to foster education in the mechanical trades. In 1903 Andrew Carnegie, who was a member of the society, provided a gift of $250,000 to renovate the building. The original top story was replaced with three stories, and the building's magnificent wrought-iron fire escapes were installed.

Henry Miller's Theater, 124–130 West 43rd Street (Allen, Ingalls & Hoffman, 1917–18). This theater was designed to the specifications of the actor/producer/director Henry W. Miller and was the venue of Miller's own productions until his death in 1926. Before its conversion into a movie house in 1969, and later into a discotheque, the theater housed such notable plays as *Born Yesterday*, *The Cocktail Party*, *Under Milk Wood*, and *Enter Laughing*.

William H. and Ada S. Moore House, 4 East 54th Street (McKim, Mead & White, 1898–1900). This marble-fronted house was commissioned by W. E. D. Stokes, builder of the Ansonia Hotel (see p. 120), but four months before its completion Stokes sold the house to Ada Moore. Moore and her husband, the Chicago industrialist William H. Moore, a founder of U.S. Steel and other large corporations, moved into one of McKim, Mead & White's most beautiful Italian Renaissance–inspired town houses.

Pierpont Morgan Library and Annex, 29–33 East 36th Street (McKim, Mead & White, 1902–07; annex, Benjamin Wistar Morris, 1927–28). When J. P. Morgan commissioned a library to house his collection of books and manuscripts, Charles McKim responded with an architectural masterpiece. McKim based his design on the attic story of the Nymphaeum of 1555, built in Rome for Pope Julius III. The facade of Tennessee marble laid up without mortar centers on an entrance in the form of a Palladian arch. To either side are lions carved by Edward Potter and roundels and panels by Andrew O'Connor and Adolph Weinman. The refined simplicity of the exterior belies the richness of the **interior**. The original library has three public rooms, each magnificently decorated. The colorful marble entrance hall is crowned by a domed ceiling adorned with murals and plasterwork by H. Siddons Mowbray, a leading muralist of the period, who derived his inspiration from the work of Raphael. The East Library is dominated by triple tiers of bookcases and is ornamented with lunettes by Mowbray. The West Library, which was Morgan's study, has been called "one of the great achievements of American interior decoration." In

Pierpont Morgan Library, 29-33 East 36th Street (McKim, Mead & White, 1902-07). View of East Room. Photo: The Pierpont Morgan Library

1927–28 a harmonious addition in the Classical Revival style was erected to the west of the original library; a glass pavilion designed by Voorsanger Mills was added to the rear in 1990–91.

Music Box Theater, 239–247 West 45th Street (C. Howard Crane & E. George Kiehler, 1920). Producer Sam Harris built this theater to house Irving Berlin's *Music Box Revues*. The "revues" ran for five years, after which time the theater housed many successful plays and musicals, including George S. Kaufman and George and Ira Gershwin's *Of Thee I Sing*, Kaufman and Edna Ferber's *Dinner at Eight* and *Stage Door*, Moss Hart and Irving Berlin's *As Thousands Cheer*, and several hits by Kaufman and Hart, including *The Man Who Came to Dinner*. The elegant English-inspired neoclassical exterior is articulated by a porch supported by four attenuated columns; the Adamesque **interior** features delicate plasterwork and murals.

New Amsterdam Theater, 214 West 42nd Street (Herts & Tallant, 1902–03). As home to the *Ziegfeld Follies*, as well as Eva Le Gallienne's Civic Repertory Theater and George White's "Scandals," this legendary theater has presented scores of great actors in memorable productions. The theater has a narrow Beaux-Arts–inspired entrance facade on West 42nd Street with a vertical sign dating from 1937, when the theater was used as a movie house. The **interior** is adorned with splendid Art Nouveau decoration. The lobby, foyers, reception room, staircases, smoking room, and auditorium contain ornate terra-cotta panels evoking theatrical themes, murals by George Peixotto, Robert Blum, and others; faience stairway balustrades; art tiles designed by Henry Mercer; and ornate plaster, stone, and wood carving. The theater has been closed for many years, and the interiors have deteriorated.

New York Central Building, now the Helmsley Building, 230 Park Avenue (Warren & Wetmore, 1927–29). The New York Central Building, set astride Park Avenue just north of Grand Central Terminal (see p. 77), was the linchpin of the Terminal City complex of hotels and office buildings sponsored by the New York Central Railroad. Designed by the same architects responsible for the exterior of the railroad terminal, this tower once dominated Park Avenue and the surrounding Midtown business district with its distinctive design and monumental pyramidal roof capped by an ornate cupola. **Interior:** The impressive lobby planned as a corridor connecting East 45th and 46th streets, echoes the grandeur of the exterior. The building's design and ornamentation celebrate the prowess of the New York Central Railroad, which had its headquarters on the premises. A sense of imperial grandeur is created by the marble walls and bronze detail, which includes extensive use of the railroad's initials. The Chinese red elevator doors open into cabs with red walls, wood moldings, gilt domes, and painted cloudscapes.

New York Public Library, Astor, Lenox and Tilden Foundation, 476 Fifth Avenue (Carrère & Hastings, 1898–1911). Carrère & Hastings's main building for the New York Public Library is perhaps the greatest masterpiece of Beaux-Arts design in the United States. The library, a private foundation housed in a city-owned building, was established in 1895 when the Astor Library (see p. 42), the Lenox Library, and the Tilden Trust (see p. 64) consolidated their holdings. The majestic building, constructed of Dorset marble from Vermont, is enormous in scale, yet its broad front stairs and projecting central pavilion are not overpowering. They draw the public into one of the world's leading research institutions. The exterior is embellished with sculpture by Edward Clark Potter (the lions), Frederick MacMonnies (the fountains), Paul Wayland Bartlett (figures above the entrances), and George Gray Barnard (the end pediments). The **interiors**, notably the main lobby (Astor Hall), staircases, and central hall, are distinguished by the outstanding quality of their design, materials, and construction. A major restoration of both the exterior and the interior was undertaken in the 1980s (Davis, Brody & Associates, architects).

New York Yacht Club, 37 West 44th Street (Warren & Wetmore, 1899–1900). This clubhouse in the Beaux-Arts style was the first building by the architects Warren & Wetmore, best known for their later work at Grand Central Terminal (see p. 77). It is one of the most lighthearted buildings of the era. As befits the home of the nation's most prestigious yacht club, the building presents a limestone facade designed on a nautical theme. The most prominent feature is the trio of windows carved to resemble the sterns of baroque galleons. Elsewhere on the ornate street front are seashells, dolphins, dripping seaweed, and other marine ornament.

Osborne Apartments, 205 West 57th Street (James E. Ware, 1883–85, enlargement of top story, 1889; addition, Alfred S. G. Taylor, 1906). The Osborne, an early luxury apartment building, is located in the area that, by the mid-1880s, was rapidly becoming the city's first center of apartment-house construction. Ware's robust Italian Renaissance–inspired building with medieval detail is clad in heavy, rock-faced blocks of red sandstone and features elegant carved ornamental panels. The building's plan—the Osborne contains duplex apartment units—is reflected in its elevations. There are 12 floors in the front and 14 toward the rear.

Palace Theater (interior), 1564–1566 Broadway (Kirchhoff & Rose, 1912–13). The legendary Palace Theater, built as a vaudeville house, has hosted a greater number of stars and a greater variety of entertainment than any other Broadway theater. Although built by Martin Beck, it was operated primarily by Beck's rival E. F. Albee of the Keith-Albee Circuit, which produced vaudeville nationwide. The first production at the Palace was a flop, but the appearance of Sarah Bernhardt in May 1913 marked the beginning of an era of unprecedented success. The Palace featured such great vaudeville stars as Bob Hope, Ed Wynn, Sophie Tucker, George Jessel, Will Rogers, Jimmy Durante, the Marx Brothers, W. C. Fields, Houdini, and Eddie Cantor. Succumbing to changes in the entertainment industry, the Palace became a movie house in 1932, but since the opening of *Sweet Charity* in 1966, it has become a theater for musicals. The theater was refurbished in 1990–91 (Fox & Fowle, architects) and reopened, appropriately, with *The Will Rogers Follies*.

Paramount Building, 1493–1501 Broadway (Rapp & Rapp, 1926–27). The theater architects Rapp & Rapp designed this dramatically massed skyscraper (at its completion, the tallest in the Times Square area) as offices for Paramount Pictures, as a home for the Paramount Theater (demolished), and as an advertisement for the Paramount Corporation. The motion picture company's trademark, a mountain encircled by five-pointed stars, is echoed in the mountainlike massing of the building and its surmounting four-faced clock, on which the hours are marked by five-pointed stars. The clock is crowned by a glass globe that, when illuminated, was visible for miles and became a focal point of the Times Square area.

Park Avenue Viaduct, also known as the Pershing Square Viaduct, Park Avenue from East 40th Street to Grand Central Terminal (Reed & Stem and Warren & Wetmore, 1917–19). Grand Central Terminal (see p. 77) was designed with complex systems for the efficient circulation of trains, surface traffic, and pedestrians. The Park Avenue Viaduct was planned by Reed & Stem as an expeditious way of moving traffic along Park Avenue and around the massive terminal. As designed by Warren & Wetmore (possibly with the assistance of Reed & Stem), the viaduct consists of three arches composed of steel girders cantilevered from granite piers; ornate iron railings run along the roadway above the arches.

Morton and Nellie Plant House, now Cartier, Inc., 651–653 Fifth Avenue and 2–4 East 52nd Street (Robert W. Gibson, 1903–05). The banker, yachtsman, and baseball club owner Morton Plant built this elegant Italian Renaissance–inspired house, which is the finest surviving mansion on Fifth Avenue south of 59th Street. The house and the adjacent **Edward and Frances Holbrook House** at 4 East 52nd Street (C. P. H. Gilbert, 1904–05) were successfully converted into a shop for the Cartier jewelry company by William W. Bosworth around 1917.

Plaza Hotel, 768 Fifth Avenue and 2 Central Park South (Henry J. Hardenbergh, 1905–07; addition, Warren & Wetmore, 1921). The Plaza's status as one of the world's great luxury hotels has been maintained since it opened in 1907. Located on a prominent site—overlooking Central Park (see p. 122), Grand Army Plaza (see p. 105), and Fifth Avenue—this elegant building was designed in a free adaptation of French Renaissance architecture, taking full advantage of the vistas provided by the surrounding open space. Warren & Wetmore's 58th Street addition is a simplified version of Hardenbergh's original design.

Plymouth Theater, 234–240 West 45th Street (Herbert J. Krapp, 1917–18). The Plymouth, planned by the Shuberts as a companion to the Broadhurst (see p. 69), has always been one of Broadway's most successful theaters. It has housed *Abe Lincoln in Illinois*, *Private Lives*, *Dial 'M' for Murder*, *The Caine Mutiny Court Martial*, *The Odd Couple*, *Plaza Suite*, and *Equus*. The Plymouth and the Broadhurst were the first designs of the prolific theater architect Herbert Krapp, and they reflect his interest in the use of patterned brickwork on the exterior and Adamesque design for the **interior**.

Public School 67, later the High School of the Performing Arts, 120 West 46th Street (C. B. J. Snyder, 1893–94). P.S. 67 is the first school known to have been designed by C. B. J. Snyder, who, as superintendent of school buildings to New York City's Board of Education for 30 years, was responsible for the design of many of the city's finest school buildings. This Romanesque Revival structure gained fame as the home of the High School of Performing Arts from the founding of the school in 1948 until 1985, when it moved to a new facility. The school's curriculum emphasizes studies in music, drama, and dance, and its graduates include Eliot Feld, Arthur Mitchell, Rita Moreno, Liza Minnelli, Al Pacino, Ben Vereen, and Edward Villella. Restoration of the building was initiated in 1991 following a fire.

Queensboro Bridge. See p. 197.

Racquet and Tennis Club, 370 Park Avenue (McKim, Mead & White, 1916–19). The Racquet and Tennis Club is one of the few survivors from the period when Park Avenue north of Grand Central Terminal was lined with luxurious masonry apartment houses and institutional buildings. In keeping with the prestige of the site chosen for its new home, the club engaged the services of McKim, Mead & White, even though by 1916 the firm's two leading designers, McKim and White, were no longer alive. A younger partner, William S. Richardson, was responsible for this project, designed in the form of an Italian Renaissance palazzo, the style that the firm had established for clubhouses almost 30 years earlier with their Century Association (see p. 70). The most interesting features of the subdued front elevation are the recessed loggia and the frieze in the form of a tennis net with crossed racquets.

Rockefeller Apartments, 17 West 54th Street and 24 West 55th Street (Harrison & Fouilhoux, 1935–37). In their simplicity, their use of industrial materials, their smooth wall surfaces, and especially their fenestration, these two brick apartment houses exemplify early International Style design in the United States. The windows consist of bands of metal sash, often grouped in curving bays, that provide 15 percent more light than required by city building codes. Commissioned by Nelson Rockefeller, these buildings represent the first of many collaborations between Rockefeller and Wallace K. Harrison.

Rockefeller Center (Associated Architects; other architects noted): **RCA Building and Lobby,** now the General Electric Building, 30 Rockefeller Plaza (1932–33); **RCA Building West,** now the General Electric Building, 1250 Sixth Avenue (1932–33); **RKO Building,** now the Amax Building, 1270 Sixth Avenue (1931–32); **Radio City Music Hall,** 1260 Sixth Avenue (1931–32); **British Empire Building,** now the British Building, 620 Fifth Avenue (1932–33); **La Maison Français,** 610 Fifth Avenue (1933); **Palazzo d'Italia,** 626 Fifth Avenue (1933–34); **International Building and Lobby,** 630 Fifth Avenue (1933–34); **International Building North,** 636 Fifth Avenue (1933–34); the former **Time-Life Building,** now 1 Rockefeller Plaza (1936–37); **Associated Press Building,** 50 Rockefeller Plaza (1938); the former **Eastern Airlines Building,** now 10 Rockefeller Plaza (1939); **U.S. Rubber Company Building,** now the Simon & Schuster Building, 1230 Sixth Avenue (1939; extension, Harrison & Abramovitz, 1954–55); **Esso Building,** now the Warner Communications Building, 75 Rockefeller Plaza (Carson & Lundin, 1946–47); **Manufacturers Hanover Trust Building,** 600 Fifth Avenue (Carson & Lundin, 1950–52); **Promenade,** also known as Channel Gardens; **Sunken Plaza; Rockefeller Plaza; and Rooftop Gardens.** Rockefeller Center, one of America's most significant architectural and urban design projects, has been copied many times, but it has never been equaled. The center, which incorporated office buildings, stores, theaters, and open space, united a sophisticated business sense with good design to create the largest privately sponsored real estate venture ever undertaken in New York City. The genesis of Rockefeller Center was the desire of John D. Rockefeller, Jr., to help the Metropolitan Opera build a new home. Rockefeller agreed to lease a large plot of land—bounded by 48th and 51st streets, Fifth and Sixth avenues—on which the new opera house would be built and where Rockefeller would erect a series of profitable office buildings. Unfortunately, the stock market crash of 1929 forced the Met to abandon the project. Despite the Depression and the withdrawal of the opera company, Rockefeller and his advisers continued to plan a large commercial complex. The layout and the design of the original buildings were handled by the Associated Architects, a group directed by Raymond Hood that included the architects Reinhard & Hofmeister, advisors to Rockefeller since the inception of the project, and Corbett, Harrison & MacMurray, specialists in skyscraper design. The plan consisted of a monumental central building—the RCA Building—surrounded by smaller office towers, low-rise buildings on Fifth Avenue that were to be leased to foreign tenants, and strategically placed open spaces such as the promenade (popularly known as the Channel Gardens because it runs between the British and French buildings) and the sunken plaza that would draw people into the underground shops. The limestone-faced buildings combine simple modern massing with a traditional artistic scheme. All of the art works in Rockefeller Center have humanistic themes—e.g., progress through science, technology and peace through international understanding. Among the most famous pieces are Paul Manship's *Prometheus*, Lee Lawrie's *Apollo*, and the RCA Building's lobby murals by Jose Maria Sert (in part replacing murals by Diego Rivera) and Frank Brangwyn. The success of the initial project led Rockefeller to plan additional buildings on sites adjacent to the original complex.

The major entertainment facility at Rockefeller Center is Radio City Music Hall. Opened in 1932, this 6,200-seat theater—the world's largest at the time of its construction—was planned by the impresario Samuel Rothafel (better known as "Roxy") for live entertainment, but soon became a movie theater in which the feature films were preceded by stage shows starring the precision dancers known as the Roxyettes (later the Rockettes). On the **interior,** the huge auditorium was planned to be as intimate as possible. It consists of a great arched proscenium in the form of a rising sun and a large orchestra with three shallow balconies. The decoration of the theater was undertaken by Donald Deskey, who created a modern, well-integrated scheme for the carpets, wall coverings, and furnishings. Like other Rockefeller Center buildings, the theater contains several major art works, including Ezra Winter's monumental foyer mural, *Fountain of Youth,* and a series of murals in the men's and women's lounges.

Rodin Studios, 200 West 57th Street (Cass Gilbert, 1916–17). Named for one of the most innovative artists living at the time, the Rodin was the latest of the series of buildings erected in Manhattan in the first years of the 20th century to provide combined studio and residential space for artists. The building contains double-height studios, most of them facing north onto 57th Street, and duplex living units at the rear. The building has a reinforced concrete frame that is clad in polychromatic rough brick with extensive iron and terra-cotta trim in a French Gothic style that complements the American Fine Arts Society (see p. 67) across the street. Cass Gilbert had previously used this style on his Woolworth Building (see p. 44). The Rodin Studios now house offices, and the duplex units have been subdivided.

Roosevelt Hospital, William J. Syms Operating Theater, 400 West 59th Street (W. Wheeler Smith, 1890–92). W. Wheeler Smith worked in conjunction with the prominent surgeon Charles McBurney to create the most advanced operating theater in the world for Roosevelt Hospital. Dr. McBurney examined modern operating facilities throughout Europe and America before he accepted a final design. Although the building has been converted internally for other hospital uses, its distinctive form (a rectangle with a semi-conical roof) and utilitarian appearance continue to express its original function.

Royale Theater, 242–250 West 45th Street (Herbert J. Krapp, 1926–27). The Royale and its neighbors, the Theater Masque (see p. 83) and the Majestic (see p. 83), were built as a trio by Irwin Chanin and all were designed in the "modern Spanish" style that he favored. The **interior** continues the Spanish-inspired detail and is particularly notable for the groin-vaulted ceiling of the auditorium, which features a large mural by Willy Pogany entitled *Lovers of Spain*. One of the most popular theaters on Broadway, the Royale has been home to *Diamond Lil* (starring Mae West), *The Magnificent Yankee*, Moss Hart's *Light Up the Sky*, Julie Andrews's American debut in *The Boy Friend*, Thornton Wilder's *The Matchmaker*, Laurence Olivier in *The Entertainer*, Tennessee Williams's *Night of the Iguana*, and *The Subject Was Roses*.

St. Bartholomew's Church (Episcopal) and Community House, Park Avenue at East 50th Street (Bertram Goodhue, 1914–19; community house, Mayers, Murray & Phillip, 1926–28). Superbly sited in a terraced garden amidst the corporate towers of Park Avenue, the Byzantine-inspired St. Bartholomew's is an outstanding example of the work of Goodhue. The church was constructed of fine materials—salmon-colored brick highlighted with bands of limestone—and is ornamented with carvings, many of them representative of the life of St. Bartholomew. The famous triple-arched entrance portal (1900–03), designed by McKim, Mead & White for the congregation's previous home on Madison Avenue, was a memorial to Cornelius Vanderbilt II; Goodhue was required to incorporate this element into his design. The entrance, with its bronze doors and carved panels, the work of Daniel Chester French and Andrew O'Connor (central bay), Herbert Adams (north), and Philip Martiny (south), was modeled on the portal to the Provençal Romanesque church of St. Gilles-du-Gard near Arles. The community house, designed by Goodhue's successor firm after his death, is completely in harmony with the church.

Church of St. Mary-the-Virgin (Episcopal) Complex, 133–145 West 46th Street (Pierre Le Brun, architect in charge, Napoleon Le Brun & Sons, 1894–95). This Midtown church complex consists of a French Gothic–inspired limestone-clad church, its flanking brick-clad clergy house and mission house, and a brick-clad rectory and lady chapel that face onto West 47th Street. The church was built for a congregation in the forefront of the American Anglo-Catholic movement, and the buildings were planned to further Anglo-Catholic worship. J. Massey Rhind's extensive sculptural decoration complements Pierre Le Brun's design. St. Mary's is thought to be the first church built with a steel frame.

St. Patrick's Cathedral (R.C.) Complex, Fifth Avenue at East 50th Street (cathedral, rectory, and cardinal's residence, James Renwick, Jr., 1853–88; lady chapel, Charles T. Mathews, 1901–06). In 1852, when New York's Roman Catholic archdiocese purchased the site for a new cathedral, the area near Fifth Avenue and 50th Street was relatively uninhabited, but by the time St. Patrick's was inaugurated in 1879 (the spires were not completed until 1888) the area had become one of the city's finest residential districts. James Renwick's design was influenced by continental Gothic buildings, in particular Cologne Cathedral. Although the marble building was not constructed exactly to Renwick's specifications (several major structural changes were made), his Fifth Avenue facade, with its three entrances and twin spires, is among the most impressive 19th-century ecclesiastical works in America. Early in the 20th century Renwick's east front was removed and reconstructed at Our Lady of Lourdes Church (see p. 149) and the present lady chapel was built.

St. Regis Hotel, 699–703 Fifth Avenue and 2 East 55th Street (Trowbridge & Livingston, 1901–04; extension, Sloan & Robertson, 1927). Planned by Col. John Jacob Astor as New York's finest luxury hotel, the St. Regis is among the most elegant Beaux-Arts buildings in the city. As befits its location on New York's most prestigious avenue, the hotel "established a new standard of excellence . . . superior to that of any hotel in this country, and probably over any hotel in the world," commented one critic on the occasion of the hotel's opening. The 1927 addition complements the original design. The hotel reopened, following an extensive refurbishing, in 1991.

St. Thomas Church (Episcopal) and Parish House, Fifth Avenue at West 53rd Street (Cram, Goodhue & Ferguson, 1906–13). St. Thomas, a major design by Cram, Goodhue & Ferguson, is a limestone-faced building that makes dramatic use of its corner site. Replacing a church that burned in 1905, the neo-Gothic design, with an asymmetrically placed tower, combines features from English and French medieval architecture. The initial plan for the church was devised by Ralph Adams Cram, but it appears to have been Goodhue who developed the idea into the magnificent building that was erected in 1911–13.

Saks Fifth Avenue, 611 Fifth Avenue (Starrett & Van Vleck, 1922–24). The department store specialists Starrett & Van Vleck designed this luxurious emporium in 1922 in a Renaissance-inspired style appropriate to the exclusive commercial character of Fifth Avenue. Saks's relocation from Herald Square to Fifth Avenue at East 50th Street marks the final chapter in the northward migration of Manhattan's large retail stores, a development that began early in the 19th century.

Scribner Building, 597 Fifth Avenue (Ernest Flagg, 1912–13). Almost two decades after moving into its building at 153–157 Fifth Avenue, between 21st and 22nd streets (see p. 61), Charles Scribner's Sons followed Manhattan's fashionable retailers to Midtown. Ernest Flagg, Charles Scribner II's brother-in-law, was again commissioned to design a store and office building for the firm. Flagg elaborated on his earlier design, which had become an identifiable image of the Scribner firm, and created a 10-story, French-inspired, limestone-fronted building with a facade that reflects the nature of the steel skeleton frame. The store retains its elegant iron shopfront. As befits a prestigious bookstore, the vaulted **interior** was designed to resemble a small library.

Seagram Building, 375 Park Avenue (Ludwig Mies van der Rohe with Philip Johnson and Kahn & Jacobs, 1956–58). The only building in New York designed by the modern master Mies van der Rohe, the Seagram Building is considered to be the greatest of the International Style skyscrapers erected in the postwar era, when this style became a symbol of corporate America. Seagram's president, Samuel Bronfman, and his daughter, the architect Phyllis Lambert, selected Mies and gave him a virtually unlimited budget for the project. The juxtaposition of the extruded bronze frame with the rectangular bronze spandrel panels and transparent glass surfaces of the curtain wall creates the tight geometry and the contrast between solid and void that typify the finest International Style design. The tower rises behind a plaza with a pair of fountains. **Interior:** The fine materials and careful detailing of the exterior are evident in the lobby, designed by Philip Johnson, with its travertine walls and floor, bronze mullions, and elevator cabs with stainless steel and bronze mesh panels. The stairs at the rear lead to the Four Seasons Restaurant (see p. 75).

Shubert Theater, 221–233 West 44th Street (Henry B. Herts, 1912–13). This is the flagship playhouse of the Shubert Organization, a major force in the construction of theaters and the production of plays in New York and elsewhere in the United States since the early 20th century. Built as a memorial to Sam Shubert, the oldest of the three Shubert brothers, the building also served as the headquarters of the Shubert theatrical empire. The theater was designed in a lavish manner with Venetian Renaissance sgraffito decoration on the exterior and, on the **interior,** elaborate plasterwork and murals by J. Mortimer Lichtenauer. The Shubert has been home to many hit productions, among them the record-breaking *A Chorus Line.*

Sidewalk Clock (see p. 62), 522 Fifth Avenue at West 44th Street (Seth Thomas Company, 1907). Installed on Fifth Avenue at West 43rd Street by the American Trust Company, this clock was moved to its present location, a block further north, in the 1930s. The clock has an unusually ornate base and is crowned by a cast-iron pineapple.

✦ **Sniffen Court Historic District**. New York City's smallest historic district consists of 10 round-arched stables erected in 1863–64 on a small court set perpendicular to East 36th Street between Lexington and Third avenues. Although the source of the court's name is obscure, it is believed that it recalls John Sniffen, a local builder. In the 1920s the modest two-story brick buildings were converted into stylish residences. One stable became the home and studio of the

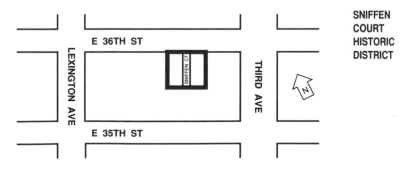

SNIFFEN COURT HISTORIC DISTRICT

sculptor Malvina Hoffman, several of whose works adorn the wall at the far end of the alley.

Moses Allen and Alice Dunning Starr House, also known as the 5 West 54th Street House (R. H. Robertson, 1897–99). The neurologist Moses Starr commissioned this meticulously detailed town house at a time when many wealthy New Yorkers were building houses in the area; it is one of five adjacent town houses erected in the late 1890s that are designated landmarks. The subtle Renaissance-inspired building has a limestone base; its upper floors are clad in Roman brick trimmed with limestone.

Tiffany & Co. Building, 397–409 Fifth Avenue (McKim, Mead & White, 1903–06). Upon the completion of this Italian Renaissance–inspired white marble palace, Tiffany & Co. became one of the first large stores to move north of 34th Street on Fifth Avenue. Stanford White's sophisticated design, closely modeled on the 16th-century Palazzo Grimani in Venice, adapted Sanmicheli's residential design to the needs of a prestigious jewelry emporium. The building now houses the offices of News World Communications and has stores on the first floor.

Town Hall, 113–123 West 43rd Street (McKim, Mead & White, 1919–21). Town Hall was built by the League for Political Education as a meeting hall for the city. It was planned to accommodate lectures, concerts, and movies and to serve as a clubhouse for members of the league. As soon as it opened, Town Hall became a popular venue for speaking engagements; guest speakers included many of the most eminent figures of the 20th century, among them Theodore Roosevelt, Henry James, Booker T. Washington, Margaret Sanger, Winston Churchill, and Woodrow Wilson. The **interior** includes a simple lobby and a Colonial Revival auditorium that is celebrated for its acoustics.

🍎 **Tudor City Historic District.** Fred F. French, one of New York's most active developers following World War I, began buying dilapidated row houses and tenements on the far east end of 42nd Street in 1925. In December of that year he announced that construction would begin on "the largest housing project ever undertaken in mid-Manhattan." French and his architectural staff, headed by H. Douglas Ives, designed a complex of apartment houses and apartment hotels with Tudor detail. The choice of a homey Tudor style, the location of the development on a bluff set apart from its surroundings, the absence of through streets, and the presence of two small private parks lent a suburban character to the complex. This ambience was appropriate since Tudor City sought to attract middle-class tenants who might have moved to the suburbs had they not been sufficiently impressed by the community's amenities and its convenient proximity to the nearby Midtown commercial district.

🍎 **Turtle Bay Gardens Historic District.** As part of a movement to reclaim the deteriorated brownstone row houses of the East Midtown area, Mrs. Walton Martin purchased 20 run-down houses on East 48th and 49th streets in 1919–20. She commissioned Edward C. Dean and William Lawrence Bottomley to renovate the houses into single-family units and apartments, to

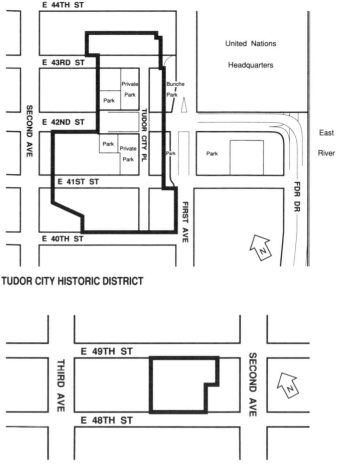

TUDOR CITY HISTORIC DISTRICT

TURTLE BAY GARDENS HISTORIC DISTRICT

redesign the facades, and to combine the rear yards into an Italian Renaissance–inspired garden. Mrs. Martin had iron turtles placed on the fence-posts and dubbed the development Turtle Bay Gardens. Ever since, the beautiful enclave has attracted people in the arts, including the architect Edward Dean, Katharine Hepburn, Mary Martin, Tyrone Power, Stephen Sondheim, Leopold Stokowski, and E. B. White.

University Club, 1 West 54th Street (McKim, Mead & White, 1896–1900). Charles McKim designed the University Club in the spirit of Italian High Renaissance palazzi. The nine-story structure is divided into three horizontal sections, each defined by the tall arched windows that light the clubhouse's major rooms (lounge, library, and dining room); subsidiary floors are subtly placed between them. The building is faced with pink Milford granite and ornamented with the seals of various universities, executed in marble by Daniel Chester French, and a large club seal by Kenyon Cox.

Villard Houses, now the Helmsley Palace Hotel and the Urban Center, 451–457 Madison Avenue and 24 East 51st Street (McKim, Mead & White, 1882–85). Commissioned by the railroad entrepreneur Henry Villard, this masterpiece of late 19th-century urban design involved the skillful combination of six brownstone houses into a single monumental U-shaped unit set around an open court. The complex is not only one of the most beautiful in New York, but was also among the first major projects in the United States to adapt specific European architectural precedents. In this case, the architect Joseph M. Wells of the McKim, Mead & White office took as a model the Palazzo della Cancelleria in Rome. The massing, arcades, window enframements, and rosette details of the Roman palace were used in the New York project, but in a novel manner, to accord with the New York site and with the demands of a late 19th-century residential commission. In the early 1970s demolition of the complex was threatened, but in 1975–76 the houses were incorporated into the Helmsley Palace Hotel and the north wing was reserved as office and gallery space for organizations involved in architectural and design issues.

13 and 15 West 54th Street Houses (Henry J. Hardenbergh, 1896–97). This pair of houses, two of five adjoining landmark town houses, was built as a speculative venture. Hardenbergh's love of Northern European architecture, evident at his famous Dakota Apartments (see p. 125), is also seen in these two residences with their banded window enframements and tapered pilasters. In 1906 No. 13 was purchased by John D. Rockefeller; it was the home of his son, John D. Rockefeller, Jr., until about 1918. Later, Governor Nelson Rockefeller of New York used the house as an office; he died here in 1979. Nelson Rockefeller purchased No. 15 in 1955 and for many years it housed the Museum of Primitive Art (now the Michael Rockefeller Collection at the Metropolitan Museum of Art).

Winter Garden Theater (interior), 1634–1646 Broadway (W. Albert Swasey, 1910–11; remodeling, Herbert J. Krapp, 1922–23). Built around 1885 as the American Horse Exchange, a stable and auction mart, this building was converted into a theater in 1910–11 for the Shuberts. The present seating arrangement and decor date largely from the remodeling of 1922–23. The enormous theater contains some of Krapp's finest Adamesque ornament. In its early years the Winter Garden attracted lavish revues; it premiered with *La Belle Paree*, which introduced Al Jolson. The revamped theater attracted both revues, such as the *Ziegfeld Follies* of 1934, which starred Fanny Brice, and a series of musicals, including *Wonderful Town*, *West Side Story*, *Funny Girl*, *Mame*, *Pacific Overtures*, and *Cats*.

59TH STREET TO 110TH STREET, EAST SIDE

Thatcher and Frances Adams House, also known as the 63 East 79th Street House (Adams & Warren, 1902–03). Designed in an English neoclassical manner for a wealthy lawyer and his wife, this brick and limestone town house is one of a group of four landmark houses located on the north side of East 79th Street.

The Arsenal, now the Administration Building of the New York City Department of Parks and Recreation, Central Park at East 64th Street (Martin E. Thompson, 1847–51). Built "to house and protect the arms of the state," the Arsenal was designed as a mock-medieval castle, complete with octagonal towers. After only a few years of use as an arsenal, the structure was converted into a police station; it later served as the first home of the American Museum of Natural History. In 1934 the building became the headquarters of New York City's Parks Department.

Vincent and Helen Astor House, now the Junior League of the City of New York, 130 East 80th Street (Mott B. Schmidt, 1927–28). One of four large adjacent landmark town houses dating from the 1920s, this limestone structure is closely modeled on Robert Adam's Society of Arts Building at the Adelphi in London. The house was erected by the millionaire real estate owner and social reformer Vincent Astor, head of the American branch of the Astor family. Astor's fortune was used to establish the Vincent Astor Fund, which benefits major social welfare projects in New York City and assists such institutions as the New York Public Library.

George F. Baker, Jr., House Complex, now (in part) the Russian Orthodox Church Outside of Russia, 67, 69, and 75 East 93rd Street (No. 75, main house, 1917–18; ballroom wing, 1928; No. 69, 1928–29; No. 67, 1931—all by Delano & Aldrich). The main section of this complex, at the corner of Park Avenue and East 93rd Street, was commissioned by the financier Francis F. Palmer. Ten years after it was begun the elegant town house was sold to George F. Baker, Jr., chairman of the First National Bank (now Citibank). Baker enlarged the house, first by the addition of a ballroom wing and garage (No. 69 East 93rd Street) and the creation of an open court to the west of the house, and later by the addition of 67 East 93rd Street, intended as a home for Baker's father, who died prior to the house's completion. The entire complex is a superb example of Delano & Aldrich's sophisticated handling of English and American 18th-century architectural forms. In 1958 the main house and its ballroom wing were converted for use as a Russian Orthodox church; a courtyard stairway was built to facilitate this new use.

R. Livingston and Eleanor T. Beeckman House, now the Permanent Mission of Yugoslavia to the United Nations, 854 Fifth Avenue (Warren & Wetmore, 1903–05). This elegant limestone dwelling, one of the few mansions still standing on Fifth Avenue, is in the style of the urban town houses erected in France during the reign of Louis XV. It was built for Robert Livingston Beeckman, a member of a prominent New York family, and was purchased by the Yugoslav government in 1946.

James A. and Florence Sloane Burden House, now the Convent of the Sacred Heart, 7 East 91st Street (Warren & Wetmore, 1902–05). William Sloane and his wife, Emily Vanderbilt Sloane, built this house and the neighboring Hammond House (see p. 106) for their daughters on land purchased from Andrew Carnegie, whose own house is across the street (see p. 99) and who acquired a significant amount of property in the neighborhood in order to regulate its development. Warren & Wetmore provided Florence Sloane and her husband, James A. Burden, Jr. (son of the founder of the Burden Ironworks), with a grand limestone-clad Beaux-Arts mansion with facades fronting both the street and the drive set between the two houses.

Mrs. Amory S. Carhart House, now Lycée Français de New-York, 3 East 95th Street (Horace Trumbauer, 1913–16). Designed to resemble a Parisian town house from the era of Louis XVI, this elegant neoclassical limestone building is the work of the Philadelphia architect Horace Trumbauer. Mrs. Carhart commissioned the house a year after her husband's death, but lived here only briefly before her own death in 1918.

✦ **Carnegie Hill Historic District**. The development of the neighborhood now known as Carnegie Hill took place in two stages. The first period of construction commenced in the 1880s when row houses built on speculation began to appear on the side streets. The second phase was inaugurated by Andrew Carnegie, who purchased the Fifth Avenue blockfront between East 90th and 91st streets in 1898 for the construction of a large mansion (p. 99). In the first decades of the 20th century other wealthy families moved to the area, building large new houses or redesigning the older row houses. The historic district contains representative examples of the popular styles of the period.

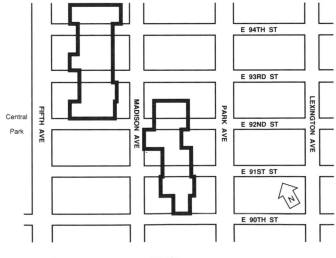

CARNEGIE HILL HISTORIC DISTRICT

Andrew and Louise Carnegie House, now the Cooper-Hewitt Museum, 2 East 91st Street (Babb, Cook & Willard, 1899–1903). After Andrew Carnegie purchased this large plot on a relatively undeveloped section of Fifth Avenue, he evicted a few squatters and demolished a riding academy and several tenements so that he could build what he envisioned as "the most modest, plainest and most roomy house in New York." The 64-room house synthesized "modest and plain" Georgian-inspired brickwork with Beaux-Arts ornament and incorporated the most advanced mechanical and structural systems of the day. Carnegie chose the site because it permitted him to lay out a large garden; the original landscape plan, probably by Schermerhorn & Foulks, is largely extant. In 1972 the mansion became the property of the Smithsonian Institution, which commissioned architect Hugh Hardy to convert the building into a museum of design. The Carnegie site also includes the Colonial Revival George L. McAlpin House at 9 East 90th Street (George Keister, 1902–03), which became the home of Carnegie's daughter in 1920.

City and Suburban Homes Company, Avenue A (York Avenue) Estate (in part), 1470–1492 York Avenue, 501–531 East 78th Street, and 502–528 East 79th Street (Harde & Short, Percy Griffin, and Philip H. Ohm, 1900–13). The Avenue A Estate was, at the time of its completion, the largest "model tenement" complex ever built. It was a project of the City and Suburban Homes Company, a limited-dividend corporation dedicated to the construction of decent affordable housing for the working poor. The company was founded and supported by some of New York's most prominent citizens, who when investing in City and Suburban shares agreed to limit their return to five percent. City and Suburban's development projects were experimental housing; thus the various buildings have different plans and room arrangements. All are clad in brick and feature modest amounts of ornament. Of special interest are the Potter Memorial buildings at 516 and 520 East 79th Street, designed in an appropriate neo-Gothic style as a memorial to the Episcopal bishop Henry C. Potter.

City and Suburban Homes Company, First Avenue Estate (in part), 1168–1200 First Avenue, 401–423 East 64th Street, and 402–416 East 65th Street (James E. Ware, James E. Ware & Son[s], and Philip H. Ohm, 1898–1915). The First Avenue Estate is the oldest extant project built by the City and Suburban Homes Company. This complex was begun before the Avenue A Estate (see above), but it was completed later. The light-colored brick buildings were designed by James E. Ware, an architect active in the design of housing for the working poor, and by City and Suburban's own architect, Philip Ohm. Since their completion, the model tenements have housed large numbers of working people in quality apartments of a sort not easily found in New York City by those with limited income.

J. William and Margaretta C. Clark House, later Automation House, now Richard Feigen & Co., 49 East 68th Street (Trowbridge & Livingston, 1913–14). The socially well-connected architecture firm of Trowbridge & Livingston designed this Colonial Revival house for the family of J. William

Clark, heir to the Clark sewing thread fortune. Restored in 1991 by Buttrick, White & Burtis, the town house has elegant Federal-inspired detail, including a pair of arched openings on the ground floor and a variety of window lintels on the upper floors.

Ogden Codman House, now Manhattan Country School, 7 East 96th Street (Ogden Codman, 1912–13). Ogden Codman, one of the most important residential architects and interior designers of the early 20th century, designed this house for himself. Codman's advocacy of French design is reflected in the facade, which is modeled after that of an 18th-century Parisian town house.

Lucy Dahlgren House, later the Pierre Cartier House, 15 East 96th Street (Ogden Codman, 1915–16). The Dahlgren House is a companion to Codman's own house nearby (see above). This French neoclassical town house was built for the socially prominent and enormously wealthy heiress Lucy Drexel Dahlgren, who apparently spent little time here. For many years the house was occupied by Pierre Cartier, founder of the jewelry firm that bears his name.

Henry P. and Kate T. Davison House, now the Consulate General of Italy, 690 Park Avenue (Walker & Gillette, 1916–17). Henry P. Davison, one of the founders of Bankers Trust, commissioned this Colonial Revival brick house, the second of four related landmark buildings that create the unique blockfront of Park Avenue between East 68th and 69th streets. The construction of these houses reflects the development of Park Avenue as a prestigious residential neighborhood following the covering of the avenue's railroad tracks around 1910. The building served as a residence until 1952, when it was converted into the Italian consulate.

Reginald and Anna DeKoven House, 1025 Park Avenue (John Russell Pope, 1911–12). The light opera composer Reginald DeKoven and his wife, the writer Anna DeKoven, commissioned this brick and limestone mansion from John Russell Pope, an architect best known for his austere classical buildings. Built after work was completed on the roofing of the Park Avenue railroad tracks, and designed in the Jacobean Revival style, the house provides evidence of Pope's wide-ranging architectural talents.

Clarence and Anne Douglass Dillon House, also known as the 124 East 80th Street House (Mott B. Schmidt, 1930). This four-story brick house, the last of the four large landmark town houses in the English neoclassical style erected on the south side of East 80th Street between 1922 and 1930, was commissioned by the financier Clarence Dillon and his wife, Anne. Their son, C. Douglas Dillon, would later serve as secretary of the treasury. The Dillon House and its neighbor, the Vincent Astor House (see p. 97), are fine examples of the sophisticated work of Mott B. Schmidt, a popular society architect who specialized in the design of residences in 18th-century revival styles.

Benjamin N. and Sarah Duke House, also known as the 1009 Fifth Avenue House (Welch, Smith & Provot, 1899–1901). Soon after its completion, this Beaux-Arts house was sold to Benjamin N. Duke, a director of the American Tobacco Company. In 1907 Benjamin's brother James purchased the house,

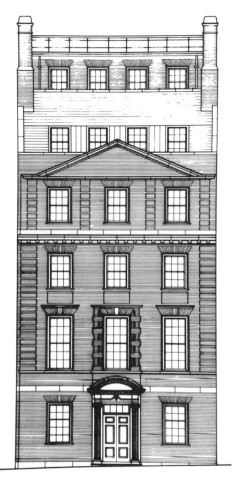

Clarence and Anne Douglass Dillon House, 124 East 80th Street (Mott B. Schmidt, 1930). Drawing: Robert Hartman

where he lived until the completion of his own nearby mansion (see below) in 1912. Since then the house has been occupied by other members of the Duke family. A superb restoration was completed in 1985.

James B. and Nanaline Duke House, now the New York University Institute of Fine Arts, 1 East 78th Street (Horace Trumbauer, 1909–12). This enormous freestanding house, modeled on the 18th-century Château Labottière in Bordeaux, is one of the most magnificent mansions in New York. Duke was born a poor farm boy in North Carolina and eventually rose to become a figure of unrivaled power in the American tobacco industry. Nanaline Duke and her daughter Doris gave the mansion to New York University in 1957, and it has been successfully adapted for use as the university's graduate school of art history.

45 East 66th Street Apartments (Harde & Short, 1906–08). The firm of Harde & Short was responsible for several of New York's most flamboyant apartment buildings in the early years of this century, including the Red House (see p. 128), Alwyn Court (see p. 67), and this impressive structure on the corner of East 66th Street and Madison Avenue. As is characteristic of the architects' work, the street facades of this building have large expanses of glazing and a profusion of French Gothic–inspired terra-cotta detail.

131–135 East 66th Street Apartments (Charles A. Platt and Simonson, Pollard & Steinam, 1905–06). This distinguished limestone-fronted building reflects the popular adaptation of the Italian Renaissance palazzo form to the

45 East 66th Street Apartments (Harde & Short, 1906–08).
Photo: Caroline Kane

New York apartment house. The cooperative was the first apartment house designed by the prestigious architect Charles A. Platt, who worked here in association with a firm that specialized in the design of buildings with double-height artists' studios and duplex living quarters. Platt himself moved into the building upon its completion.

130–134 East 67th Street Apartments (Rossiter & Wright, 1907). This building, on the corner of Lexington Avenue and East 67th Street, was designed as a pendant to the adjacent apartment house at 131–135 East 66th Street (see above). Like its neighbor, the East 67th Street structure is a cooperative building, faced in limestone and designed in the Italian Renaissance style; it does not, however, contain double-height studios.

11 East 70th Street House (John H. Duncan, 1909–10). Of the five landmark town houses on this block, No. 11 is the only one built on speculation. The builder Cornelius Luyster, Jr., commissioned the dwelling from the well-known architect John Duncan, who designed a subdued residence in the French neoclassical style.

161–179 and 166–182 East 73rd Street Buildings (Nos. 161 and 163, Thomas Rae, 1896–97; Nos. 165 and 167, George L. Amoroux, 1903–04; No. 171, 1860; No. 173, Hobart H. Walker, 1893; No. 175, 1860; No. 177–179, Charles F. Hoppe, 1906; No. 166, Richard M. Hunt, 1883–84; No. 168, Charles W. Romeyn, 1899; No. 170, Frank Wennemer, 1890–91; No. 172–174, Frank Wennemer, 1889; No. 178, John H. Friend, 1902; No. 180, William Schickel & Co., 1890–91; No. 182, Andrew Spense Mayer, 1890). Beginning in the final decades of the 19th century, as the blocks of the Upper East Side between Fifth and Park avenues were being transformed into streets of mansions and town houses erected for New York's wealthiest citizens, many of the streets to the east were redeveloped with carriage houses. These carriage houses were erected in locations that were convenient to the large houses but sufficiently far away that the smells and noise of the stables did not mar the quality of life on the residential streets. In the years immediately preceding these developments, East 73rd Street between Lexington and Third avenues was lined with modest row houses erected around 1860; two of these buildings, Nos. 171 and 175 have survived. In 1883 Richard Morris Hunt designed the first private carriage house on the street, a Romanesque Revival building at No. 166, built for Henry G. Marquand, for whom Hunt also designed a lavish mansion on Madison Avenue. The 10 carriage houses that followed were erected either by individuals for their own use or by speculative builders who sold the structures to nearby residents. The most distinguished of these is No. 168, a neo-Flemish building complete with stepped gable and strapwork ornament designed for banker William Baylis. Since only the very wealthy could afford to maintain a private carriage house, most people who owned horses boarded them in commercial stables such as the five-story Romanesque Revival building at No. 182. In the early years of the 20th century, the majority of the carriage houses and stables were converted for automotive use. In this same period, commercial garages, such as the handsome building in the Beaux-Arts style at No. 177–179, began to appear in the neighborhood. By the 1920s, as the maintenance of a private garage became prohibitively expensive, most of the carriage houses were converted into private residences. At the same time, the two surviving row houses were rehabilitated, each by a prominent New York architect for his own residence—Erastus D. Litchfield at No. 171 and Francis L. Pell at No. 175.

157, 159, 161, 163, and 165 East 78th Street Houses (1861). These five brick houses with Italianate elements survive from a row of 11 erected by the builder Henry Armstrong at the time when the Upper East Side was just beginning to attract middle-class homeowners. Nos. 163 and 165 have been combined into a single residence.

208, 210, 212, 214, 216, and 218 East 78th Street Houses (1861–65). These six narrow Italianate row houses, erected as part of a speculative venture that included the construction of 15 identical red brick houses, were built just after the streets of Yorkville were opened in 1860. The unusual, elliptically arched doors and windows on the facades lend a rhythmic pattern to the streetscape.

146, 148, 150, 152, 154, and 156 East 89th Street Houses (Hubert, Pirsson & Co., 1886–87). Six houses survive from an original group of 10 picturesque Queen Anne dwellings erected by William Rhinelander, whose family had acquired this land in 1812. The narrow houses were designed as a unit with richly textured facades, projecting oriels, and a continuous mansard roof pierced by gables, dormers, and tall brick chimneys.

17 East 90th Street House (F. Burrall Hoffman, Jr., 1917–19). This handsome Colonial Revival brick house with an unusual street-level arcade was commissioned by Robert and Charlotte Fowler, who apparently never lived here, since the property was sold in 1919.

120 and 122 East 92nd Street Houses (1859 and 1871). These two vernacular frame houses recall the period before intense urbanization altered the semirural character of the Upper East Side. Each of the houses has a deep front porch, heavy window surrounds, and a bracketed cornice—all typical features of Italianate design.

160 East 92nd Street House (attributed to Albro Howell, carpenter-builder, 1852–53). One of the few residences to survive from the period when Yorkville was a country village, this vernacular frame house is surprisingly well preserved. The original Corinthian columns of the front porch were replaced around 1930.

East River Houses, later the Shively Sanitary Tenements, now the Cherokee Apartments, 507–523 East 77th Street and 508–522 East 78th Street (Henry Atterbury Smith, 1910–11). The East River Houses were erected in response to two of New York City's most pressing social problems—a serious tuberculosis epidemic and the need for affordable housing. These "model tenements," sponsored by Mrs. William K. Vanderbilt, were intended to house working people, especially families in which a member suffered from tuberculosis. The idea for this complex was conceived by Henry Shively, a physician and an expert on consumption. The tenements were designed by architect and housing reformer Henry Atterbury Smith, with large central courts, triple-sash windows, balconies supported by Guastavino vaults, and open stair towers—all features maximizing the amount of sunlight and fresh air that reached each apartment. The buildings underwent an extensive exterior restoration in 1989–90.

Ernesto and Edith Fabbri House, now the House of the Redeemer, 7 East 95th Street (Egisto Fabbri and Grosvenor Atterbury, 1914–16). Edith Fabbri, a great-granddaughter of Cornelius Vanderbilt, and her husband, the Italian count Ernesto Fabbri built this L-shaped, Italian Renaissance–inspired house; his family's coat of arms, an arm holding a hammer, is visible in the iron gate at the courtyard. Although Atterbury is the architect of record, it is apparently Count Fabbri's brother, the Italian architect and interior designer Egisto Fabbri, who was responsible for the actual design. In 1949 Mrs. Fabbri transferred the property to the House of the Redeemer, an Episcopal retreat center.

998 Fifth Avenue Apartments (McKim, Mead & White, 1910–14). This magnificent Italian Renaissance–inspired building was the first luxury apartment house erected on Fifth Avenue north of 59th Street. The expansive simplex and duplex units appealed to an elite clientele, and the building was rapidly rented. The limestone-clad structure became the model for hundreds of buildings later erected on Fifth, Park, and other avenues.

Oliver D. and Mary Pyne Filley House, now the Spanish Institute, 684 Park Avenue (McKim, Mead & White, 1925–26). The last of the four landmark Colonial Revival town houses on this block, this house was built for the daughter and son-in-law of Percy and Maud Pyne—for whom McKim, Mead &

White had designed the adjacent house (see p. 113) 16 years earlier—on the site of the Pynes' garden.

Henry Clay and Adelaide Childs Frick House, now the Frick Collection and Frick Art Reference Library, 1 East 70th Street and 10 East 71st Street (Carrère & Hastings, 1913–14; library, John Russell Pope, 1931–35; garden addition, Harry Van Dyke, John Barrington Bayley, and G. Frederick Poehler, 1977; garden, Russell Page). The palatial residence of the steel magnate Henry Clay Frick, built on the entire Fifth Avenue blockfront formerly occupied by the Lenox Library, was planned by Thomas Hastings both as a residence and a gallery for the display of Frick's great art collection. Modeled on 18th-century French sources, the house is placed on a terrace set back from Fifth Avenue and surrounded by a retaining wall, thus heightening the structure's formal monumentality. Following the death of Adelaide Frick in 1931, the house was enlarged and converted into a museum, which opened to the public in 1935. This conversion, as well as the construction of the adjoining reference library, was undertaken by John Russell Pope several years before he designed the National Gallery in Washington.

Gracie Mansion, East End Avenue at 88th Street (attributed to Ezra Weeks, 1799–1804; Susan B. Wagner wing, Mott B. Schmidt, 1965–66). In 1793 the Scottish-born Archibald Gracie settled in New York, where he established a successful mercantile business. In 1798 Gracie began purchasing land on Horn's Hook, a small peninsula jutting into the East River at Hell Gate; here he erected a country house overlooking the river. The house was expanded in 1802–04. Gracie sold the property in 1823, and it had several owners before being acquired by the city's Department of Parks in 1896. In 1924 the house was converted for use by the Museum of the City of New York. A major renovation was undertaken by the architect Aymar Embury II in 1934–36, following the museum's move to Fifth Avenue. Gracie Mansion became the official home of the mayor of New York City in 1942. Mott B. Schmidt added a wing to the house in 1965–66, and a major restoration by Charles A. Platt Partners was completed in 1985 .

Grand Army Plaza Scenic Landmark, Fifth Avenue at 59th Street (Carrère & Hastings, 1913–16). A modest plaza was laid out on this site as part of the design of Central Park (see p. 122). Although Richard Morris Hunt had proposed a formal plaza for the site as early as 1863, it was the sculptor Karl Bitter's 1898 proposal for a Parisian-inspired plaza that was eventually acted upon. In 1912 Joseph Pulitzer bequeathed $50,000 for the erection of a fountain and a competition was held for the design. In 1913 the project was awarded to Thomas Hastings, who closely followed Bitter's plan. Hastings laid out one of the most urbane public spaces in the city: a formal, axial, elliptical space divided in half by 59th Street. The plaza is a setting for Hastings's Pulitzer Fountain, which is crowned by Bitter's bronze statue of Pomona, goddess of abundance. North of 59th Street is Augustus Saint-Gaudens's masterful General Sherman Monument set on a base by Charles McKim. This statue, which had been unveiled in 1903, was moved in order to align with the new fountain. The fountain was restored and the Sherman statue regilded in 1988–90.

Solomon R. Guggenheim Museum, 1071 Fifth Avenue (Frank Lloyd Wright, 1956-59). View of skylight. Photo: Caroline Kane

Solomon R. Guggenheim Museum, 1071 Fifth Avenue (Frank Lloyd Wright, 1956–59). Established by Solomon R. Guggenheim as a repository of non-objective (i.e., abstract) art, the Guggenheim Museum is housed in one of the most acclaimed buildings of the 20th century. The museum is the major New York City work of the American master Frank Lloyd Wright and is often considered to be the crowning achievement of his later career. The building's organic form, a reversed spiral, was intended as a reflection of the natural shapes to be found across the street in Central Park. The **interior**, with its vast open space and spiraling cantilevered ramp punctuated by exhibition alcoves, is among Wright's most spectacular. In the basement is a circular auditorium also designed by Wright. In 1989–92 an addition designed by Charles Gwathmey was constructed and Wright's building was restored.

John Henry and Emily Vanderbilt Sloane Hammond House, 9 East 91st Street (Carrère & Hastings, 1902–03). This grand house, designed in the 16th-century Roman manner, and its neighbor, the Burden House (see p. 98), were erected for the daughters and sons-in-law of William and Emily Vanderbilt Sloane on land that the Sloanes had purchased from Andrew Carnegie. The beautifully proportioned limestone-clad mansion is among the most impressive residential designs of Carrère & Hastings.

Edward S. and Mary Stillman Harkness House, now the Commonwealth Fund, 1 East 75th Street (Hale & Rogers, 1907–09). Built by the son of one of the six original partners in the Standard Oil Company, the Harkness House is an Italian Renaissance–inspired mansion faced entirely with marble. Following the death of Mary Harkness in 1950, the house became the headquarters of the Commonwealth Fund, a philanthropic foundation that Edward Harkness's mother had founded in 1918. The building is surrounded by a spectacular cast- and wrought-iron fence that has been restored.

Cyril and Barbara Rutherford Hatch House, 153 East 63rd Street (Frederick J. Sterner, 1917–19). Shortly after their marriage, the New York socialites Barbara Rutherford (daughter of Mrs. William K. Vanderbilt) and Cyril Hatch commissioned this handsome Mediterranean-inspired town house. Following the Hatches' divorce in 1920, the spacious house, which has an interior court-yard, was occupied by Charles Dillingham, owner of the Globe Theater (see p. 77) and one of the country's most prominent theatrical producers, and then by Charles L. Lawrence, a pioneer in aeronautical engineering. In 1940 the property was purchased by Louise Hovick, better known as the burlesque queen Gypsy Rose Lee.

♣ **Henderson Place Historic District.** The 24 picturesque Queen Anne houses of this district survive from an enclave of 32 houses built in 1881 by the developer John C. Henderson for "persons of moderate means." Architects Lamb & Rich composed each blockfront as a unit, emphasizing the ends with small towers and effectively grouping the houses in pairs. As is characteristic of the Queen Anne style, the massing is dynamic and the facades are richly textured. The houses are built of brick, rough stone, and slate and are enlivened by projecting bays and oriels, small-paned windows, and a roof line with an eccentric silhouette of gables, dormers, mansards, and stout towers.

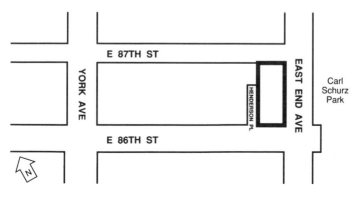

HENDERSON PLACE HISTORIC DISTRICT

Church of the Holy Trinity (Episcopal) Complex, 316–332 East 88th Street (Barney & Chapman, 1897–99). Serena Rhinelander donated this church as a memorial to her father and grandfather, building it on land that had been in her family since 1798. Holy Trinity was planned as a settlement church, run by the affluent St. James Parish on Madison Avenue, to minister to the poorer residents of Yorkville. The complex—consisting of the church, the parsonage, and St. Christopher House, all of French Gothic inspiration—was built of rich tawny brick with extensive terra-cotta trim and is set around a landscaped court anchored by one of New York's most beautiful towers. The church was built three years after Barney & Chapman designed the similarly styled but simpler Grace Chapel (see p. 44).

John H. and Caroline Iselin Residence, also known as the 59 East 79th Street House (Foster, Gade & Graham, 1908–09). Socially prominent lawyer John Iselin and his wife commissioned this house, which is stylistically unusual in its combination of Northern Renaissance and French classic forms, and lived here until 1919. It is one of four adjacent landmark town houses constructed early in the 20th century when East 79th Street became an especially prestigious residential address.

Oliver Gould and Mary Brewster Jennings House, now Lycée Français de New-York, 7 East 72nd Street (Flagg & Chambers, 1898–99). The Jennings House and the neighboring Sloane House (see p. 116) are two of the finest Beaux-Arts residences in New York City; they lend a note of Parisian elegance to Manhattan's Upper East Side. Appropriately, both houses were designed by French-trained architects and both are now owned by a French school. Built for a wealthy businessman and his family, the limestone-fronted Jennings House displays a rich surface texture, with vermiculated blocks on the ground floor and rusticated stonework above. The house is crowned by a particularly bold convex mansard with exuberant copper detail.

Otto and Addie Kahn House, now the Convent of the Sacred Heart, 1 East 91st Street (J. Armstrong Stenhouse with C. P. H. Gilbert, 1913–18). British architect J. Armstrong Stenhouse worked with C. P. H. Gilbert to create this magnificent limestone mansion, modeled on the 15th-century Palazzo della Cancelleria in Rome. The client, the banker Otto Kahn, was one of New York's most generous patrons of the arts; he twice aided in saving the Metropolitan Opera, backed many American theatrical organizations, and sponsored the American tours of such European institutions as Stanislavsky's Moscow Art Theater and Diaghilev's Ballet Russe. Since 1934 the house has served as the Convent of the Sacred Heart's prestigious school for girls.

Knickerbocker Club, 2 East 62nd Street (Delano & Aldrich, 1913–15). The exclusive Knickerbocker Club, founded in 1871 in reaction to the relaxation of admissions standards at other private men's clubs, commissioned this clubhouse in 1913. The architects Delano & Aldrich specialized in the design of refined adaptations of 18th- and early 19th-century American and English architecture, as can be seen in this elegant brick building and in several nearby landmark houses. A restoration of the club was completed in 1991.

Alvin W. and Angeline Krech House, also known as the 17 East 70th Street House (Arthur C. Jackson, 1909–11). The Krech family's French neoclassical limestone home is one of five landmark early 20th-century town houses that lend a dignified character to the north side of East 70th Street. Alvin Krech was, according to his obituary, "one of the prominent figures in American finance and industry," serving as chairman of the Equitable Trust Company and as a railroad administrator.

William Goadby and Florence Baker Loew House, now the Smithers Alcoholism Center of Roosevelt Hospital, 56 East 93rd Street (Walker & Gillette, 1930–31). The scale and austere geometry of this monumental limestone mansion are reminiscent of late 18th-century English design. William Loew was a wealthy stockbroker and socialite with the financial resources to build this mansion during the Depression. The site was acquired soon after Loew's brother-in-law George Baker purchased the house across the street (see p. 97). The facade of the Loew House, with its concave front and refined fluted arches, is among the most unusual in New York. Following Loew's death in 1955 the house was acquired by the theatrical producer Billy Rose, who lived here until his death in 1966.

1261 Madison Avenue Apartments (Buchman & Fox, 1900–01). This elegant Beaux-Arts apartment house has a characteristic limestone facade with a mansard roof, iron balconies, and three-dimensional carved detail. Its construction in 1900 reflected a change in the character of the area now known as Carnegie Hill, as imposing new apartment houses intended for affluent residents joined the neighborhood's earlier tenements and row houses.

1321 Madison Avenue House (James E. Ware, 1890–91). This Queen Anne house with a towering pyramidal roof was originally the end building of a row of five brownstone-fronted dwellings. The brick facade on East 93rd Street has a prominent entrance set above a massive stone stoop.

Metropolitan Club, 1–11 East 60th Street (McKim, Mead & White, 1891–94; addition, Ogden Codman, 1912). The 19th-century architecture critic Montgomery Schuyler described the Metropolitan Club as "the largest, most imposing, and most luxurious of the clubhouses of New York." This building, designed in the Italian Renaissance style, is a masterpiece of late 19th-century American architecture and a major example of the design skills of Stanford White. The Metropolitan Club was founded in 1891 by a group of prominent New Yorkers disgruntled by the rejection of several of their friends from membership in the Union Club. The marble exterior of the new club was specifically planned to be as unostentatious as possible, with rich detail limited to the interior. Since the club wished to have a lounge overlooking Central Park, the entrance is on the side, through elaborate gates and a court demarcated by a two-story wing with a shallow niche. The east side of the court is flanked by an earlier row house (11 East 60th Street) redesigned for the club in 1912.

Metropolitan Museum of Art, Fifth Avenue at East 82nd Street (major wings by Vaux & Mould, 1874–80; Thomas Weston with Arthur L. Tuckerman, associate, 1864–66; Richard Morris Hunt, 1894–95; Richard Howland Hunt and George B. Post, 1895–1902; McKim, Mead & White, 1904–26; Kevin Roche, John Dinkeloo & Associates, 1971–90). In their original design for Central Park (see p. 122), Frederick Law Olmsted and Calvert Vaux sited the Metropolitan Museum of Art on a plot west of Fifth Avenue at 82nd Street. The original museum building, a High Victorian Gothic structure designed by Vaux and Jacob Wrey Mould (and now partially visible as the inner wall of the Lehman Wing), was built into the park landscape. As the Metropolitan expanded its collections, a series of wings were added. The early wings, such as Weston and Tuckerman's south wing (now visible in the Petrie Sculpture Court), were built into the landscape; the focus changed, however, with the design of Richard Morris Hunt's Beaux-Arts central pavilion (completed by Richard Howland Hunt following his father's death in 1895) on Fifth Avenue. The avenue frontage was completed by McKim, Mead & White's north and south wings. **Interior:** The vestibule, Great Hall, and stairway were designed by Richard Morris Hunt, and construction was supervised by his son, with George B. Post as consulting architect. The entrance ensemble provides a fitting introduction to the expanded museum. Beginning in 1904 the Metropolitan undertook further additions on Fifth Avenue. These additions by McKim, Mead & White represent a simplified version of Hunt's design. Kevin Roche, John Dinkeloo & Associates prepared a master plan for the museum in 1971; the last of their modern stone-and-glass wings was completed in 1990. Their American Wing, built at the northwest corner of the complex, incorporates the facade of the former Bank of New York (Martin E. Thompson, 1823–25), which was saved from destruction and moved to the museum in 1924.

🍎 **Metropolitan Museum Historic District.** Located across Fifth Avenue from Central Park and the Metropolitan Museum of Art, this district traces the three main stages of residential development on the Upper East Side. Many modest row houses were built on speculation on the district's side streets in the 1870s and 1880s, especially after the Third Avenue Elevated began operation in 1878. The area was then transformed into one of New York's most exclusive residential neighborhoods beginning in the 1890s, when the city's financial and social elite constructed mansions and town houses. Especially fine examples of these houses can be seen on East 78th and 79th streets. In the second decade of the 20th century, such luxury apartment houses as 998 Fifth Avenue (see p. 104) began to replace the mansions. This development has continued into recent years, with the construction of 1001 Fifth Avenue (1978–80), whose early postmodern facade was designed by Philip Johnson.

Grafton W. and Anne Minot House, also known as the 11 East 90th Street House (A. Wallace McCrea, 1929). The present austere facade of this house was inspired by 18th-century French designs. It replaces the original Beaux-Arts front designed by Barney & Chapman and built in 1902–03 for William and Louise McAlpin. A. Wallace McCrea specialized in this type of townhouse modernization.

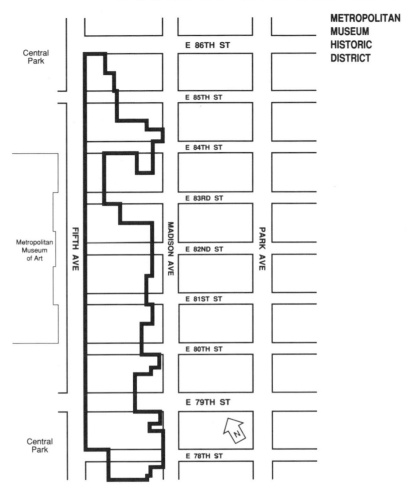

John Chandler and Corinne deB. Moore House, also known as the 15 East 70th Street House (Charles I. Berg, 1909–10). This house in the French neo-classical style is one of five adjacent landmarks erected on land that had been owned by James Lenox and the Lenox estate until 1907, when plots were sold to individuals who erected new town houses.

Dave Hennen and Alice Morris House, also known as the 19 East 70th Street House, now the Knoedler Gallery (Thornton Chard, 1909–10). This especially austere early Italian Renaissance–inspired limestone building, one of five adjacent landmark town houses built on land previously owned by the wealthy landholder and philanthropist James Lenox, was erected for a client who would later become the U.S. ambassador to Belgium.

Lewis Gouverneur and Nathalie Bailey Morris House, 100 East 85th Street (Ernest Flagg, 1913–14). Flagg designed this idiosyncratic house for a descendant of a prominent colonial New York family. The town house is massed in three sections, all oriented toward East 85th Street: the main residential block, a rear wing with a garage at street level, and a stairway wing recessed behind a narrow court. Appropriate to Morris's lineage, the design combines American Colonial detail with the massing and the free use of 18th-century forms favored by the English architect Richard Norman Shaw.

Lewis Spencer and Emily Morris House, also known as the 116 East 80th Street House (Cross & Cross, 1922–23). The design of this house, the earliest of four adjoining landmark town houses, was based closely on 18th-century London residences. Especially notable features are the house's projecting central pedimented pavilion and the brick arches of the ground-floor windows.

Mount Sinai Dispensary, also known as the 149–151 East 67th Street Building, now the Kennedy Child Study Center (Buchman & Deisler and Brunner & Tryon, 1889–90). Mount Sinai Hospital, the oldest Jewish hospital in New York City, first opened a dispensary for the treatment of outpatients in 1875. As the demand for services grew, this Italian Renaissance–inspired structure, faced in brick, stone, and terra cotta, was erected to house both an enlarged dispensary and the hospital's nursing school. The design is the combined work of two prominent Jewish architecture firms.

Municipal Asphalt Plant, now the Asphalt Green Recreational Center, Franklin Delano Roosevelt Drive at East 90th Street (Kahn & Jacobs, 1941–44). The asphalt plant, built adjacent to the FDR Drive, was the first successful American use of the parabolic arch form in reinforced concrete. The radical design was based on principles that Robert Allan Jacobs had studied while working for Le Corbusier in France. The plant ceased operations in 1968 and, after standing vacant for several years, was converted into a recreation center by Hellmuth, Obata & Kassabaum and Pasanella + Klein.

Museum of the City of New York, 1220–1227 Fifth Avenue (Joseph J. Freedlander, 1928–30). Designed in a Georgian Colonial style—an appropriate choice for this museum, which specializes in local history—this brick building with a white marble base and trim is massed around a courtyard that opens onto Fifth Avenue and Central Park. The museum was incorporated in 1923 and was originally housed in Gracie Mansion (see p. 105). The city donated the site between East 103rd and 104th streets, but funds for construction were privately subscribed.

New York Public Library, Yorkville Branch, 222 East 79th Street (James Brown Lord, 1902). The Palladian-inspired Yorkville Library was the first of numerous branch libraries throughout the city built as a result of Andrew Carnegie's 1901 gift to the New York Public Library (see p. 148). This facility had been planned many years earlier by the New York Free Circulating Library, which explains the choice of James Brown Lord as architect; Lord had previously designed the Free Circulating Library's Bloomingdale Branch (see p. 127).

Municipal Asphalt Plant, now the Asphalt Green Recreational Center, Franklin Delano Roosevelt Drive at East 90th Street (Kahn & Jacobs, 1941–44). Photo: Carl Forster

Gustav and Virginia Pagenstrecher House, also known as the 21 East 70th Street House, now Hirschl & Adler Galleries (William J. Rogers 1918–19). The last of the five landmark town houses to be erected on the north side of East 70th Street, the Pagenstrecher House is a limestone structure designed in an austere French neoclassical style. At the second floor a pair of tall round-arched windows is set in deep reveals.

Park East Synagogue (Congregation Zichron Ephraim), 163 East 67th Street (Schneider & Herter, 1889–90). Park East is a late manifestation of the use of Moorish forms in synagogue design (see Central Synagogue, p. 70). The congregation was organized in 1888 by Rabbi Bernard Drachman, who believed in the importance of adapting Orthodox practices and traditions to American customs. This conviction was a direct response to the increasing popularity of Reform Judaism, especially among the German Jews settling in substantial numbers on the Upper East Side in the late 19th century. This synagogue's architectural style was seen as a link between 19th-century Judaism and the flowering of Jewish culture in Moorish Spain.

Percy and Maud H. Pyne House, now the Center for Inter-American Relations, 680 Park Avenue (McKim, Mead & White, 1906–12). Charles McKim designed this house for the financier and philanthropist Percy Pyne and his wife in 1906, but construction did not begin until 1910, when the railroad tracks along Park Avenue were finally covered. The house was one of the earliest mansions on Park Avenue, and set a Colonial Revival precedent that was followed by the three succeeding town houses on this block, erected between 1916 and 1926. In 1965 demolition began on this house and its two neighbors, the Filley and Sloane houses (see pp. 105 and 116). In response to a public outcry, the Marquesa de Cuevas, a granddaughter of John D. Rockefeller, purchased the houses at the last minute and donated them to various organizations.

Queensboro Bridge. See p. 197.

Regis High School, 55 East 84th Street (Maginnis & Walsh, 1913–17). Designed to harmonize in scale with the Church of St. Ignatius Loyola (see p. 115), directly across the street, Regis is an imposing five-story Classical Revival limestone building with street fronts on both East 84th and East 85th streets. The school was founded by the Jesuits in 1912 to provide a liberal arts education to gifted Catholic men.

George and Sarah Rives House, also known as the 67–69 East 79th Street House, now the Greek Consulate General (Carrère & Hastings, 1907–08). Modeled on the late 17th-century town houses built on the Place Vendôme in Paris, this house is one of four landmark residences on the north side of East 79th Street. The house was commissioned by the lawyer, statesman, and historian George Rives and his second wife, Sarah. In 1962 the Greek architect Pierre Zannettos altered the top two floors of the house and added a sixth story.

John S. and Catharine C. Rogers House, now the New York Society Library, 53 East 79th Street (Trowbridge & Livingston, 1916–17). The most impressive of the four landmark town houses on the north side of East 79th Street, the Rogers House was built for a wealthy lawyer and his wife. The limestone structure, whose design is based on Italian Renaissance prototypes, has housed the New York Society Library since 1937.

Sara Delano Roosevelt and Franklin and Eleanor Roosevelt Houses, now the Sara Delano Roosevelt Memorial House, 47–49 East 65th Street (Charles A. Platt, 1907–08). This double town house of unified English Georgian–inspired design has a single central entrance. Access to the individual units was gained through doors in the vestibule; Sara Roosevelt lived to the left and her son and daughter-in-law lived to the right. It was in his fourth-floor bedroom in this house that Franklin Roosevelt convalesced from polio in 1921–22. After Sara's death in 1941 the building was purchased for use by nearby Hunter College.

St. Cecilia's Church (R.C.) and Regina Angelorum, 112–120 East 106th Street (church, Napoleon Le Brun & Sons, 1883–87; Regina Angelorum, Neville & Bagge, 1907). Founded in 1873, St. Cecilia's was one of the first Roman Catholic churches in East Harlem. The facade of this Romanesque Revival structure reflects the architects' masterful use of brick and terra cotta, especially evident in the arched panel depicting St. Cecilia, the patron saint of music, playing an organ. The Regina Angelorum was designed to complement the church; its facade unified two earlier buildings, which were to be used as a convent and a home for working girls (now a convent and day nursery).

Church of St. Ignatius Loyola (R.C.), 980 Park Avenue (Schickel & Ditmars, 1895–1900). As is characteristic of Jesuit churches, the design of St. Ignatius Loyola is modeled on the Jesuits' Renaissance churches in Rome. The symmetrically massed, limestone-faced structure rests on the rough stone base (visible on East 84th Street) of an earlier church, dedicated to St. Lawrence O'Toole, that was begun in 1884 but never finished.

St. Jean Baptiste R.C. Church, 1067–1071 Lexington Avenue (Nicholas Sirracino, 1910–13). St. Jean Baptiste, built to serve a largely French-Canadian Roman Catholic congregation, is an impressive example of Italian Mannerist–inspired design. Of special note on this limestone-faced church are the Corinthian portico, paired towers, and dome. Construction was funded by the streetcar magnate Thomas Fortune Ryan, who, it is said, sought to replace a smaller building in which he had once been forced to stand during mass.

St. Nicholas Russian Orthodox Cathedral, 15 East 97th Street (John Bergesen, 1901–02). St. Nicholas, the diocesan seat of the Russian Orthodox Church in North America, was built with funds collected throughout the Russian empire. With its five onion domes, polychromatic detail, and *kokoshniki* (ogival pediments), the design derives from 17th-century Baroque churches in Moscow. The "Moscow Baroque" style was revived in Russia in the late 19th century and was adapted for this New York site by an architect of Russian descent.

Church of St. Vincent Ferrer (R.C.) Complex, 869 Lexington Avenue and 141–151 East 65th Street (church, Bertram Goodhue, 1914–18; priory, William Schickel, 1880–81; Holy Name Society Building, Wilfred E. Anthony, 1930; school, Elliot L. Chisling—Ferrenz & Taylor, 1948). Shortly after completing St. Thomas Church (see p. 92), Bertram Goodhue received the commission for this Roman Catholic church erected by the Dominican order. Goodhue's design uses academic Gothic forms in a free manner. The austere exterior is faced in Plymouth granite with white limestone carvings by Lee Lawrie that appear to grow organically from the massive stonework. Immediately south of the church is the older priory, a Victorian Gothic design that is one of the few surviving examples of the ecclesiastical work of the architect William Schickel. In the 20th century the church complex expanded along East 65th Street with the construction of the neo-Gothic Holy Name Society Building and St. Vincent Ferrer School.

Seventh Regiment Armory, 643 Park Avenue (Charles W. Clinton, 1877–79). The socially prominent Seventh Regiment was formed in 1806 and in 1824 became the first regiment to adopt the term *National Guard*. In 1874 the city leased this Park Avenue site to the regiment, which raised the money to build a monumental new armory. Clinton, a Seventh Regiment veteran, designed the armory with a 187-by-290-foot drill shed and an administration building in the form of a medieval fortress. The building became a prototype for the later medieval-inspired armories that appeared in large numbers in New York (see pp. 116, 125, 186, and 204) and throughout the country.

Sidewalk Clocks (see p. 62).

783 Fifth Avenue at East 59th Street (E. Howard Clock Company, 1927). Located in front of the Sherry Netherland Hotel, this clock was probably installed around the time the hotel opened in 1927.

1501 Third Avenue at East 84th Street (E. Howard Clock Company, late 19th century). This unusual sidewalk clock, designed in the form of a giant pocket watch, was erected by the jeweler Adolph Stern in front of his shop at 1508 Third Avenue. When the business relocated across the street in the 1920s, the clock was also moved. At some point after 1900 arms were placed above the watch fob; these once supported the three golden balls that are a traditional symbol of a pawnbroker.

Henry T. and Jessie Sloane House, now Lycée Français de New-York, 9 East 72nd Street (Carrère & Hastings, 1894–96). Henry T. Sloane, son of the founder of the W. & J. Sloane furniture store, commissioned this luxuriant Beaux-Arts house from the French-trained architects Carrère & Hastings. Sloane and his wife lived here only briefly before their scandalous divorce in 1898. After being briefly occupied by Joseph Pulitzer, the house was purchased by James Stillman, president of National City Bank. The house and its complementary neighbor, the Oliver Gould Jennings House (see p. 108), are now occupied by the Lycée Français.

William and Frances Crocker Sloane House, now the Italian Cultural Institute, 686 Park Avenue (Delano & Aldrich, 1916–19). Delano & Aldrich excelled at the design of Colonial Revival buildings, and this house, designed for the president of the prominent W. & J. Sloane furniture store, is a characteristic example. It is one of four stylistically related landmark houses on this block and one of three saved from demolition in 1965 (see Pyne House, p. 113).

Abigail Adams Smith Museum, 421 East 61st Street (1799). In 1795 Col. William S. Smith and his wife, Abigail, the daughter of John and Abigail Adams, established the estate of Mount Vernon along the East River. In 1798, before all the estate buildings were complete, the Smiths were forced to sell their property to William T. Robinson; it was Robinson who constructed the combined coach house and stable that is now the Abigail Adams Smith Museum. The building's conversion into a hotel in 1826 entailed substantial alterations to the interior and the construction of a veranda. The Colonial Dames of America purchased the property in 1924 and converted the hotel into a museum that has been open to the public since 1939.

Squadron A Armory, Madison Avenue between East 94th and 95th streets (John R. Thomas, 1893–95). The picturesque, battlemented Madison Avenue facade is all that remains of the monumental Squadron A Armory, which once occupied the entire block between Madison and Park avenues. The facade was saved when the remainder of the building was demolished in 1966, and it now serves as the entrance to the playground of the Hunter College High School.

Willard and Dorothy Whitney Straight House, later the National Audubon Society, now the International Center of Photography, 1130 Fifth Avenue (Delano & Aldrich, 1913–15). This imposing English Georgian Revival house was commissioned by Willard Straight, a diplomat and financier who specialized in Far Eastern affairs. While working as a Far East expert for J. P. Morgan & Co., Straight founded India House (see Hanover Bank, p. 18), a club whose members were involved with foreign ventures. With the financial assistance of his wife, Straight later founded *The New Republic* and *Asia* magazines. The Straights' house is one of Delano & Aldrich's boldest designs. Of special note are the ocular windows on the upper story, which are modeled after similar windows on the wing of Hampton Court Palace designed by Sir Christopher Wren.

🍎 **Treadwell Farms Historic District**. Once part of the farm of Adam Treadwell, the older brother of Seabury Tredwell [sic], whose house (see Old Merchant's House, p. 49) is now a museum, this district was transformed by speculative builders into a neighborhood of modest row houses in 1868–76. Later in the 19th century the neighborhood deteriorated, but it was rediscovered after World War I by affluent New Yorkers searching for housing convenient to the new Midtown commercial area. Between 1919 and 1922 almost every house in the district was altered; many of the facades were simplified by the removal of stoops and other projecting features. In 1930 Martin Hedmark designed the Swedish Baptist Church (now Trinity Baptist) at 250 East 61st Street in an unusual Scandinavian Modern style; the church features exceptional brickwork.

Emily Trevor House, also known as the 15 East 90th Street House (Mott B. Schmidt, 1927–28). This red brick house, with its carefully detailed limestone portico and trim, is an essay in English 18th-century design. It was built for the sister of John B. Trevor, whose house is located on East 91st Street (see below).

John B. and Caroline Trevor House, 11 East 91st Street (Trowbridge & Livingston, 1909–11). The Trevor House is the smallest of the four landmark town houses on the north side of East 91st Street. The simple French neoclassi-

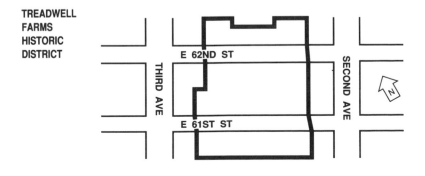

TREADWELL FARMS HISTORIC DISTRICT

E 62ND ST

E 61ST ST

THIRD AVE

SECOND AVE

N

cal residence is faced with limestone articulated by a trio of arched openings on the main floor and is crowned by a mansard roof.

🍎 **Upper East Side Historic District**. This district is composed largely of the mansions, town houses, apartment houses, institutional buildings, and private carriage houses erected by or for New York City's wealthiest citizens in the first decades of the 20th century. The earliest wave of development in the district occurred in the 1870s, when brownstone and brick row houses were constructed by speculative builders for sale to middle-class residents; this movement was spurred by the opening of the Third Avenue Elevated in 1878. Many of these houses were demolished or redesigned in the late 19th and early 20th centuries when a more affluent constituency transformed the streets north of 59th Street. It was in these years that the city's financial and social elite commissioned substantial town houses from many of the nation's finest architects, who created notable examples of Beaux-Arts, Italian Renaissance, French Renaissance, and Colonial Revival design. In addition, the neighborhood's new residents donated money for the construction of fine new churches, synagogues, and private clubs. Some of the wealthiest families also built or purchased private carriage houses, most of them located on the blocks east of Park Avenue. The era of opulent town houses was brief, however, lasting only about 25 years. After World War I the maintenance of private homes became prohibitively expensive, and luxurious apartment houses were built on Fifth and Park avenues. Madison Avenue, which had been a residential street, became a commercial thoroughfare at this time, as the lower floors of old houses were converted into elegant shops.

Virginia Graham Fair Vanderbilt House, now Lycée Français de New-York, 60 East 93rd Street (John Russell Pope, 1930–31). Mrs. Vanderbilt was a society leader, a racehorse breeder, the ex-wife of William K. Vanderbilt, and the daughter of Senator James Fair of Nevada, who made his fortune tapping the Comstock lode and Big Bonanza mine. The limestone house resembles the great private *hôtels* built in Paris during the reign of Louis XV. Appropriately, it is one of several French-inspired residences in the neighborhood that now house a French school.

Gertrude Rhinelander Waldo House, now the Polo/Ralph Lauren Store, 867 Madison Avenue (Kimball & Thompson, 1895–98). Designed in the style of the early French Renaissance châteaux of the Loire Valley, this enormous limestone mansion was built by an eccentric society matron who never lived in the house. Rather, she resided across the street, and the house remained empty until 1920, when it was converted for commercial use. Ralph Lauren instituted a major rehabilitation of the property in 1984.

Felix and Frieda S. Warburg House, now the Jewish Museum, 1109 Fifth Avenue (C. P. H. Gilbert, 1906–08). Gilbert, who specialized in mansions in the style of François I, designed similar limestone-faced, Loire Valley châteaux–inspired houses for Isaac D. Fletcher (on Fifth Avenue at East 79th Street, now in the Metropolitan Museum Historic District), F. W. Woolworth (demolished), and Felix Warburg. In 1944 Frieda Warburg donated the house

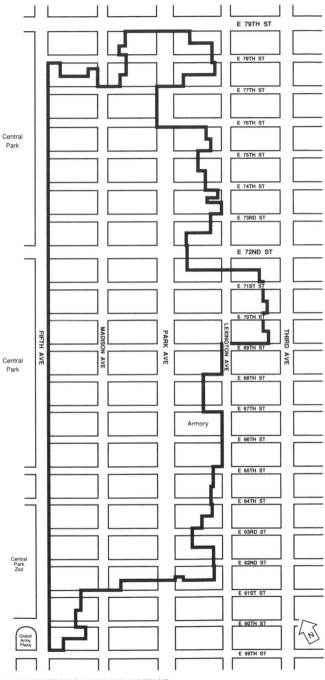

UPPER EAST SIDE HISTORIC DISTRICT

as a permanent home for the Jewish Museum. In 1990 work began on an addition by Kevin Roche that echoes the design of the original house.

George and Martha Whitney House, also known as the 120 East 80th Street House (Cross & Cross, 1929–30). The town house commissioned by George Whitney is the most elaborate of the four adjacent landmark houses on East 80th Street, all modeled on 18th-century London residences. Whitney was an internationally famous financier who served for many years as the head of J. P. Morgan & Co.

Payne and Helen Hay Whitney House, now the Office of Cultural Services, Embassy of France, 972 Fifth Avenue (McKim, Mead & White, 1902–09). Financier Oliver H. Payne commissioned this house as a wedding gift for his nephew Payne Whitney and Whitney's bride, Helen Hay. The bowfronted marble mansion is one of Stanford White's most successful Italian High Renaissance–inspired designs. The Republic of France acquired the building in 1952.

59TH STREET TO 110TH STREET, WEST SIDE

American Museum of Natural History, Central Park West at West 77th Street (Vaux & Mould, 1874–77; south and part of west elevation, Cady, Berg & See, 1888–1908; east wing, Trowbridge & Livingston, 1912–34; Theodore Roosevelt Memorial Hall, John Russell Pope, 1931–34; Hayden Planetarium, Trowbridge & Livingston, 1934; library, Kevin Roche, John Dinkeloo & Associates, 1990–92). Five years after the museum's incorporation in 1869, construction began on a spacious site known as Manhattan Square with Vaux & Mould's High Victorian Gothic building, now barely visible in a court at the west side of the site. In 1888 Cady, Berg & See prepared a master plan for the institution that envisioned a monumental Romanesque Revival complex to be constructed of pink granite; only the south front and a portion of the west front (undertaken by the architect Charles Volz) were completed. In 1912 Trowbridge & Livingston began planning a series of Classical Revival pavilions, and in 1934 they added the Moderne–style Planetarium. John Russell Pope's Theodore Roosevelt Memorial Hall, now the museum's main entrance, is in the form of a massive triumphal arch. The **interior** of Memorial Hall is among New York's great monumental spaces, with a barrel-vaulted ceiling, giant Corinthian columns, and rich marble walls and floors, all reminiscent of the grandeur of ancient Rome. The room, reopened in 1991 following a restoration by the Roche firm, contains a series of murals by William A. Mackay that depict events in Roosevelt's life.

Ansonia Hotel, 2101–2119 Broadway (Paul E. M. DuBoy, 1899–1904). The largest and most exuberant of the multiple dwellings in the Beaux-Arts style erected on the Upper West Side at the turn of the century, the Ansonia was built as an apartment hotel (i.e., a building with residential suites that lack kitchens) by W. E. D. Stokes, a major developer in the area. Stokes advocated all-masonry fireproof construction, including soundproof partitions between floors and

Ansonia Hotel, 2101–2119 Broadway (Paul E. M. DuBoy, 1899–1904). Photo: Caroline Kane

apartments, a feature that has attracted many distinguished musicians, singers, and conductors.

Apthorp Apartments, 2201–2219 Broadway (Clinton & Russell, 1906–08). The Astor estate commissioned this monumental apartment house, which covers an entire square block of the Upper West Side. Clinton & Russell's adaptation of an Italian Renaissance palazzo includes a large, landscaped central courtyard separated from the street by handsome iron gates.

Association Residence for Respectable Aged Indigent Females, now the New York City American Youth Hostel, 891 Amsterdam Avenue (Richard Morris Hunt, 1881–83; addition, Charles A. Rich, 1907–08). The Association for the Relief of Respectable Aged Indigent Females, one of New York City's first charitable institutions, was chartered in 1814 to aid those who were left poor widows by the Revolutionary War and the War of 1812. As the association's clients grew in number, a large new home was needed; in 1881 the Amsterdam Avenue blockfront between West 103rd and 104th streets was purchased. This building is among the few extant structures in New York City designed by Richard Morris Hunt; it is also a rare example of 19th-century institutional architecture that has been successfully adapted to a new use. The design of the Gothic-inspired brick-and-stone building clearly reflects Hunt's knowledge of contemporary French design. The conversion to New York's first youth hostel was completed in 1990 (Larsen Associates, architect).

William and Clara Baumgarten House, 294 Riverside Drive (Schickel & Ditmars, 1900–01). This Beaux-Arts town house near West 102nd Street is one of the few luxury residences of its type to survive on Riverside Drive. The limestone structure was commissioned by William Baumgarten, who served as head of the famous interior design firm of Herter Brothers and later established his own decorating company.

Beacon Theater (interior), 2124 Broadway (Walter W. Ahlschlager, 1927–28). The lavishly appointed lobbies, stairways, and auditorium of the Beacon, with their eclectic Greek, Roman, Renaissance, and Rococo detail, are characteristic of the great movie palaces built in the 1920s. The Beacon, one of the last surviving movie palaces in New York City, is now used primarily for concerts.

Belleclaire Hotel, 2171–2179 Broadway (Emery Roth of the firm Stein, Cohen & Roth, 1901–03). The earliest known design by Roth, the Belleclaire is among the fine apartment hotels erected on the Upper West Side at the turn of the century. The design is unusual in its use of ornamental motifs inspired by contemporary Secessionist design in Central Europe in combination with more traditional French Beaux-Arts motifs.

Belnord Apartments, 201–225 West 86th Street (H. Hobart Weekes, 1908–09). Built at a time when apartment houses were becoming the most popular type of residence on the Upper West Side, the Belnord, designed in the Italian Renaissance style, is an enormous building, encompassing an entire city block. The three main entrance arches on West 86th Street lead to a large landscaped courtyard.

Beresford Apartments, 211 Central Park West (Emery Roth, 1928–29). The Italian Renaissance–inspired Beresford, with its three prominent octagonal towers, is one of the masterpieces of the famed apartment-house designer Emery Roth. The building is among the most prominent elements of Central Park West's distinctive skyline.

Central Park Scenic Landmark, Fifth Avenue to Central Park West, 59th Street to 110th Street (Frederick Law Olmsted and Calvert Vaux, designed 1858). One of the great manmade monuments of the 19th century, Central Park was the first large-scale public park in the United States, and its success influenced park design all across the country. The design embodies 19th-century attitudes toward nature and the ideals of a democratic society. The park was planned as a naturalistic landscape in which urban dwellers could mingle and find respite from the pressures of life. Olmsted and Vaux transformed a rugged, swampy wasteland into a bucolic setting of meadows, lakes, and forests punctuated with modest buildings designed by Vaux. Four separate road and path systems wend their way through the park: pedestrian walkways, carriage drives, bridle paths, and transverse roads that carry crosstown traffic. These systems pass over and under one another by way of stone and cast-iron bridges of exceptional beauty. Major restoration projects undertaken since the 1970s have returned much of Central Park to its original glory.

354 and 355 Central Park West Houses (Gilbert A. Schellenger, 1892–93). These two survivors from a row of five neo-Renaissance dwellings are rare examples of row houses built on Central Park West.

⚜ **Central Park West—West 73rd–74th Streets Historic District.** Now entirely subsumed within the Upper West Side—Central Park West Historic District (see p. 133), this square block contains some of the finest residential design on the Upper West Side. The earliest buildings in the district are 18 row houses on West 73rd Street, which survive from a row of 28 designed by Henry J. Hardenbergh in 1882–85 for Edward S. Clark, president of the Singer [Sewing Machine] Manufacturing Co., in a style compatible with the nearby Dakota Apartments (see p. 125). Clark's grandson Ambrose Clark developed much of West 74th Street in 1902–04 with a long neo-Georgian row designed by Percy Griffin. The Clarks sold the Central Park West frontage in 1902, and Clinton & Russell's elegant Langham Apartments in the Beaux-Arts style was erected in 1904–07.

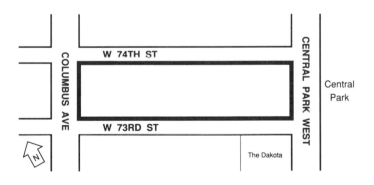

CENTRAL PARK WEST—WEST 73RD–74TH STREETS HISTORIC DISTRICT

⚜ **Central Park West—76th Street Historic District**. This small historic district is now located entirely within the Upper West Side—Central Park West Historic District (see p. 133). Row houses began to appear on West 76th Street in 1887; by 1900, 44 of them had been built within the district. Central Park West retains examples of the three types of buildings erected on that avenue at the turn of the century: the Kenilworth (Townsend, Steinle & Haskell, 1906–08), a Beaux-Arts–style apartment house designed for upper-middle-class

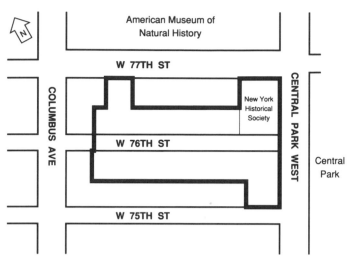

CENTRAL PARK WEST—76TH STREET HISTORIC DISTRICT

families; the neo-Gothic Church of the Divine Paternity (now Fourth Universalist Society; William A. Potter, 1897–98); and the New-York Historical Society (see p. 127), one of two major museums located along the park. The district also includes Harde & Short's Studio Building (1907–09) at 44 West 77th Street, an apartment house that contains two-story artist's studios and duplex residential units.

Central Savings Bank, now the Apple Bank for Savings, 2100–2108 Broadway (York & Sawyer, 1926–28). York & Sawyer, the leading architects of banks in New York City in the 1920s, were responsible for several banks in the Italian Renaissance palazzo style. The freestanding Central Savings Bank is the grandest of these, with its massive rusticated limestone facades and magnificent ironwork crafted by Samuel Yellin of Philadelphia.

Century Apartments, 25 Central Park West (Irwin Chanin, 1931). The twin-towered Century, a sophisticated example of residential Art Deco design in New York, is a major element of Central Park West's distinctive skyline. Much of the Century's aesthetic interest lies in the successful manipulation of such features as brickwork, windows, bays, and balconies and the spare use of ornament to highlight such features as entrances, setbacks, and towers.

Chatsworth Apartments and Annex, 340 and 344 West 72nd Street (John E. Scharsmith, 1902–04 and 1905–06). Prominently sited at the southern end of Riverside Park and Drive, the Beaux-Arts Chatsworth and its annex were built to house the affluent families moving into Upper West Side apartment houses at the turn of the century. The Chatsworth originally offered such amenities as a conservatory, a sun parlor, a café, a billiards room, a barber shop, a beauty salon, and electric bus service along West 72nd Street to and from Central Park.

Claremont Stables, now the Claremont Riding Academy, 175 West 89th Street (Frank A. Rooke, 1892). Designed in the Romanesque Revival style, the Claremont is the oldest functioning commercial stable in Manhattan. The building was erected as a livery stable for the rental of horses and carriages.

Dakota Apartments, 1 West 72nd Street (Henry J. Hardenbergh, 1880–84). One of New York's best-known buildings, the Dakota was erected at a time when the Upper West Side was sparsely populated. The building was commissioned by Edward S. Clark, president of the Singer [Sewing Machine] Manufacturing Company and an active West Side developer. Hardenbergh's interest in Northern European architecture is evident in the building's somewhat Germanic design, with its picturesque gables rising above Central Park. In plan, the Dakota has a central courtyard with an entrance in each corner; this plan became a prototype for other early New York City apartment houses.

Dorilton Apartments, 171 West 71st Street (Janes & Leo, 1900–02). Perhaps the most flamboyant apartment house in New York, the Dorilton is an enormous Beaux-Arts pile with striking French-inspired sculptural decoration and an iron gate reminiscent of those that guard French palaces. The Dorilton was erected to cater to the prosperous upper-middle-class families who were moving into apartment houses on the Upper West Side in increasing numbers in the early years of the 20th century.

Eldorado Apartments, 300 Central Park West (Margon & Holder with Emery Roth, 1929–31). The Art Deco Eldorado is the northernmost of the four great twin-towered apartment buildings that line Central Park West. It is believed that Margon & Holder designed the Art Deco detailing but that Emery Roth, one of the leading apartment house designers of the period, was responsible for the plan and massing, which closely resemble Roth's contemporaneous work on the San Remo Apartments (see p. 132).

First Battery Armory, later the 102nd Medical Battalion Armory, now the Capital Cities / ABC, Inc., Studios, 56 West 66th Street (Horgan & Slattery, 1900–03). The First Battery, founded in 1867, was a largely German-American volunteer unit of the National Guard. The unit was one of several in New York City that built medieval-inspired armories at the turn of the century. This relatively small building has a lively facade, with turrets, crenellations, and other castlelike features, some functional and others merely decorative.

First Church of Christ, Scientist, 1 West 96th Street (Carrère & Hastings, 1899–1903). New York City's oldest Christian Science congregation erected this magnificent church, which is built entirely of Concord granite. The building was designed by Carrère & Hastings shortly after they won the competition for the New York Public Library (see p. 86). The church displays a rare combination of English Baroque massing (not unlike the churches of Nicholas Hawksmoor) and French Beaux-Arts detail.

Interborough Rapid Transit System Control House, Broadway at West 72nd Street, and **Interborough Rapid Transit System Underground Stations,** 59th Street—Columbus Circle, 72nd Street, and 79th Street. See p. 18.

Kent Automatic Parking Garage, later the Sofia Brothers Warehouse, now the Sofia Apartments, 33–43 West 61st Street (Jardine, Hill & Murdock, 1929–30). This flamboyant brick and polychromed terra-cotta Art Deco building was erected as a parking garage that employed a patented automatic parking system: an electrical "parking machine" engaged each car by its rear axle and towed it from an elevator to a parking spot. Unfortunately, the novel system failed. The building served as a more conventional garage until 1941, when it became the Sofia Brothers Warehouse. In 1983–84 the warehouse was converted into luxury apartments.

Philip and Maria Kleeberg House, 3 Riverside Drive (C. P. H. Gilbert, 1896–98). The Kleebergs' elegant town house, designed in the French Renaissance style, is one of four landmark residences located at the gateway to Riverside Drive. Gilbert's design for this limestone-fronted house takes full advantage of its wide curving lot, incorporating a recessed bay above the entrance, a large projecting bay, and a fourth-story loggia.

John B. and Isabella Leech House, 520 West End Avenue (Clarence True, 1892). The Leech residence is an unusual work by the prolific West Side architect/developer Clarence True. The corner house combines Romanesque, Gothic, and Elizabethan forms and is enlivened by superb carved detail. Built for a wealthy cotton broker, the house is a rare example of an individually designed single-family town house on West End Avenue.

Majestic Apartments, 115 Central Park West (Irwin S. Chanin, 1930–31). The Majestic is one of the four great twin-towered apartment buildings that define the Central Park West skyline. This Art Deco building is the earlier of Irwin Chanin's two Central Park West apartment houses and is somewhat simpler than the nearby Century (see p. 124). The towers are a response to a 1929 building regulation that limited the height of an apartment building's street wall but permitted tall towers on large plots.

Marseilles Hotel, 2689–2693 Broadway (Harry Allan Jacobs, 1902–05). The Marseilles is among the most prominent of the grand apartment hotels erected at the turn of the century on the Upper West Side. The Beaux-Arts building—with its limestone base, brick facing, terra-cotta trim, and mansard roof—was built in anticipation of the opening of an IRT subway station at West 103rd Street.

Master Building, 310–312 Riverside Drive (Harvey Wiley Corbett of the firm Helmle, Corbett & Harrison, with Sugarman & Berger, associated architects, 1928–29). This innovative mixed-use structure is a significant work by Corbett, an influential designer of skyscrapers. The building was planned as a 29-story apartment hotel that would incorporate the Nicholas Roerich Museum—including galleries, a library, and an auditorium (now a theater)—on its ground floor. The building is among the finest Art Deco high-rise structures in New York

City. Among its notable features are the patterned brickwork that varies from dark to light as the building rises, the dramatic setbacks and irregular massing of the upper floors, the ornamental crown, and the innovative use of corner windows.

Midtown Theater, now the Metro Theater, 2624–2626 Broadway (Boak & Paris, 1932–33). In the 1920s and 1930s Broadway on the Upper West Side was lined with neighborhood movie theaters. The Art Deco Midtown is not only one of the few still functioning, but it also has one of the finest theater facades in New York. The street front is clad entirely in colored terra cotta, primarily beige and black. The focus of the design is a medallion with a bas relief of figures and masks representing comedy and tragedy. The marquee, with its horizontal chrome banding, is largely original.

New York Cancer Hospital, later the Towers Nursing Home, 455 Central Park West and 32 West 106th Street (Charles C. Haight, 1884–86, and additions, 1889–90). Founded in 1884, the New York Cancer Hospital was the first institution in the United States (and the second in the world, after the London Cancer Hospital) dedicated exclusively to the study and treatment of cancer. Haight's design was inspired by Le Lude, one of the great Renaissance châteaux of the Loire Valley. The five massive round towers were planned to provide a maximum amount of light and air to the wards and to facilitate nursing supervision from the center of each ward; it was also thought that the shape prevented air stagnation and the accumulation of dirt and germs in corners. The building is now vacant, awaiting conversion to residential use.

New York Free Circulating Library, Bloomingdale Branch, now the Ukrainian Academy of Arts and Sciences, 206 West 100th Street (James Brown Lord, 1898). The Bloomingdale Branch Library was commissioned by the New York Free Circulating Library, an organization established in 1878 by wealthy New Yorkers to provide for the "moral and intellectual elevation of the masses." In order to serve the increasingly populous Upper West Side the library erected this fireproof steel-frame structure designed in the French classical style. The library became a branch of the New York Public Library in 1901; in 1961 the building was sold to a private organization for use as a research facility devoted to the study of Ukrainian culture.

New-York Historical Society, 170 Central Park West (York & Sawyer, 1903–08; wings, Walker & Gillette, 1937–38). This museum and research facility, designed in a severe Classical Revival style, was built to house a rich repository of art work and historical material relating primarily to the history of New York City and New York State and collected since the organization of the society in 1804. The granite-faced central pavilion with its Ionic colonnade is complemented by end wings added several decades later.

New York Society for Ethical Culture, 2 West 64th Street (Robert D. Kohn, 1909–10). The Ethical Culture meetinghouse is among a small group of exceptional buildings designed by Robert Kohn in the Secessionist mode, a reform style that developed in Vienna at the turn of the century. The austere geometry and abstract classicism of Viennese design are evident in this structure and in Kohn's New York Evening Post Building (see p. 34). For both buildings Kohn's wife, Estelle Rumbold Kohn, provided sculptural decoration.

Normandy Apartments, 140 Riverside Drive (Emery Roth & Sons, 1938–39). The Normandy is a masterpiece of the apartment-house specialist Emery Roth. Overlooking the Hudson River, this twin-towered building is the last of Roth's major prewar apartment houses. The building combines the Italian Renaissance forms that Roth had perfected at the Beresford (see p. 122) and the San Remo (see p. 132) on Central Park West with new Moderne features such as streamlined corners and concave entrances featuring mosaic detail.

Pomander Walk, 3–22 Pomander Walk, 261–267 West 94th Street, and 260–274 West 95th Street (King & Campbell, 1921). One of the most surprising residential enclaves in New York City, Pomander Walk consists of 16 two-story neo-Tudor houses facing onto a private walk and 11 additional houses on West 94th and West 95th streets. This picturesque complex was built by the restaurateur and developer Thomas Healy in an attempt to recreate the village atmosphere evoked in Lewis Parker's popular play *Pomander Walk*.

Frederick and Lydia Prentiss House, 1 Riverside Drive (C. P. H. Gilbert, 1899–1901). One of three extraordinary town houses at the southernmost end of Riverside Drive, designed by the prolific architect C. P. H. Gilbert, this limestone-fronted Beaux-Arts structure is set on a curved lot and has two visible facades, one of which fronts a triangular court shared with the neighboring Sutphen House (see p. 133).

Red House, 350 West 85th Street (Harde & Short, 1903–04). With its combination of French Gothic and Renaissance elements, the Red House recalls early 16th-century residences in the style of François I. This red brick and white terra-cotta building is the first of the four major French Gothic–inspired apartment houses designed by Harde & Short and is a reflection of the changing character of the Upper West Side in the early years of the 20th century when apartment houses began to supplant row houses as the dominant type of residence.

Isaac L. and Julia B. Rice House, now the Yeshiva Ketana of Manhattan, 346 West 89th Street (Herts & Tallant, 1901–03). The Rice mansion is one of only two freestanding houses that survive on Riverside Drive. The noted theater architects Herts & Tallant designed this mansion for the lawyer, writer, and chess expert Isaac Rice and his wife, Julia, a physician who, although she never practiced, was involved in medical issues and was responsible for the creation of quiet zones around New York City hospitals. Villa Julia, as the Rices called their home, combines Georgian and Beaux-Arts forms in a highly individualistic manner. In 1908 C. P. H. Gilbert undertook alterations (most barely visible) for the second owner, Solomon Schinasi, a partner in the tobacco firm of Schinasi Brothers (see Morris and Laurette Schinasi House, p. 132).

103, 104, 105 and 107–109 Riverside Drive and 332 West 83rd Street Houses (Clarence True, 1898–99). The architect/developer Clarence True erected these five houses as part of a row of six (No. 102 has been demolished), using his signature "Elizabethan Revival" mode of design, which combined English and French Renaissance forms; the idiosyncratic style is unique to True's residential work on the Upper West Side. The facades of Nos. 103 and 104 were redesigned by Clinton & Russell and rebuilt in 1910–11 in a manner that recalled the original, after a lawsuit brought by a neighboring property owner forced the removal of the original stoops and bowfronts, which encroached on the public way. The facades of Nos. 105 and 107–109 were redesigned by Bosworth & Holden and Tracy, Swartwout & Litchfield, respectively, and rebuilt in the same years.

◀ **Riverside Drive—West 80th–81st Street Historic District.** This small historic district illustrates, in microcosm, the early residential development of the West End section of New York's Upper West Side. Development began on West 81st Street in 1891, with the construction of a row of five transitional Romanesque Revival / neo-Renaissance row houses designed by Charles Israels. Two years later Israels designed an additional row on West 80th Street. Another wave of row-house construction occurred in 1897–99, when the architect/developer Clarence True built the houses on and adjacent to Riverside Drive. These large brick and stone row houses are characteristic of True's Northern European–inspired designs. Contemporaneous with the row houses are three modest French flats erected on West 80th Street for middle-class families. In 1926 one of True's houses was demolished and replaced by a 16-story neoclassical apartment building.

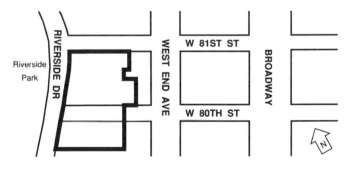

RIVERSIDE DRIVE—WEST 80TH–81ST STREET HISTORIC DISTRICT

◀ **Riverside Drive—West 105th Street Historic District.** This small district built on the gentle slope leading to Riverside Drive consists of residences erected in 1899–1902. The cohesive quality of the district's row houses and town houses is the result of five factors: the brief construction span; the use of English basements with entries at or near the sidewalk level; the use of similar materials, predominantly limestone, to create a unified streetscape; the exuberant Beaux-Arts detail chosen by all four architecture firms active in the district

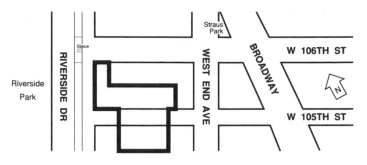

RIVERSIDE DRIVE—WEST 105TH STREET HISTORIC DISTRICT

(Janes & Leo, Mowbray & Uffinger, Hoppin & Koen, and Robert D. Kohn); and the covenants that required buildings of "suitable character and such as are a benefit to the neighborhood."

🍎 **Riverside Drive—West End Historic District.** The West End section, the portion of the Upper West Side located west of Broadway, developed somewhat later than the area near Central Park, which was served by the elevated trains running along Columbus Avenue. Although the earliest buildings in the district are row houses dating from 1884, development did not begin in earnest until three years later. Between 1887 and 1897, row houses were built on speculation along the length of West End Avenue and adjacent side streets. Notable examples include the neo-Renaissance rows designed by Thom & Wilson in yellow brick on West 89th and 90th streets, the two surviving blockfronts on West End Avenue between West 90th and 91st streets, and several groups designed by Clarence True on West End Avenue at West 91st and 92nd streets. Early in the 20th century elegant apartment houses began to be built in the district, many of them replacing the rows on West End Avenue. Architects who specialized in apartment-house design were responsible for some of the district's finest multiple dwellings, notably the Chautauqua (Schwartz & Gross, 1911; 574 West End Avenue), with its Sullivanesque ornament, and the Evanston (George and Edward Blum, 1910; 610 West End Avenue), with its unusual terra-cotta and iron detail. In the 1920s grand apartment houses were erected on Riverside Drive; the massing of these buildings follows the curve of the drive.

Riverside Park and Riverside Drive Scenic Landmark, West 72nd Street to St. Clair Place (Frederick Law Olmsted, 1873–75; additions, Clifton Lloyd, 1934–37). Riverside Park was initially established in 1865 as a way of increasing real estate values on the Upper West Side. Riverside Drive was laid out as a separate entity in 1870. Three years later the city's Parks Department asked Olmsted, the landscape architect of Central Park (see p. 122) and Prospect Park (see p. 178), to draw up a formal plan for the park and drive. It was Olmsted's idea to treat the two as a single entity that would take advantage of the natural beauty of the site. The curving drive was landscaped with trees, walkways, and

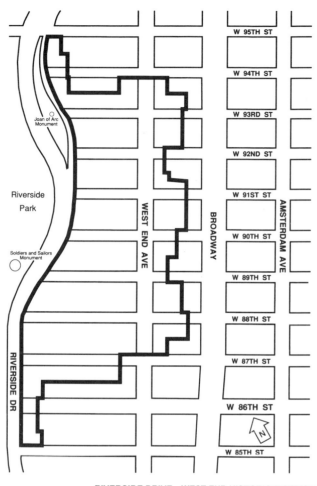

RIVERSIDE DRIVE—WEST END HISTORIC DISTRICT

viewing sites, and the hillside leading down toward the New York Central's railroad tracks and the Hudson River was planted. The wide straight walkway within the park (located on top of the railroad tracks) and the paths and playgrounds alongside the river were not part of Olmsted's design but were laid out by Clifton Lloyd at the time of the construction of the Henry Hudson Parkway, during Robert Moses's tenure as Parks Commissioner. Since the late 19th century Riverside Drive has acquired some of New York's finest monuments. The most prominent of these are Grant's Tomb (see p. 142) and the Soldiers' and Sailors' Monument (see p. 132). On a more modest scale are such important works of public sculpture as Anna Hyatt Huntington's *Joan of Arc* at West 93rd Street and Karl Bitter's *Franz Sigel* at West 106th Street.

St. Agnes Church Parish House. See Trinity School (p. 133).

St. Paul's Methodist Episcopal Church and Parish House, now the Church of St. Paul and St. Andrew (United Methodist), 540 West End Avenue (Robert H. Robertson, 1895–97). The design of St. Paul's Methodist Episcopal Church and parish house reflects a major shift from the picturesque Romanesque Revival to a style dominated by Classical and Renaissance-inspired forms. With its bold octagonal campanile, tiled buttresses, and singular terra-cotta detail, St. Paul's exemplifies the eclecticism of the 1890s in its combination of elements from many different sources, including Early Christian, early Italian Renaissance, Spanish Renaissance, and German Romanesque architecture.

San Remo Apartments, 145–146 Central Park West (Emery Roth, 1929–30). Soaring over Central Park, the San Remo is one of the most significant components of the Central Park West skyline. The building was designed by Emery Roth at the pinnacle of his career as a designer of apartment houses. The San Remo and the nearby Beresford (see p. 122) are examples of Roth's sophisticated adaptation of Italian Renaissance forms to high-rise residential design.

Morris and Laurette Schinasi House, 351 Riverside Drive (William B. Tuthill, 1907–09). This flamboyant marble residence, one of only two freestanding mansions surviving on Riverside Drive, was built by a wealthy cigarette manufacturer and partner in the tobacco firm of Schinasi Brothers. The early 16th-century French Renaissance style popular for the châteaux along the Loire was adapted here to an urban setting overlooking the Hudson.

Shearith Israel Synagogue (the Spanish and Portuguese Synagogue), 99 Central Park West (Brunner & Tryon, 1896–97). As the Jewish population in the United States expanded, especially in the second half of the 19th century, debate arose over the appropriate style for synagogues. In the post–Civil War years, Moorish-inspired designs were popular. Late in the century, after archaeologists discovered the ruins of the Second Temple in Jerusalem, built during the Roman occupation of Palestine, this classical monument became the model for new synagogues. Congregation Shearith Israel is believed to have been the first to adopt this style when it erected its new home on Central Park West. Shearith Israel, founded in 1654 by Sephardic Jews who arrived in New York from a Dutch colony in Brazil, is the oldest Jewish congregation in North America. This synagogue is the fourth erected by the congregation since it built its initial home in 1730.

Soldiers' and Sailors' Monument, Riverside Drive at West 89th Street (Stoughton & Stoughton with Paul E. M. DuBoy, 1897–02). The Soldiers' and Sailors' Memorial Arch (see p. 184) in Brooklyn and this monument on Riverside Drive are physical manifestations of the nostalgia for the Civil War era that swept across the United States in the late 19th century as the horrors of the war faded into history. Although a Civil War monument was proposed as early as 1869, it was not until 1897 that enough interest was generated to hold a design competition. The monument was originally intended for Grand Army Plaza, near the entrance to Central Park; the design that won the competition needed to be reworked when the site was changed to Riverside Drive. Construction of the marble monument and its related terraces began in 1900. The cylindrical building is an enlarged version of the Hellenistic Monument of Lysicrates in Athens.

John and Mary Sutphen House, 311 West 72nd Street (C. P. H. Gilbert, 1901–02). The Sutphen House and the neighboring Kleeberg and Prentiss houses (see pp. 126 and 128) are all French-inspired limestone-fronted dwellings built on oddly shaped lots in accordance with restrictive covenants that required the construction of high-quality residences. These restrictions were inaugurated by John Sutphen's father, who once owned the entire Riverside Drive frontage between West 72nd and West 73rd streets.

Trinity School (including the former St. Agnes Parish House), 121–147 West 91st Street (school, Charles C. Haight, 1893–94; parish house, William A. Potter, 1888–92). Trinity School, established in 1709, followed New York's population north until it settled on the Upper West Side in 1894. Haight designed an English Collegiate Gothic structure not unlike his contemporaneous work at Yale. The building incorporates large windows that maximize natural light and air circulation. Adjacent to the school is the Romanesque Revival, granite-and-red-sandstone parish house originally built for use by Trinity Church's St. Agnes Chapel. When the church was demolished in 1944, the parish house was converted into classrooms.

⚜ Upper West Side—Central Park West Historic District. Extending westward from the western edge of Central Park, this large district evokes the distinctive qualities of the Upper West Side, from its powerful iconography of twin towers along Central Park West to its active commerce along Columbus Avenue to its residential side streets. The district is defined by a large concentration of architecturally distinctive buildings erected on the Upper West Side during the 50 years in which substantial development occurred in the neighborhood. The inauguration of the Ninth Avenue Elevated in 1879 along what is now Columbus Avenue opened the vast unoccupied regions of the Upper West Side to speculative development, and hundreds of neo-Grec, Romanesque Revival, Queen Anne, and neo-Renaissance row houses were built on the side streets between Central Park West and Amsterdam Avenue, while tenements and French flats for middle-class citizens were constructed along Amsterdam and Columbus avenues and on the adjoining streets. A few grand apartment houses such as the Dakota (see p. 125) were built in this early period, but most apartment-house construction in the district dates to the turn of the century, when the neighborhood's great Beaux-Arts buildings were erected. Beginning in 1902, West 67th Street was transformed into a unique enclave of apartment houses, most designed in a neo-Gothic mode with duplex studio spaces for artists. In the 1920s many large apartment houses and apartment hotels were built along Central Park West and other streets in the district, but most construction ceased with the advent of the Great Depression in 1929. During the entire span of development, important institutional buildings were also erected, including museums, churches, and synagogues.

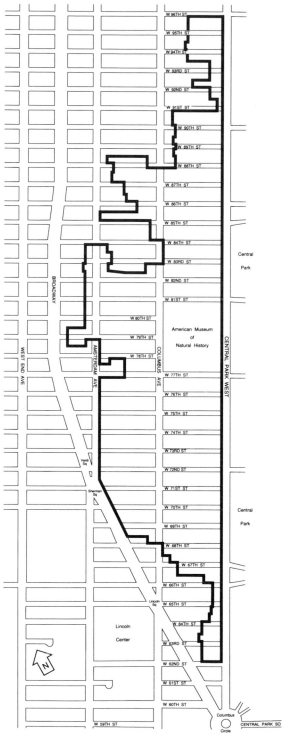

**UPPER WEST SIDE—
CENTRAL PARK
WEST HISTORIC
DISTRICT**

Upper West Side—Central Park West Historic District. The north side of West 78th Street between Amsterdam and Columbus avenues. Houses built in 1890 (Thom & Wilson, architects). Photo: Caroline Kane

Verdi Square Scenic Landmark, Broadway and Amsterdam Avenue at West 72nd Street. This small triangular park is dominated by a statue of Giuseppe Verdi, commissioned by New York's Italian community from the Sicilian sculptor Pasquale Civiletti and unveiled in 1906. The granite pedestal is encircled by figures representing characters from four of Verdi's operas.

Charles A. Vissani House, 143 West 95th Street (James W. Cole, 1889). Appropriately, this Gothic Revival town house was commissioned by the Very Reverend Charles A. Vissani, the first Commissary General of the Holy Land for the United States. It housed not only Vissani but also a group of Franciscan priests who worked with him in his mission to develop interest in the preservation of the holy places in Jerusalem and Palestine. The building has been divided into apartments.

🍎 **West 71st Street Historic District.** This small, nearly block-long district on a quiet cul-de-sac ends in a wall that separates the street from the railroad tracks to the west. The district consists of 33 row houses, erected in six groups over only a three-year period (1893 to 1896), a single town house of 1903–04, and an apartment building erected in 1924. The block's cohesive quality results

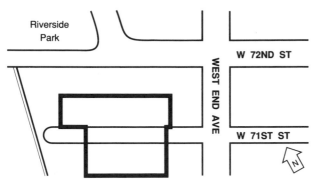

WEST 71ST STREET HISTORIC DISTRICT

from the consistent use of Renaissance-inspired detail on all of the masonry row houses.

309 West 72nd Street House, also known as the William E. Diller House (Gilbert A. Schellenger, 1899–1901). William E. Diller, a physician and an active builder of single-family houses, erected this impressive Renaissance Revival town house as a speculative venture. Built on a site with restrictive covenants that required high-quality construction, the house complements the neighboring residences commissioned by the Kleeberg, Prentiss, and Sutphen families (see pp. 126, 128, and 133).

332 West 83rd Street House. See p. 128.

316, 318, 320, 322, 324, and 326 West 85th Street Houses (Clarence True, 1892). This row of six brick houses trimmed with Maynard red sandstone is among the most unusual designed by Clarence True. The houses were commissioned by Charles Judson, with whom True shared a business address. The well-preserved row is of note for the Spanish tile used on the rectangular oriels and projecting false roofs and for its brickwork laid in a rusticated manner to echo the rusticated stonework on the entrance level.

329, 331, 333, 335, and 337 West 85th Street Houses (Ralph S. Townsend, 1890–91). Townsend's row of five Queen Anne/Romanesque Revival brick-and-brownstone houses was erected in the decade when much of the Upper West Side west of Broadway was emerging as a desirable residential neighborhood.

254 West 102nd Street House. See below.

854, 856, and 858 West End Avenue and 254 West 102nd Street Houses (Schneider & Herter, 1892–93). These four Queen Anne/Romanesque Revival brownstone houses are the sole surviving examples of a type of site planning commonly employed on West End Avenue corners in the 1890s, when this street was being developed with speculative row houses for upper-middle-class buyers. Each of these groups featured residences along the avenue, a prominent corner house, and an additional house facing the side street.

West End Collegiate Church and Collegiate School, West End Avenue at West 77th Street (Robert W. Gibson, 1892–93). The West End Collegiate Church traces its roots back to the organization of the first church in New Amsterdam in 1628. Appropriately, when the church built on the Upper West Side, a style evocative of Dutch Renaissance architecture was chosen. The massing and the use of stepped gables, strapwork ornament, and finials are reminiscent of the design of the early 17th-century Butcher's Market in Haarlem, the Netherlands. The school building, erected to house the oldest private secondary school in America, founded in 1638, was built as a part of the church complex; the Collegiate School is now an independent institution.

⚫ **West End—Collegiate Historic District**. Named for the nearby West End Collegiate Church (see above), this historic district consists primarily of row houses that developers built on speculation in the last 15 years of the 19th century. Many of the city's most talented architects specializing in row-house design—including C. P. H. Gilbert, Lamb & Rich, and Clarence True—were active in the district, creating blockfronts with an eclectic blend of Italian, French, Flemish Renaissance, and other stylistic forms. Lamb & Rich's 1891 blockfront in the François I style on the west side of West End Avenue between West 76th and West 77th streets is among the most beautiful on the Upper West Side. In the first decades of the 20th century several apartment houses were built in the district, reflecting the decline in row-house construction as land values rose and as the apartment house became an increasingly acceptable residential alternative for affluent New Yorkers.

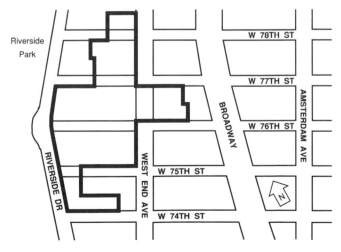

WEST END—COLLEGIATE HISTORIC DISTRICT

North of 110th Street

Apollo Theater, originally Hurtig & Seamon's New (Burlesque) Theater, 253 West 125th Street (George Keister, 1913–14). The Apollo became famous in the 1930s when the theater began to feature black entertainers. Today it is world-renowned as a center for the display of African-American performing talent. In recognition of the Apollo's importance in the history of American entertainment and, more specifically, its central role in the presentation of major African-American performers, both the exterior and the **interior** of the theater have been designated as landmarks.

Astor Row, 8–62 West 130th Street (Charles Buek, 1880–83). The 28 houses of Astor Row were erected in three campaigns on land owned by William Astor. The coherent blockfront of brick houses with wooden porches is unique in New York City. Nos. 8–22 were built in freestanding pairs, while the remaining 20 houses are linked at their rear sections. The entire row is undergoing rehabilitation in 1992.

🖤 **Audubon Terrace Historic District.** Established on the former estate of artist and naturalist John James Audubon, Audubon Terrace is one of America's first planned cultural centers. The complex was conceived by Archer M. Huntington, philanthropist, Spanish scholar, and heir to the Southern Pacific Railroad fortune. In 1904 Huntington founded the Hispanic Society of America and commissioned his cousin Charles P. Huntington to design a gallery and library for a site on West 155th Street, just west of Broadway. The Hispanic Society (1904–08) was soon joined by the American Numismatic Society (1907), the American Geographical Society (1911; now housing Boricua College), the Museum of the American Indian (1915–22), and the Spanish-language Church of Our Lady of Esperanza (1912), all designed by Huntington. Later the American Academy of Arts and Letters and the National Institute of Arts and Letters (now the American Academy and Institute of Arts and Letters) moved into a building designed by McKim, Mead & White (1921–23) at the west end of the complex; Cass Gilbert designed an auditorium and art gallery addition for these organizations in 1928. All of the buildings share a unified

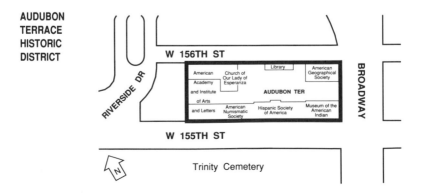

Italian Renaissance style and are set around a plaza embellished with sculpture by Archer Huntington's wife, Anna Hyatt Huntington.

James A. and Ruth M. Bailey House, now the M. Marshall Blake Funeral Home, 10 St. Nicholas Place (Samuel B. Reed, 1886–88). The circus impresario James A. Bailey (of the famed Barnum & Bailey Circus) commissioned this flamboyant Romanesque Revival limestone house with Flemish gables. At the time of its construction the house was located in a relatively undeveloped neighborhood and enjoyed fine views to the east, toward Long Island Sound.

City College, now City College North Campus, City University of New York, Convent Avenue between West 138th and West 140th streets (George B. Post, 1897–1930). What is now City College was founded as the Free Academy in 1847 and was located on Lexington Avenue near East 23rd Street. Renamed in 1866, the college purchased the site of its uptown campus along Convent Avenue in 1897. After Post won the design competition for the new campus, this Collegiate Gothic complex was erected. All of the early campus buildings and the three original gates—at West 138th, 139th, and 140th streets—were constructed of dark Manhattan schist, excavated on the site, and trimmed with contrasting white terra cotta. The buildings are: Main Building (now Shepard Hall), 1903–08; Chemistry Building (now Baskerville Hall), 1903–08; Mechanic Arts Building (now Compton Hall), 1903–08; Technology Building (now Goethals Hall), 1928–30; Townsend Harris Hall, 1903–06; and Gymnasium (now Wingate Hall), 1903–08.

The Cloisters, Fort Tryon Park (Charles Collens of Allen, Collens & Willis, 1934–39). The Cloisters, located in the midst of Fort Tryon Park (see p. 142), was designed by the Boston architect Charles Collens to house a portion of the Metropolitan Museum of Art's medieval art collection and to incorporate fragments from various cloisters and other medieval buildings that had been collected by the sculptor George Gray Barnard and had been purchased for the museum by John D. Rockefeller, Jr. The building, designed to resemble a French Romanesque abbey, has a tall tower that is an important focal point in the Fort Tryon Park landscape.

Columbia University, Broadway at West 116th Street. In 1891 Columbia College announced that it would abandon its campus on East 49th Street and Park Avenue and move to the site of New York Hospital's Bloomingdale Insane Asylum. In December 1893 Charles McKim was chosen as architect of the new campus; designs were prepared in 1894. McKim's axial plan, inspired by Beaux-Arts concepts, called for a central library symmetrically flanked by classroom buildings, a chapel, and an assembly hall, and a student center to the rear of the library, all to be built on a raised platform. Much of this plan was completed, and several of the structures are now designated landmarks. As Columbia grew, land to the south and east was purchased and McKim, Mead & White enlarged the campus plan.

 Casa Italiana, 1151–1161 Amsterdam Avenue (McKim, Mead & White, 1926–27). Casa Italiana is located on the east campus, acquired by

Columbia early in the 20th century. William M. Kendall, a partner in McKim, Mead & White, was responsible for this building, appropriately styled to copy a 15th-century Roman palazzo. Constructed to house the university's center for Italian studies, Casa Italiana was primarily funded by wealthy New Yorkers of Italian descent, notably members of the Paterno family—leading real estate developers.

Low Memorial Library (McKim, Mead & White, 1894–98). Charles McKim's monumental domed library is at the heart of the Columbia campus. The building is raised above its surroundings on a series of plazas linked by stairways and commands the main entrance to the academic precinct. Modeled on the Roman Pantheon, the library is the only building on the original Columbia campus that is faced entirely in stone. The library was a gift from Columbia's president Seth Low as a memorial to his father, the China trader Abiel Abbot Low. The grandeur of the exterior is continued on the **interior**, which features a vestibule marked by a pair of Connemara marble columns and an enormous domed octagonal rotunda supported by four great piers and 16 columns of green Vermont marble. The library's collections were moved to a new building in 1934 and Low became an administrative center.

St. Paul's Chapel (Howells & Stokes, 1904–07). St. Paul's Chapel was a gift of Olivia and Caroline Phelps Stokes, in memory of their parents, and was designed by their nephew, I. N. Phelps Stokes, and his partner John Mead Howells. The building, a magnificent example of Northern Italian Renaissance design, is faced with burned brick, limestone, and terra cotta and is surmounted by a tile roof.

Croton Aqueduct System. On July 4, 1842, amidst great fanfare, the Croton Aqueduct was inaugurated, providing New Yorkers with pure water brought from the Croton Reservoir in northern Westchester County. Water was piped from the reservoir to the Harlem River, where it passed over High Bridge (a temporary pipe served the system until the bridge was completed in 1848) and ran down Tenth Avenue to a receiving reservoir at 79th Street (a site now in Central Park) and finally to the famous Egyptian Revival distributing reservoir on Fifth Avenue at West 42nd Street (the site of the New York Public Library). As the city grew, the water system was expanded. In 1872 the High Bridge Water Tower was constructed as part of a northern Manhattan reservoir. By the 1870s it was clear that the original Croton system could not meet New York City's water needs and the New Croton Aqueduct was proposed. Work on the new aqueduct, begun in 1883, included the construction of a major gatehouse at West 135th Street. After the turn of the century New York City's water system expanded dramatically with the construction of the Catskill and Delaware water systems. Although the Croton systems still provide New York with water, only the gatehouse remains in active use.

High Bridge, spanning the Harlem River between West 170th Street, the Bronx, and High Bridge Park, Manhattan (John J. Jervis, 1838–48; addition, 1860; replacement of central piers, 1923). Upon its completion, High Bridge was hailed as a feat of engineering. The stone arches of the bridge were modeled after such ancient Roman aqueducts as the Pont du Gard in southern France. The aqueduct on the bridge carried Croton water from the Bronx to Manhattan via two 36-inch mains. In 1860 a 90-inch main was installed atop the earlier two and the walls of the bridge raised. In 1923 the navy removed the central piers and replaced them with a steel arch in order to improve navigation on the Harlem River. The aqueduct is no longer in use.

High Bridge Water Tower, High Bridge Park (John B. Jervis, 1866–72). This 200-foot-high granite water tower was erected with a 47,000-gallon tank that provided gravity pressure for Manhattan's water supply, a necessity by the early 1870s as the use of flush toilets increased. Water was pumped into the tank from an adjacent reservoir, which was replaced by a swimming pool in 1934. Fifteen years later the tower was removed from service. In 1989–90 the stonework was cleaned and restored and the cupola, which had burned, was reconstructed (William Hall Partnership, architects).

135th Street Gatehouse, West 135th Street at Convent Avenue (Frederick S. Cook, 1884–90). The granite and brownstone gatehouse is the most impressive local architectural feature of the New Croton Aqueduct. The building was erected to regulate the flow of water from both the new and old Croton Aqueduct systems. Although relatively small, the building looms like an impregnable medieval fortress, symbolically protecting New York's vital water supply.

Dunbar Apartments, West 149th Street to West 150th Street between Frederick Douglas and Adam Clayton Powell, Jr.,boulevards (Andrew J. Thomas, 1926–28). The Dunbar was the first major nonprofit cooperative apartment complex built specifically for African-Americans. Financed by John D. Rockefeller, Jr., the Dunbar consists of six five- and six-story walk-up buildings set around a landscaped central courtyard. Named for the poet Paul Laurence Dunbar, the cooperative (now rental buildings) attracted many of the most prominent members of the Harlem community, including W. E. B. DuBois, A. Philip Randolph, Paul Robeson, and Bill ("Bojangles") Robinson.

Dyckman House, Broadway at West 204th Street (c. 1785; restoration, Alexander M. Welch, 1915–16). The only farmhouse in the Dutch Colonial style surviving in Manhattan, the Dyckman House is constructed of fieldstone, brick, and wood and contains the gambrel roof, spring eaves, and porch typical of rural Dutch buildings. The house replaced an earlier building erected by the Dyckmans that was burned in the Revolutionary War. In 1915, when the house was threatened with demolition, two Dyckman sisters initiated a restoration project (under the architectural direction of the husband of one of the women), and presented the house to the city.

17 East 128th Street House (c. 1864). In the mid-19th century northern Manhattan was dotted with hundreds of wooden houses, few of which survive. This French Second Empire example is one of a handful of buildings still standing that relate to Harlem's early history as a rural village. The house is

Dyckman House, Broadway at West 204th Street (c. 1785; restoration, Alexander M. Welch, 1915–16). Photo: Carl Forster

remarkably well preserved; it retains its original stoop, decorated porch, double doors, shutters, and multicolored slate roof.

Fort Tryon Park Scenic Landmark (Olmsted Brothers, 1930–35). Fort Tryon Park is an outstanding example of the work of Olmsted Brothers, the successor firm to that founded by Frederick Law Olmsted. The park occupies a portion of the site of the Revolutionary War Battle of Washington Heights; after the war the land was parceled into several country estates. John D. Rockefeller, Jr., began buying the estates in 1917 with the intention of creating a park. In 1930 he presented Fort Tryon Park to the city. The park contains varied landscape features, among them a magnificent heather garden, and takes full advantage of its spectacular setting overlooking the Hudson River and the Palisades. In addition to the parkland, Rockefeller also purchased a collection of medieval art, housed at the time in a nearby stable, and donated it to the Metropolitan Museum of Art. The museum built the Cloisters, located within the park, for display of the collection (see p. 139).

Graham Court Apartments, 1923–1937 Adam Clayton Powell, Jr., Boulevard (Clinton & Russell, 1899–1901). Commissioned by William Waldorf Astor, whose family had owned this site in Harlem since the 1860s, Graham Court is one of the grandest courtyard apartment houses in New York and became the prototype for the Apthorp Apartments (see p. 121). The building, designed in the Italian Renaissance style, offers evidence of Harlem's early development as an affluent urban neighborhood.

General Ulysses S. Grant Tomb, now the General Grant National Memorial, Riverside Drive at West 122nd Street (John H. Duncan, 1891–97).

Dramatically sited near the north end of Riverside Park, Grant's Tomb is among the most impressive Classical Revival monuments of its period. Begun six years after Grant's death in 1885, the tomb was erected at a time of increasing nostalgia for the Civil War era with money contributed by some 90,000 people, including many African-Americans. Duncan's granite monument was modeled on reconstructions of one of the great classical tombs, the Mausoleum of Halicarnassus. The **interior**, incorporating a domed rotunda and dominated by a central crypt with twin sarcophagi (for Grant and his wife), was inspired by the Invalides, the final resting place of Napoleon, in Paris.

🍎 **Hamilton Heights Historic District.** Located immediately north of City College (see p. 139), the Hamilton Heights Historic District consists almost entirely of row houses and churches erected between 1886 and 1906. The land was once part of Alexander Hamilton's estate, and Hamilton's own house (see p. 144) is preserved at 287 Convent Avenue. The area remained undeveloped until the 1880s, when the new elevated railroads brought it within commuting distance of downtown commercial districts. Speculative developers erected houses in a wide range of styles, including some remarkable examples of Flemish and Dutch Revival at 452–466 and 453–467 West 144th Street (William E. Mowbray, 1886–90). Three important churches anchor the edges of the district; architecturally, the most notable is R. H. Robertson's St. Luke's Episcopal Church (1892–95), 285 Convent Avenue at West 141st Street. The

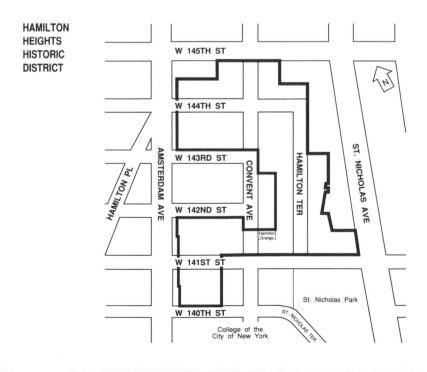

Harlem River Houses, West 151st to 153rd streets, Macombs Place to Harlem River Drive (Archibald Manning Brown, chief architect, 1936–37). Photo: Carl Forster

latest building erected in the district, the Art Deco–style Ivey Delph Apartments at 19 Hamilton Terrace, was designed by Vertner W. Tandy, the first African-American architect registered in New York State.

Alexander Hamilton House, the Grange, now the Hamilton Grange National Monument, 287 Convent Avenue (John McComb, Jr., 1801–02). Alexander Hamilton's country house, designed in the Federal style, once stood on a 35-acre tract. In 1889, when the house was threatened with demolition, it was moved to its present location and somewhat altered. The Grange later served as the rectory for the adjacent St. Luke's Episcopal Church. It was purchased by a preservation organization in 1924, opened to the public nine years later, and donated to the U.S. Department of the Interior in 1962.

Harlem Courthouse, 170 East 121st Street (Thom & Wilson, 1891–93). One of the most impressive buildings in East Harlem, the former Harlem Courthouse is an idiosyncratic Romanesque Revival brick structure with an octagonal tower and a four-faced clock. The building was erected to house the New York City Police Court and District Court, but, after the reorganization of the court system in 1962, other city agencies moved into the building.

Harlem River Houses, West 151st to West 153rd streets, Macombs Place to Harlem River Drive (Archibald Manning Brown, chief architect, 1936–37). Harlem River Houses was the first federally funded housing project in New York City. Built in 1936 as "a recognition in brick and mortar of the special and urgent needs of Harlem," the project was an attempt to provide high-quality housing for African-American working people. The four- and five-story

Langston Hughes House, 20 East 127th Street (Alexander Wilson, 1869). Langston Hughes lived and worked here between 1947 and his death in 1967. Photo: Carl Forster

buildings of the nine-acre complex are set around large open areas that are land-scaped with walkways as wide as streets, recreation sites, and lawns. The human scale, generous open space, and careful detailing of the project set a standard for public housing that has rarely been matched. Among the architects of Harlem River Houses was John Louis Wilson, Jr., one of the first African-American architects registered in New York State.

Langston Hughes House, 20 East 127th Street (Alexander Wilson, 1869). Langston Hughes, one of the leading figures of the Harlem Renaissance, lived on the top floor of this Italianate brownstone from 1947 until his death in 1967. Hughes wrote many works while residing on East 127th Street, including his humorous pieces documenting the life of the common man in Harlem (as represented by Jess B. Semple) and a series of books exploring aspects of African-American culture.

Interborough Rapid Transit System Underground Stations, 110th Street and 116th Street—Columbia University, and **Interborough Rapid Transit System, Manhattan Valley Viaduct,** Broadway from West 122nd to West 135th streets. See p. 18.

Chapel of the Intercession (Episcopal), now the Church of the Intercession Complex, Broadway at West 155th Street (Bertram Goodhue of the firm Cram, Goodhue & Ferguson, 1910–14). The Church of the Intercession, a chapel of Trinity Church until 1976, is a remarkable complex of English Gothic inspiration, consisting of the main church, with its gabled front and tall tower, and a full cloister, vicarage, vestry, and parish house to the rear. Intercession has been called "the quintessential Goodhue church," and was the architect's own favorite; he is, in fact, buried in the north transept.

Jeffrey's Hook Lighthouse, also known as the Little Red Lighthouse, Fort Washington Park (1880; reconstruction, 1921). Erected in Sandy Hook, New Jersey, in 1880, this small conical iron lighthouse was moved to Jeffrey's Hook on Manhattan's Hudson River shore in 1921. The lighthouse, located beneath the George Washington Bridge, is best known as the subject of the children's book *The Little Red Lighthouse and the Great Gray Bridge*, written by Hildegarde Swift and published in 1942. Threatened with demolition after being taken out of service in 1951, the lighthouse was saved after an outcry from children led to its acquisition by New York City's Parks Department.

☙Jumel Terrace Historic District. This small historic district consists largely of row houses erected adjacent to the Roger Morris House (see p. 147) after the former Morris estate was sold in 1882 by the heirs of Madame Eliza Jumel. In that year the estate's carriage drive (now Sylvan Terrace) was built up with 20 two-story wooden houses. Restored in 1979–81, these houses are among the few surviving examples of the frame dwellings once common in northern Manhattan. The remainder of the district contains Queen Anne, Romanesque Revival, and neo-Renaissance row houses erected between 1890 and 1902.

Metropolitan Baptist Church, originally the New York Presbyterian Church, 151 West 128th Street (John R. Thomas, 1884–85; additions, Richard R. Davis, 1889–90). Although built in two sections, this church reads as a single unified

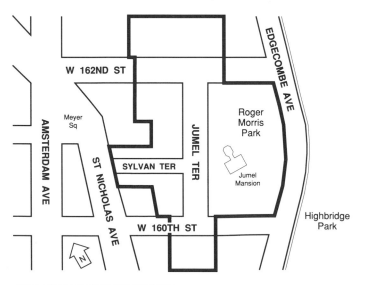

JUMEL TERRACE HISTORIC DISTRICT

Jumel Terrace Historic District. View of Sylvan Terrace about 1900. Houses built in 1882 (Gilbert Robinson, Jr., architect). Photo: Landmarks Preservation Commission collection

structure. John R. Thomas was responsible for the chapel and lecture room on West 128th Street, while the main sanctuary on Adam Clayton Powell Boulevard is attributed to the Harlem architect Richard Davis (who may have used Thomas's unexecuted design). The unusual building combines Romanesque-inspired massing and rough-textured stonework with such Gothic features as pointed arches and flying buttresses. In 1918 the building was sold to the Metropolitan Baptist Church, a reflection of the changing character of Harlem as it developed into America's most important African-American community. Metropolitan was one of the first black congregations established in Harlem and remains one of the most prestigious churches in the community.

Roger and Mary Philipse Morris House, Mount Morris, also known as the Morris-Jumel Mansion, West 160th Street at Edgecombe Avenue (1765; remodeling, c. 1810). Mount Morris was built as a summer villa by the British military officer Roger Morris and his American-born wife, Mary Philipse Morris. The house is an early example of the use of Palladian forms in North America; the double-height portico with a triangular pediment was an especially innovative feature in 1765. Historically, the house is famed for having served as Gen. George Washington's headquarters for more than a month in 1776. Later used by the British, the house was confiscated at the end of the war. In 1810 Stephen Jumel, a wealthy French emigré merchant, purchased the property and moved in with his wife (formerly his mistress), Eliza Bowen. The Jumels undertook some remodeling, including the addition of the handsome entrance in the Federal style. The house was purchased by New York City in 1903 and converted into a museum; operations were handed over to a women's group known as the Washington Headquarters Association. The mansion contains some of the finest Georgian **interiors** in America, including what is generally believed to be the country's first octagonal room.

🍎 **Mount Morris Park Historic District.** The streets of this district are lined with substantial masonry row houses interspersed with institutional buildings of exceptional quality, all reflecting Harlem's development as an affluent residential community following the extension of transit lines into the area around 1880. Initially, construction the neighborhood was closely linked to Mount Morris Park (renamed Marcus Garvey Park in 1973 in honor of one of the first black nationalist leaders). Almost every street in the district contains fine examples of row houses in the neo-Grec, Romanesque Revival, and neo-Renaissance styles. Several major buildings belonging to religious institutions line Lenox Avenue, and on the corner of Lenox and West 123rd Street is the Harlem Club (1888–89; now a church), designed by Lamb & Rich in the Romanesque Revival style.

New York Public Library: Branch Libraries. In the late 19th century most of the city's public libraries were run by private organizations such as the New York Free Circulating Library (see p. 127). The New York Public Library, founded in 1895, had an endowment devoted to its research facility and lacked the financial resources to organize and run a circulating system. Andrew Carnegie solved the problem in 1901 when he offered the New York Public Library a gift of more than five million dollars for the construction of 65 branch libraries. Because land in Manhattan was expensive, almost all of the libraries were conceived as relatively narrow midblock structures and a general plan was devised that could easily be adapted to most of these sites. Each library was to be three stories tall, with a Renaissance-inspired limestone facade. This basic arrangement had been successfully employed by the Free Circulating Library (these libraries were merged into the public library system). Many of the finest library buildings erected as a result of Carnegie's donation were designed by Charles McKim of the firm McKim, Mead & White.

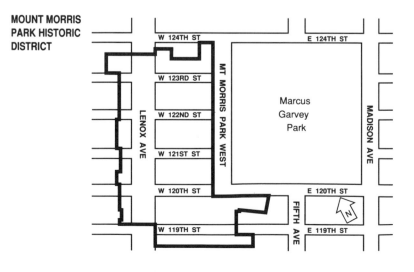

MOUNT MORRIS PARK HISTORIC DISTRICT

Hamilton Grange Branch, 503 West 145th Street (McKim, Mead & White, 1905–06). Features of the Palazzo Farnese in Rome are evident in this library's beautifully proportioned rusticated facade, with its alternating triangular and segmental window pediments and elegant iron railing.

115th Street Branch, 203 West 115th Street (McKim, Mead & White, 1907–09). The emphatic rustication on the facade of this library is reminiscent of that on the Palazzo Strozzi in Florence. A flamboyant shield bearing the seal of New York is balanced by a pair of putti above the central window on the ground floor.

135th Street Branch, now the New York Public Library, Schomburg Center for Research in Black Culture, 103 West 135th Street (McKim, Mead & White, 1903–05). The 135th Street Branch was one of the first new libraries completed with money from the Carnegie grant. The building's design is loosely based on Sanmicheli's Palazzo Canossa in Verona. Early in the 1920s, in response to changes in the surrounding Harlem neighborhood, the branch librarian Ernestine Rose began compiling a small collection of black literature and history books; in 1925 the branch was renamed the 135th Street Branch Division of Negro Literature. A year later the famed Schomburg Collection—a treasure trove of material on black culture and history, amassed by Arthur Schomburg—was purchased for the library. The facility was renamed for Schomburg in 1972, and eight years later a new building to house the research collection was completed on an adjacent site. The original building was restored in 1990 and is used by the Schomburg Center for exhibitions.

Eglise de Notre Dame (R.C.) and Rectory, Morningside Drive at West 114th Street (Daus & Otto, 1909–10, and Cross & Cross, 1914; rectory, Cross & Cross, 1913–14). Daus & Otto's imposing limestone sanctuary, dedicated to Our Lady of Lourdes, was completed in 1910. The austere nave, front elevation, and rectory, designed by Cross & Cross, were completed four years later. The formal French neoclassical design, with its pedimented Corinthian portico, was originally intended to be crowned by a dome (never executed) modeled on that of the Pantheon in Paris.

Our Lady of Lourdes (R.C.) Church, 467 West 142nd Street (O'Reilly Brothers, 1902–04). This Roman Catholic church, one of the oddest buildings in New York, is composed of pieces salvaged from three of the city's most prominent mid-19th-century landmarks and combined by Cornelius O'Reilly. Much of the High Victorian Gothic facade is a reconstruction of Peter B. Wight's famous National Academy of Design (1863–65), which stood at Fourth Avenue and East 23rd Street. The rear of the church consists of the original east end of James Renwick's St. Patrick's Cathedral (see p. 91), which was replaced in 1902–04 by a new lady chapel. The stone pedestals that flank the front steps come from the A. T. Stewart mansion (John Kellum, 1864–69), which stood at Fifth Avenue and 34th Street.

St. Andrew's Church (Episcopal), 2067 Fifth Avenue (Henry M. Congdon, 1872–73; enlargement, 1889–90). St. Andrew's is one of the finest Victorian

Gothic churches in New York City and one of the few 19th-century Protestant churches in Harlem that is still occupied by its original congregation. Henry Congdon designed St. Andrew's for a site on East 127th Street between Park and Lexington avenues, but by the late 1880s the congregation had outgrown the building. Congdon was rehired to dismantle the structure and supervise its reconstruction and enlargement on this more prestigious site at the corner of Fifth Avenue and East 127th Street.

St. Martin's Episcopal Church Complex, originally Holy Trinity Episcopal Church, Rectory, and Parish House, 230 Lenox Avenue (William A. Potter, 1887–89). Known as St. Martin's Episcopal Church since 1928, this prominent Harlem church is generally considered the finest Romanesque Revival religious complex in the city. The church and its related buildings have massive rough-hewn granite walls pierced by large rectangular and round-arched windows trimmed with brown sandstone. The complex is compactly planned; the parish house faces Lenox Avenue and the sanctuary, with its tall square bell tower, and rectory are to the rear.

♣ **St. Nicholas Historic District.** This district is an outstanding example of late 19th-century urban design in New York City. The four blockfronts, each a unified streetscape, were conceived by the developer David H. King "on such a large scale and with such ample resources as to 'Create a Neighborhood' independent of surrounding influences." King worked with three distinguished architecture firms. James Brown Lord designed the Colonial Revival red brick row on the south side of West 138th Street; Bruce Price was responsible for the Colonial Revival yellow brick rows on the north side of West 138th and the south side of West 139th streets; and McKim, Mead & White designed the Italian Renaissance–inspired row in dark brown mottled brick on the north side of West 139th Street. Service alleys, an extremely rare feature in New York City, run behind each row. These elegantly appointed houses were initially sold to affluent merchants and professionals. As Harlem evolved into America's preeminent black community, the houses were sold to middle-class African-Americans, including prominent entertainers, doctors, and politicians, and the area became known as Strivers' Row, a reference to the aspirations of many of the neighborhood's residents.

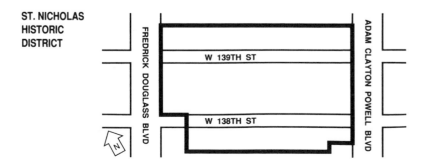

ST. NICHOLAS HISTORIC DISTRICT

FREDRICK DOUGLASS BLVD

W 139TH ST

W 138TH ST

ADAM CLAYTON POWELL BLVD

N

32nd Police Precinct Station House, later the 30th Police Precinct Station House, 1854 Amsterdam Avenue (Nathaniel D. Bush, 1871). After Bush became the police department's first architect in 1862, he designed a series of Italianate and French Second Empire brick precinct houses. When the 32nd Precinct Station House was built, the area around it was still largely rural and the structure, with its large mansard roof and handsome iron cresting, was among the most conspicuous in the vicinity. The building is currently vacant.

369th Regiment Armory, 2360 Fifth Avenue (drill shed, Tachau & Vought, 1921–24; administration building, Van Wart & Wein, 1930–33). One of the last New York City armories to be constructed, the 369th Regiment was built in two separate campaigns. The massive administration building is unusual in its combination of Art Deco features with the medieval motifs common to armory design. The armory is the home of the renowned African-American regiment known as the "Harlem Hell Fighters."

Union Theological Seminary, encompassing Brown Memorial Tower, James Tower, and James Memorial Chapel, Broadway at Reinhold Niebuhr Place (Allen & Collens, 1908–10). This Protestant seminary, founded in 1836, followed Columbia University (see p. 151) to Morningside Heights, purchasing two entire square blocks along Broadway between West 120th (now Reinhold Niebuhr Place) and 122nd streets in 1905, primarily with money donated by D. Willis James, a wealthy importer and manufacturer (for whom James Tower is named). A 1906 design competition was won by the Boston firm of Allen & Collens with its appropriate English Perpendicular Gothic–style entry. The landmark elements—the two tall towers and the chapel that faces onto Claremont Avenue—are the three most significant features of the campus.

University Heights Bridge. See p. 216.

Washington Bridge, spanning the Harlem River between West 181st Street, Manhattan, and University Avenue, the Bronx (Charles C. Schneider and Wilhelm Hildenbrand, 1886–89; modifications, Union Bridge Company, William J. McAlpine, Theodore Cooper, and DeLemos & Cordes, with Edward H. Kendall, consulting architect; enlargement and reconstruction, 1989–92). The Washington Bridge is an important monument of 19th-century American engineering; its complex design and construction history includes the contributions of many engineers and architects. The bridge consists of arcaded masonry approaches leading to a pair of steel, cast-iron, and wrought-iron arches supported by masonry piers. The bridge was the first major link between Manhattan and the Bronx. A reconstruction and widening of the roadway was undertaken in the late 1980s.

Watch Tower, Marcus Garvey Park (attributed to James Bogardus, 1855). Rising from a rocky outcropping in what was originally known as Mount Morris Park, this three-tiered cast-iron structure, with its spiral staircase and octagonal lookout, is the only surviving fire tower in New York City. The iron is thought to have been cast in the foundry of James Bogardus. Use of the tower was discontinued in 1878, after the installation of fire alarm boxes.

BROOKLYN

⚫ **Albemarle-Kenmore Terraces Historic District.** This small historic district, nestled behind the grounds of the Flatbush Reformed Dutch Church (see p. 167), consists of two cul-de-sacs lined with houses designed by the local firm of Slee & Bryson. Albemarle Terrace (1916–17) has charming Colonial Revival brick row houses, while the Garden City–inspired Kenmore Terrace (1917–18, with two houses from 1919–20) is an early example of the influence of the automobile on American architecture; each house on the south side of Kenmore Terrace incorporates a garage into the ground story.

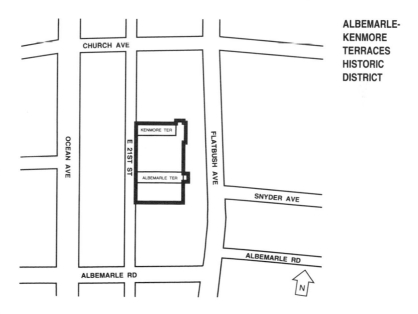

ALBEMARLE-KENMORE TERRACES HISTORIC DISTRICT

Boys' High School, 832 Marcy Avenue (James W. Naughton, 1891–92). See p. 156. Photo: Caroline Kane

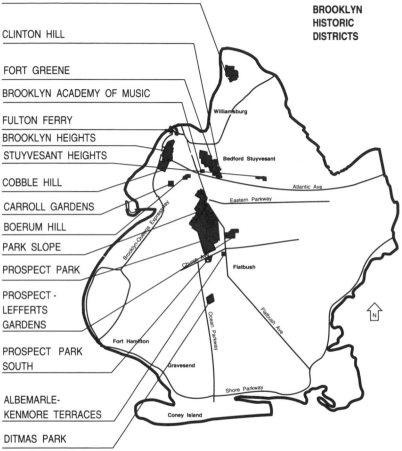

GREENPOINT

CLINTON HILL

FORT GREENE

BROOKLYN ACADEMY OF MUSIC

FULTON FERRY
BROOKLYN HEIGHTS
STUYVESANT HEIGHTS

COBBLE HILL

CARROLL GARDENS

BOERUM HILL

PARK SLOPE

PROSPECT PARK

PROSPECT -
LEFFERTS
GARDENS

PROSPECT PARK
SOUTH

ALBEMARLE-
KENMORE TERRACES

DITMAS PARK

**BROOKLYN
HISTORIC
DISTRICTS**

Williamsburg

Bedford Stuyvesant

Atlantic Ave

Eastern Parkway

Brooklyn-Queens Expressway

Church Ave

Flatbush

Fort Hamilton

Ocean Parkway

Flatbush Ave

Gravesend

Shore Parkway

Coney Island

N

Alhambra Apartments, 500–518 Nostrand Avenue and 29–33 Macon Street (Montrose Morris, 1889–90). The earliest of the three major apartment houses designed by Morris for the developer Louis F. Seitz (see Imperial Apartments, p. 172, and Renaissance Apartments, p. 182) and an early example of a Brooklyn apartment house for affluent middle-class tenants, the Alhambra displays rich textural contrasts and is notable for its six towers, steep roof slopes, gables, loggias, arcades, and lively terra-còtta detail. The building is currently vacant.

Antioch Baptist Church, originally the Greene Avenue Baptist Church and Church House, 828 and 826 Greene Avenue (church, Lansing C. Holden and Paul F. Higgs, 1887–92; church house, Langston & Dahlander, 1891–93). The Greene Avenue Baptist Church built this Romanesque Revival / Queen Anne building at a time when this section of Bedford-Stuyvesant was being rapidly developed as a row-house neighborhood. The manner in which the midblock church is massed to resemble a group of row houses reflects the architect's effort to design a building that would fit within its urban context. Holden prepared a design, but only the extant basement can be definitively attributed to him. The upper church is either a new design by Higgs or an adaptation by Higgs of Holden's original scheme. The church was sold in 1950 to the Antioch Baptist Church, an African-American congregation established in downtown Brooklyn in 1918. The church has hosted many leaders of the civil rights movement, including Martin Luther King, Jr., as well as many important politicians and notable African-Americans. The Romanesque Revival church house is one of a row of seven houses designed in 1891.

Astral Apartments, 184 Franklin Street (Lamb & Rich, 1885–86). The Astral is a significant example of "model tenement" design. Erected by Charles Pratt and named for the "astral oil" manufactured by one of his companies in a nearby Greenpoint refinery, the building was planned as quality affordable housing for 95 families. Each apartment contained adequate windows, a toilet, hot and cold running water, and other amenities not usually provided for working-class families in the 19th century. The building was designed in the Queen Anne style by a Manhattan firm often engaged by the Pratt family.

John and Altje Baxter House, also known as Stoothoff-Baxter-Kouwenhoven House, 1640 East 48th Street (wing, c. 1747; main house, 1811). The small wing of this house was probably erected by Wilhelmus Stoothoff. His granddaughter Altje married John Baxter, and in 1811 they moved the small building, connecting it to a new larger house. The entire house was reoriented on the lot around 1900. The steeply pitched roof, projecting eaves, and end chimneys are typical features of Dutch Colonial design.

🍴 **Boerum Hill Historic District.** Located just south of busy Atlantic Avenue, Boerum Hill is a homogeneous district composed primarily of row houses with brick or brownstone facades. Designed in the Greek Revival and Italianate styles, most of the houses were erected between the 1840s and the early 1870s. The district contains exceptionally long rows for this period, enhancing the cohesive quality of the blockfronts.

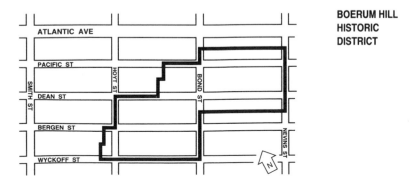

BOERUM HILL
HISTORIC
DISTRICT

Boys' High School, 832 Marcy Avenue (James W. Naughton, 1891–92; additions, C. B. J. Snyder, c. 1905–10). In the late 19th century Boys' High School was considered one of the most important public schools in Brooklyn; its new home was therefore conceived as a major architectural monument visible throughout much of central Brooklyn. The focus of this Romanesque Revival building is its dynamic roofline, with gables, dormers, round tower, and lofty corner campanile, all modeled on the public buildings of Henry Hobson Richardson. The school initially housed 782 students in 22 classrooms; as enrollment increased, several additions were constructed early in the 20th century. Boys' High and the nearby Girls' High (see p. 170) were organized in 1878 as separate departments of the Central Grammar School.

🍎 **Brooklyn Academy of Music Historic District.** Although primarily a residential district of Italianate brick and brownstone row houses erected in the 1850s and 1860s, this district contains several uncommon buildings, including a row of cast-iron residential structures with ground-floor stores on Fulton Street (built 1882); the Brooklyn Academy of Music, one of Brooklyn's preeminent cultural institutions, housed in an Italian Renaissance–inspired structure clad in brick, marble, and terra cotta and designed by Herts & Tallant in 1907; and the Williamsburgh Savings Bank tower (see p. 188).

Brooklyn Bridge, spanning the East River between Cadman Plaza, Brooklyn, and City Hall Park, Manhattan (John, Washington, and Emily Roebling, 1867–83). The Brooklyn Bridge, one of the great engineering feats of the 19th century, was the first physical link between the independent cities of Brooklyn and New York (they merged in 1898). It not only became the world's longest suspension bridge but was also an aesthetic triumph, with its intricate web of cables and its bold Gothic-inspired piers serving as symbolic portals to the two cities. Conceived by John A. Roebling, who had previously designed suspension bridges in Cincinnati and Pittsburgh, the project was taken over by his son Washington after Roebling died from an injury sustained during construction. Even when Washington Roebling was later paralyzed by caisson disease, he continued, with the help of his wife, Emily, to oversee the project from the

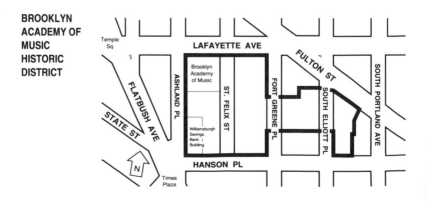

BROOKLYN ACADEMY OF MUSIC HISTORIC DISTRICT

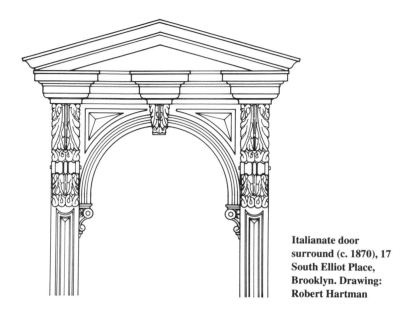

Italianate door surround (c. 1870), 17 South Elliot Place, Brooklyn. Drawing: Robert Hartman

window of a house in Brooklyn Heights. In 1972–73 the bridge was repainted in historically accurate colors. The pedestrian walkway was rebuilt in 1981–83, and the cables have been undergoing rehabilitation since 1989.

Brooklyn Central Office, Bureau of Fire Communications, 35 Empire Boulevard (Frank J. Helmle, 1913). Designed in a Florentine Early Renaissance style, this elegant building serves as a communications center for the New York City Fire Department. Helmle was responsible for many of Brooklyn's finest early 20th-century Renaissance-inspired landmarks including buildings in Prospect Park (see p. 178) and Winthrop Park (see p. 188) and several Roman Catholic churches.

Brooklyn City Hall, now Brooklyn Borough Hall, 209 Joralemon Street (Gamaliel King, 1845–48; alterations, Vincent Griffith and Stoughton & Stoughton, 1898). Brooklyn's City Hall is an imposing Greek Revival structure. The exterior of the Tuckahoe marble building, with its Ionic portico and crisp window enframements, remained unaltered until its original cupola was destroyed by fire in 1895. The architects Vincent Griffith and Stoughton & Stoughton designed a new cast-iron cupola in 1898, the same year that Brooklyn was consolidated into Greater New York and the building became Borough Hall. A restoration of the building was completed in 1989 under the direction of the architecture firm Conklin Rossant; the copper shingles of the cupola were meticulously reconstituted by the French firm Les Metalliers Champenois (which also restored the Statue of Liberty) and a crowning figure of justice, planned in 1898, was finally installed.

Brooklyn City Railroad Company, 8 Cadman Plaza West (Fulton Street) (1860–61). Established in 1853, the Brooklyn City Railroad Company operated horse-car lines that brought people to and from the Fulton Ferry terminal. The company's headquarters building is an Italianate brick structure with granite trim and a cast-iron storefront. It has been converted into apartments.

Brooklyn Fire Headquarters, 365–367 Jay Street (Frank Freeman, 1892). The former headquarters of the Brooklyn Fire Department, designed by one of Brooklyn's most talented 19th-century architects, is a masterpiece of the Romanesque Revival. This powerful building is distinguished by its massive entrance arch and richly textured elevation, clad in rock-faced red sandstone and gold Roman brick and trimmed with terra cotta. The building is now an apartment house.

⚜ Brooklyn Heights Historic District. Following the establishment of the steam-powered Fulton Ferry in 1814, the Heights became the first area of Brooklyn to be urbanized. In the 1820s elegant houses in the Federal style were erected in the north Heights. These houses were followed in later decades by mansions and row houses in the Greek Revival, Gothic Revival, Italianate, Queen Anne, Romanesque Revival, and other styles. In the 1880s elegant apartment houses began to appear in the neighborhood, notably on Montague and Pierrepont streets. The Heights also contains an exceptional group of institutional buildings, among them Richard Upjohn's Congregational Church of the Pilgrims (1844–46; now Our Lady of Lebanon R.C. Church), the first round-arched Early Romanesque Revival building in the United States; Minard Lafever's Gothic Revival Church of the Holy Trinity (Episcopal) (1844–47;

Brooklyn Heights Historic District. The southeast corner of Middagh and Willow streets. Federal house built in 1829. Photo: Caroline Kane

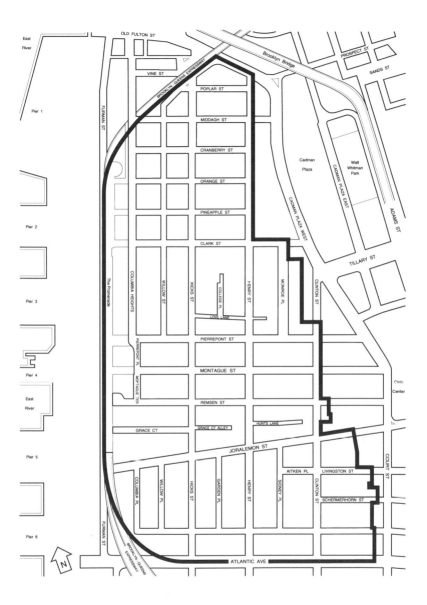

BROOKLYN HEIGHTS HISTORIC DISTRICT

Brooklyn Heights Historic District. A Gothic Revival house at 131 Hicks Street (built in 1848). Drawing: Robert Hartman

now St. Ann and the Holy Trinity), with its early stained-glass windows, and his Packer Collegiate Institute (1853–56); James Renwick's High Victorian Gothic masterpiece, the former St. Ann's Episcopal Church (1866–67); Joseph C. Wells's Plymouth Church (Congregational) (1849), erected for the fiery abolitionist preacher Henry Ward Beecher; and George B. Post's Long Island Historical Society (1878–81; now the Brooklyn Historical Society, see p. 173), one of the earliest buildings to make extensive use of ornamental terra cotta. In 1965 Brooklyn Heights became the first historic district designated by the Landmarks Preservation Commission.

Brooklyn Museum, 200 Eastern Parkway at Washington Avenue (McKim, Mead & White, 1893–1915; removal of front stairs, 1934–35). In 1893 McKim, Mead & White won a competition for the new home of the Brooklyn Institute of Arts and Sciences. The firm's winning entry proposed a monumental Classical Revival structure, only a small portion of which was eventually erected. The building is enhanced by extensive sculptural embellishment undertaken by a group of artists supervised by Daniel Chester French. The museum was originally entered via a grand flight of stairs leading to the Ionic portico; these stairs were removed in 1934–35. The museum, housing one of the country's finest art collections, is especially famous for its American, Egyptian, and African holdings.

Brooklyn Navy Yard. The Brooklyn Navy Yard was established in 1801 and rapidly grew into one of the busiest naval stations on the eastern seaboard. Some 400 ships were fitted out at the navy yard during the Civil War, and during World War II the yard employed more than 70,000 people. Although the navy yard is now an industrial center, most of its early buildings are extant.

Commandant's House, Hudson Avenue at Evans Street (1805–06). The design of this frame house has often been attributed to the Boston architect Charles Bulfinch working in association with John McComb, Jr., but there is no evidence to support this attribution. The house is among the most elegant structures in the Federal style in New York. Of special note are the porches supported by slender colonnettes and the pair of especially fine fan-lit entranceways. The house was the residence of Matthew Perry when he served as commanding officer of the shipyard in the 1840s.

Dry Dock #1, Dock Street at the foot of 3rd Street (William J. McAlpine, chief engineer, 1840–51). The construction of Dry Dock #1 was one of the great feats of 19th-century American engineering. At a cost of more than two million dollars, the dry dock was constructed of granite from Maine and Connecticut that was laid under the supervision of the master mason Thornton MacNess Niven.

Surgeon's House, Flushing Avenue opposite Ryerson Street (True W. Rollins and Charles Hastings, builders, 1863). This mansarded, French Second Empire house, built for the chief surgeon of the nearby naval hospital (see below), was erected during the Civil War, a period when the Brooklyn Navy Yard experienced extensive growth.

U.S. Naval Hospital, Hospital Road (Martin E. Thompson, 1830–38; wings, 1840 and c. 1862). Designed by one of the most prominent architects of the pre–Civil War period, the former U.S. Naval Hospital is an austere yet impressive Greek Revival Westchester marble structure distinguished by the eight square stone piers along its main facade. The building is vacant.

🍎 **Carroll Gardens Historic District.** This small district of row houses set behind deep front yards retains much of its 19th-century character. The impression of space is the result of the surveyor Richard Butts's plan devised in 1846, which created building lots with unusually deep front yards and a street pattern that protects President and Carroll streets from through traffic. All of the brownstone row houses in the district were erected between 1869 and 1884 by local builders.

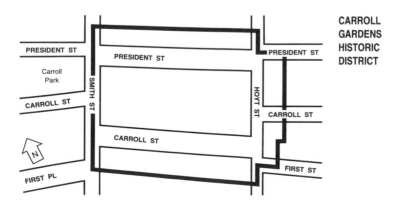

CARROLL GARDENS HISTORIC DISTRICT

Carroll Street Bridge, spanning the Gowanus Canal (Robert Van Buren, chief engineer; George Ingram, engineer in charge, 1888–89). One of the oldest bridges in New York City and the oldest of the four known American examples of a "retractile" bridge, the Carroll Street Bridge rolls horizontally onto land whenever a ship needs to pass along the Gowanus Canal. The superstructure was manufactured by the New Jersey Steel and Iron Company, a subsidiary of Cooper, Hewitt & Company, one of the country's foremost iron and steel producers. The bridge was restored in 1989 by engineers in the city's Department of Transportation.

♦**Clinton Hill Historic District.** Clinton Hill is unusual in that it is one of the few residential neighborhoods in Brooklyn whose several phases of development are all still visible. Clinton Avenue was laid out in 1832 as a wide boulevard for large suburban residences; several of these houses survive. In the 1860s urban development invaded the area and long rows of Italianate brick and brownstone houses were erected. Grand Avenue, Cambridge Street, and St. James Place contain some of New York's most intact mid-19th-century rows. In the 1870s Clinton Avenue and Washington Avenue began to attract many of Brooklyn's wealthiest citizens, notably Charles Pratt and his sons, who erected imposing mansions. These mansions and late 19th-century row houses were designed by prominent Manhattan architects and by such talented Brooklyn architects as William Tubby and Montrose Morris. By the early 20th century apartment houses began to be built in the historic district. The mix of row houses, mansions, and apartment buildings, designed in a variety of styles, contribute to the unique character of Clinton Hill's streets.

Queen Anne terracotta panel (Parfitt Brothers, 1882), 410 Clinton Avenue, Brooklyn. Drawing: Robert Hartman

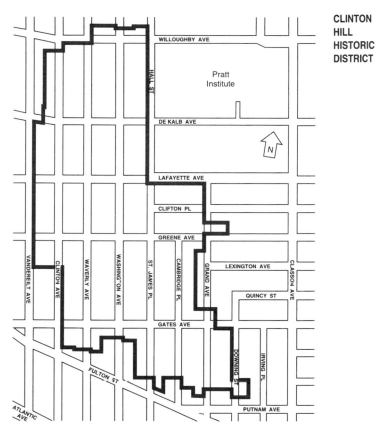

CLINTON HILL HISTORIC DISTRICT

WILLOUGHBY AVE

Pratt Institute

HALL ST

DE KALB AVE

N

LAFAYETTE AVE

CLIFTON PL

GREENE AVE

VANDERBILT AVE

CLINTON AVE

WAVERLY AVE

WASHINGTON AVE

ST. JAMES PL

CAMBRIDGE PL

GRAND AVE

LEXINGTON AVE

CLASSON AVE

QUINCY ST

GATES AVE

DOWNING ST

IRVING PL

FULTON ST

PUTNAM AVE

ATLANTIC AVE

🍎 **Cobble Hill Historic District.** The inauguration in 1836 of service on the South Ferry, linking Atlantic Avenue and Whitehall Street across the East River, led to the development of what at the time was farmland into a middle-class residential neighborhood. The row houses of Cobble Hill are primarily Greek Revival and Italianate in style; most are faced with brick or brownstone and feature high stoops with exceptionally fine ironwork. The district also includes two "model tenement" complexes that are among the most significant housing erected in the United States in the 19th century. The Home and Tower buildings, on Hicks Street at Baltic Street, designed by William Field & Son in 1876 and 1878 respectively, were erected by the Brooklyn businessman Alfred T. White as decent affordable housing for working people. The apartments were designed to provide plumbing and sufficient light and air, amenities that are often taken for granted today. Behind the Tower Apartments, stretching along Warren Place, White built two rows of 11½-foot-wide houses facing onto a common garden.

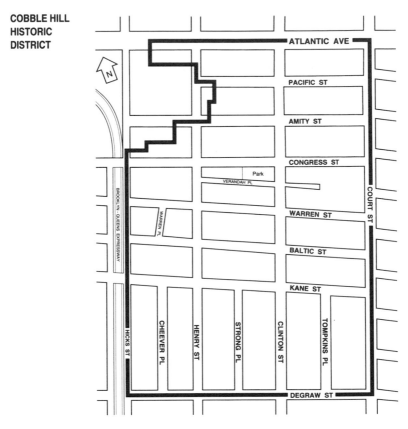

COBBLE HILL HISTORIC DISTRICT

ATLANTIC AVE

PACIFIC ST

AMITY ST

CONGRESS ST

Park

VERANDAH PL

WARREN ST

BALTIC ST

KANE ST

COURT ST

BROOKLYN - QUEENS EXPRESSWAY

WARREN PL

HICKS ST

CHEEVER PL

HENRY ST

STRONG PL

CLINTON ST

TOMPKINS PL

DEGRAW ST

William B. Cronyn House, also known as the 271 Ninth Street House (1856–57). This French Second Empire suburban villa was erected by a wealthy Wall Street merchant. The stucco-covered house is especially notable for its central cupola lighted by a clerestory and its slate mansard roof with end pavilions and iron cresting. When the house was built, the surrounding area was largely open farmland, but by the the end of the 19th century the neighborhood had become industrialized and the house served as the headquarters for Charles M. Higgins's India ink company. Today the house is once again in residential use.

The Cyclone, 834 Surf Avenue (Harry C. Baker, inventor, and Vernon Keenan, engineer, 1927). The Cyclone at Coney Island, one of America's most famous roller coasters (it has been called "the world's best"), is one of a vanishing breed of wood-track coasters. The Cyclone is a gravity ride. A chain pulls the three-car train to the top of the first plunge; the train then runs on its own momentum, reaching a speed of up to 68 miles per hour as it proceeds through nine drops and six curves.

The Cyclone, 834 Surf Avenue (Harry C. Baker, inventor, and Vernon Keenan, engineer, 1927). Photo: Janet Adams

🍎 **Ditmas Park Historic District.** Following the success of Prospect Park South (see p. 178), much of Flatbush was developed with freestanding suburban homes. Ditmas Park was a real estate venture planned by the developer Lewis H. Pounds in 1902. Pounds graded the land, divided the area into lots, and planted the magnificent trees that still grace the streets. He then erected houses or sold lots to other builders. Most of the houses in the district are wood-frame structures in the Colonial Revival style, although there are also a few examples of neo-Tudor and neo-Renaissance design and a handsome row of Arts and Crafts bungalows. The most prominent building in the district is the imposing neo-Georgian Flatbush Congregational Church, designed in 1910 by the Boston architects Allen & Collens working in collaboration with the local architect Louis Jallade. The adjacent parish house, designed by Whitefield & King and built in 1899, is an unusual seven-sided Shingle Style structure.

Eastern Parkway Scenic Landmark, between Grand Army Plaza and Ralph Avenue (Frederick Law Olmsted and Calvert Vaux, 1870–74). Eastern Parkway was part of a regional system envisioned by Olmsted and Vaux in 1866 as a means of introducing open space, fresh air, and greenery into the city's residential neighborhoods. The idea of a tree-lined boulevard with a central roadway flanked by access roads was new to the United States; Olmsted coined the term *parkway* in 1868 to describe this new type of urban thoroughfare. Although the parkway originally terminated at Ralph Avenue, it was intended as part of a system that would eventually run eastward from Prospect Park to the East River and then, on the other side of the river, continue to

DITMAS PARK
HISTORIC
DISTRIC

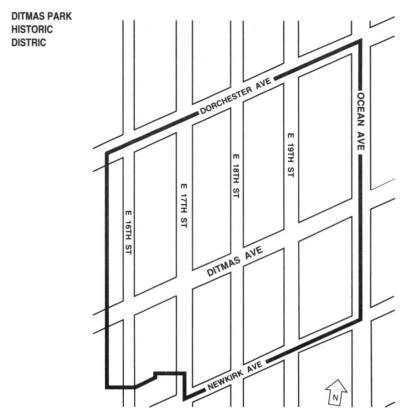

Central Park and the Hudson River; to the south the system extends via Ocean Parkway (see p. 174) to the Atlantic shore.

Emmanuel Baptist Church, 279 Lafayette Avenue (Francis H. Kimball, 1886–87; chapel, Ebenezer L. Roberts, 1882–83; school, 1925–27). The construction of the imposing Emmanuel Baptist was financed largely by Charles Pratt, a Standard Oil vice president and Brooklyn's wealthiest citizen, who resided nearby. Built of a light-colored Ohio sandstone, the church recalls the medieval Gothic cathedrals of France. The complex consists of a towered chapel on St. James Place; the sanctuary, which is Kimball's largest ecclesiastical design; and the neo-Gothic school building to the west of the church.

Erasmus Hall Academy, now Erasmus Hall Museum, in the courtyard of Erasmus Hall High School, 911 Flatbush Avenue (1786). Erasmus Hall, the first secondary school chartered by the New York State Board of Regents, was originally a private school for boys. Founded with the assistance of Alexander Hamilton, Aaron Burr, John Jay, and others, the school was housed in this Federal-period wooden building until Erasmus Hall High School, the surrounding Collegiate Gothic complex, was erected early in the 20th century.

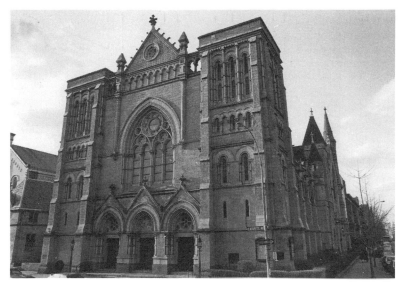

Emmanuel Baptist Church, 279 Lafayette Avenue (Francis H. Kimball, 1886–87).
Photo: Caroline Kane

First Free Congregational Church, later the Bridge Street A.W.M.E. Church, now Polytechnic Institute, 311 Bridge Street (1846–47). A rare surviving Greek Revival church structure in Brooklyn, this building first served as a Congregational church. Just seven years after its completion it was sold to Brooklyn's oldest African-American congregation, the African Wesleyan Methodist Episcopal Church. This congregation, which soon became known as the Bridge Street A.W.M.E. Church, occupied the building for 84 years before moving to Bedford-Stuyvesant. The building eventually became a factory and was rehabilitated by Polytechnic Institute after it acquired the property in 1968.

Flatbush Reformed Dutch Church Complex, 890 Flatbush Avenue (church, Thomas Fardon, 1793–98; cemetery, first burial, 17th century; parsonage, at 2101–2103 Kenmore Terrace, 1853; church house, Meyer & Mathieu, 1923–24). This church, the third to be erected at this location, occupies the site in longest continuous use for religious purposes in New York City. The stone-and-brick building in the Federal style has an elegant clock tower and steeple. To the south and west is a cemetery that contains the graves of members of local families; familiar names include Vanderbilt, Lott, Lefferts, Cortelyou, and Bergen. The parsonage is an exceptional example of a vernacular house in a transitional style, with both Greek Revival and Italianate features. A Colonial Revival brick church house completes the complex.

Flatbush Town Hall, 35 Snyder Avenue (John Y. Culyer, 1874–75). Designed in a High Victorian Gothic style by Culyer, an engineer, this brick and stone structure, with its prominent tower and gables, is a reminder of the period when

Flatbush was an independent community. The building, which was restored in the late 1980s after years of standing vacant, is currently used by the New York City Board of Education.

Flatlands Dutch Reformed Church, Kings Highway at East 40th Street (1848). With its simple clapboard siding, multipaned windows, and tall steeple, the Flatlands church is a notable example of rural Greek Revival design. The church, which is the third building to occupy this site, was restored after a fire in 1977.

🍎 **Fort Greene Historic District.** The streets of this district are lined with brick and brownstone row houses designed in the styles popular in the 25-year period (1855 to 1880) during which the area was transformed from a landscape of farms and shanties into a prestigious residential neighborhood. The district contains especially fine Italianate and French Second Empire rows. Its focus is Fort Greene Park, designed by Frederick Law Olmsted and Calvert Vaux in 1867 on the site of a Revolutionary War fort. In the center of the park is

FORT GREENE
HISTORIC
DISTRICT

Fort Greene Historic District. A French Second Empire house at 179 Washington Park (Joseph H. Townsend, c. 1866). Drawing: Robert Hartman

McKim, Mead & White's Prison Ship Martyrs' Monument of 1906–09, an enormous Doric column commemorating the American patriots who died on British prison ships in nearby Wallabout Bay during the Revolutionary War.

Fort Hamilton Casemate Fort, now the Officers' Club, Whiting Quadrangle (1825–31). Fort Hamilton and its companion, Fort Wadsworth on Staten Island (see p. 224), were erected to protect the Narrows at the entrance to New York Harbor. The granite casemate fort, erected as part of the Totten system of seacoast fortifications, is an impressive example of 19th-century military architecture. The fort was altered in 1937–38 when it was converted for use as an officers' club.

Friends Meeting House, 110 Schermerhorn Street (attributed to Charles T. Bunting, 1857). Consistent with Quaker taste, the Brooklyn Friends Meeting House is a beautifully proportioned but severely simple brick structure. It is articulated by tall multipaned windows that allow light to flood the second-floor meeting room.

 Fulton Ferry Historic District. The development of Fulton Ferry, Brooklyn's only commercial area designated a historic district, is closely related to the advent of steam-powered ferry service between Brooklyn and Manhattan in 1814. The success of the ferry and resultant commuter traffic led business owners to erect new commercial structures. Among the district's notable early buildings are the Greek Revival Long Island Insurance Company (1835) at 5–7 Front Street, thought to be New York City's earliest surviving office building; the row of Greek Revival stores at 7–23 Fulton Street, erected after the street was widened in 1835; the cast-iron Long Island Safe Deposit Company

**FULTON FERRY
HISTORIC
DISTRICT**

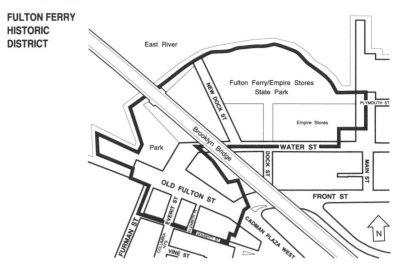

(1868–69) at Fulton and Front streets; and the Italianate Brooklyn City Railroad Building (see p. 158). The most impressive building on Fulton Street is the former Eagle Warehouse, a massive Romanesque Revival brick structure designed in 1893 by Frank Freeman. Throughout much of the 19th century the district's waterfront was lined with stores and warehouses used for the storage of produce and other goods that were shipped through the port. The monumental Empire Stores at 53–83 Water Street, with their round-arched openings and iron shutters, are among the handful of port warehouses that survive. The opening of the Brooklyn Bridge (see p. 156) in 1883 doomed the ferry and the economic life of Fulton Street, but the area began to revive in the 1970s through the rehabilitation and adaptive use of many of the buildings in the district.

Gage & Tollner Restaurant, 372 Fulton Street (building, c. 1875; restaurant design, 1892). One of Brooklyn's most celebrated restaurants, Gage & Tollner opened at a nearby location in 1879. The restaurant moved to this brownstone building in 1892, at which time a new wooden shopfront was added and the **interior** was redesigned. The dining room retains an authentic 19th-century character, with cherry wood trim, original furnishings and mirrors, Lincrusta (an imitation leather) wall covering, and graceful gaslight fixtures.

Girls' High School, now the Board of Education Brooklyn Adult Training Center, 475 Nostrand Avenue (James W. Naughton, 1885–86, and rear addition, 1891; Macon Street addition, C. B. J. Snyder, 1912). The roots of Girls' High School extend back to the organization of the Central Grammar School, Brooklyn's first public high school, in 1878. As the student population increased, a new school was erected on Nostrand Avenue between Halsey and Macon streets. Only the Girls' Department of Central Grammar School moved to this facility; the Boys' Department later moved to Boys' High School (see p.

156). The Nostrand Avenue building, popularly known as Girls' High School (the name was made official in 1891), is the oldest surviving structure in New York City erected as a high school. The design of the Victorian Gothic building focuses on the central entrance pavilion with its tall cupola.

Gravesend Cemetery, Gravesend Neck Road at McDonald Avenue (c. 1650s–). Gravesend was the first English settlement in the New Netherlands and the first European community in the New World established by a woman—Lady Deborah Moody. This small cemetery of 1.6 acres may date back to the 1650s, but all of the gravestones predating the 18th century have been lost.

🍎 **Greenpoint Historic District.** Unlike Brooklyn's other 19th-century residential historic districts, Greenpoint was not settled by people who commuted to Manhattan. Rather, development in Greenpoint was closely linked to the prosperity of the nearby industrial waterfront. The district contains a wide variety of buildings, reflecting the varied income levels of the local residents. Houses range from early examples of flats to modest frame dwellings to

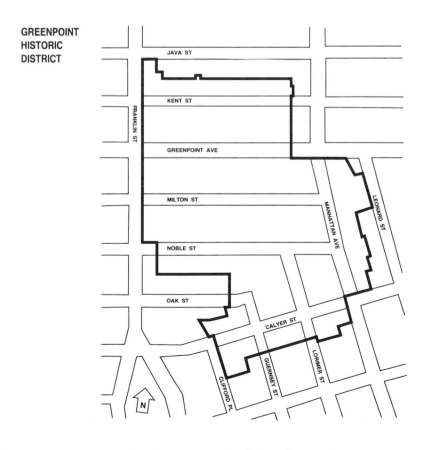

impressive masonry row houses. Construction boomed in the 1860s and early 1870s, and it was in these decades that some of the district's finest houses were erected. Among them are a large number of Italianate brick row houses with cast-iron window lintels and door hoods that were probably cast in local Greenpoint foundries. Also within the district are some of the most impressive ecclesiastical buildings in eastern Brooklyn.

Green-Wood Cemetery Gates, Fifth Avenue at 25th Street (Richard Upjohn & Son, 1861–65). The design of these spectacular Gothic Revival gates is generally attributed to R. M. Upjohn, as opposed to his more famous father, Richard Upjohn. The gates and adjoining pavilions are intricately carved from New Jersey brownstone. Above the pair of entrance arches are four panels of Nova Scotia sandstone carved with scenes evoking the themes of death and resurrection.

Hanson Place Baptist Church, now the Hanson Place Seventh Day Adventist Church, 88 Hanson Place (George Penchard, 1857–60). This unusual church building combines the austere round-arched brick forms of the Early Romanesque Revival, a style popular with Protestant denominations in the 1850s, with a grand Corinthian temple front. A restoration of both the exterior and the interior was undertaken in the late 1970s.

Imperial Apartments, 1198 Pacific Street and 1327–1339 Bedford Avenue (Montrose Morris, 1892). The success of the Alhambra Apartments (see p. 154) led the developer Louis F. Seitz to commission this apartment house and the Renaissance (see p. 182) in 1892. The light-colored brick building, with its terra-cotta trim, metal bay windows, tall arcades, and round corner tower, is an important presence on Grant Square. This relatively early example of a prestigious apartment house in Brooklyn was built at a time when hundreds of handsome row houses were being erected on the surrounding streets of the Crown Heights neighborhood.

Interborough Rapid Transit System Underground Station, Borough Hall. See p. 18.

Howard E. and Jessie Jones House, also known as the 8200 Narrows Avenue House (J. Sarsfield Kennedy, 1916–17). Arts and Crafts design is rare in New York City, and this house built of boulders is a striking example of the type. Erected for a successful shipping merchant, the house is set on a large landscaped plot and contains a series of homey details, including an asphalt roof designed to simulate thatch.

Kings County Savings Bank, 135 Broadway (King & Wilcox, 1868). This former bank, built of light-colored sandstone, is one of New York's most magnificent French Second Empire buildings. The baroque quality of the design is accented by a projecting entrance portico, recessed loggias, a pair of projecting corner pavilions on the side facade, and beautifully executed carving on the ground floor. The building is currently vacant.

Peter Lefferts House, also known as the Lefferts Homestead, Flatbush Avenue near Empire Boulevard (1777–83). Peter Lefferts built this farmhouse in the traditional Dutch Colonial style to replace an earlier dwelling that was burned by American troops during the Battle of Brooklyn in 1776. Originally located on Flatbush Avenue between Maple and Midwood streets, the house was moved to Prospect Park (see p. 178) in 1918 in order to save it from destruction; it is now a house museum.

Lincoln Club, now Mechanics Temple, Independent Order of Mechanics of the Western Hemisphere, 65 Putnam Avenue (Rudolph L. Daus, 1889). The former home of the Lincoln Club is a flamboyant Queen Anne brick, stone, and terracotta structure designed by one of Brooklyn's most original late 19th-century architects. The club was organized in 1878 by a group of affluent local gentlemen who sought to band together for social purposes and to further the interests of the Republican Party (political activities were soon dropped). The Lincoln Club disbanded in 1931. In the 1940s the clubhouse was acquired by the Mechanics. This is a rare example of a 19th-century clubhouse that still serves its original social function.

Edwin Clarke and Grace Hill Litchfield House, Grace Hill, also known as Litchfield Villa, now the Brooklyn Headquarters of the New York City Department of Parks and Recreation, Prospect Park West at 5th Street, Prospect Park (A. J. Davis, 1854–57). The lawyer and railroad financier Edwin Clarke Litchfield purchased much land in Brooklyn in the 1850s. At the crest of Prospect Hill, Litchfield erected one of the finest Italianate villas in the United States. Originally clad in stucco tinted to simulate stone, the building has a picturesque silhouette; its towers and projecting bays were planned to take advantage of views of the surrounding landscape and of New York Harbor. On the south side is a porch supported by columns with corncob capitals. Part of the house's grounds were incorporated into Prospect Park when the park site was acquired (see p. 178), and the house was converted in 1913 for use by the Parks Department.

Long Island Historical Society (interior), now the Brooklyn Historical Society, 128 Pierrepont Street (George B. Post, 1878–81). Organized in 1863, the Long Island Historical Society soon grew into a leading library and museum of local history. Fourteen architects entered a design competition for the society's building in 1878. Post's Renaissance-inspired design won, and the new building, the first in New York to exploit ornamental terra cotta extensively, was dedicated in January 1881. This building is located within the Brooklyn Heights Historic District. It contains one of New York's great 19th-century interiors. The second-floor library retains its original furnishings and stained-glass windows; outstanding architectural features include columns, a gallery railing, and other woodwork carved of ash. The library houses an important collection of books, prints, photographs, and other material relating to Brooklyn.

Hendrick I. Lott House, 1940 East 36th Street (east wing, 1720; main section and west wing, 1800). The Lott family first settled in what is now Brooklyn in 1652. In 1720 Johannes Lott erected a small house in the village of Flatlands.

Eighty years later his grandson Hendrick built a new house that incorporated the earlier building as its east wing. The house, designed in traditional Dutch Colonial style, remains on its original site and is virtually unaltered on the exterior, retaining its gambrel roof, spring eaves, and shingled siding. The large site gives a sense of the house's original setting.

Magnolia Grandiflora and Magnolia Tree Earth Center, 677, 678, and 679 Lafayette Avenue (tree, c. 1885; houses, 1880–83). This magnificent tree, which grows at the northern edge of its species' range, was planted around 1885 from a slip brought from North Carolina. The tree has become a symbol for the revitalization of the Bedford-Stuyvesant community; it stands in front of three late 19th-century houses that have been converted into a center for environmental education.

New England Congregational Church, now Light of the World Church, 179 South Ninth Street (Thomas Little, 1852–53). In the 19th century numerous rural New Englanders settled in Brooklyn and built new Congregational churches. The former New England Congregational Church is one of these and is a rare example of an Italianate brownstone church building. The design and scale of the church, which occupies a midblock site, help to integrate the building into the surrounding urban fabric.

New Lots Reformed Dutch Church, now New Lots Community Church, 630 New Lots Avenue (1823–24). This simple wood building, with Gothic-inspired pointed windows and its modest cupola, was erected to serve a small farming community.

New Utrecht Reformed Church, 18th Avenue at 83rd Street (1828). Reusing rubble stone from an earlier octagonal church of 1699 in its construction, the New Utrecht church is attractively sited on a landscaped plot. The building has Gothic pointed arches, a square tower, and a pedimented front elevation articulated by a beautifully proportioned roundel window in the Federal style.

Ocean Parkway Scenic Landmark, between Church Avenue and Seabreeze Avenue (Frederick Law Olmsted and Calvert Vaux, 1874–76). Ocean Parkway was planned as part of an extensive system of parkways that would extend the rural beauty of Prospect Park into Brooklyn's residential neighborhoods and that were eventually to connect with Manhattan's Central Park. The road—with its central drive, landscaped malls, bridle path (now paved), pedestrian promenade, and narrow access roads—originally ran from the park to Coney Island and was a companion to Eastern Parkway (see p. 165). The northernmost section was destroyed in the 1950s for the construction of the Prospect Expressway.

Parachute Jump, Riegelmann Boardwalk at West 16th Street (James H. Strong, inventor, and Elwyn E. Seelye & Co., engineers, 1939). Originally constructed at the New York World's Fair of 1939–40, the Parachute Jump was rebuilt in 1940 at Coney Island's Steeplechase Park, where it continued to thrill riders for 28 years. Although the jump has long been closed, the tapered steel structure with its radiating crown remains one of the borough's most visible landmarks.

🍎 **Park Slope Historic District.** Park Slope is situated along the western edge of Prospect Park (see p. 178). Located several miles from Brooklyn's 19th-century ferry terminals, Park Slope owes its development as a prestigious neighborhood to the opening of the Brooklyn Bridge (see p. 156) in 1883; the convenience of commuting over the bridge permitted people to live in locations that were farther from Manhattan than previously developed areas. The Slope contains a mix of mansions, row houses, apartment houses, and institutional buildings, almost all of which were erected in the final decades of the 19th century and the first years of the 20th century. These include some of the most outstanding Romanesque Revival and Queen Anne residences in the United States. The brick and stone houses on Carroll Street and Montgomery Place designed by C. P. H. Gilbert in the late 1880s are especially distinguished. The district's fine institutional structures include a cluster of three churches at St. John's Place and Seventh Avenue, the imposing Classical Revival Beth Elohim

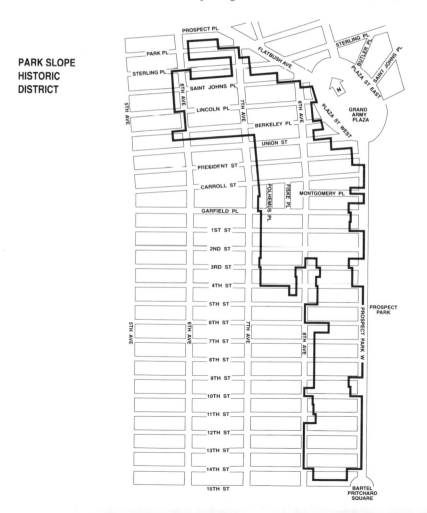

PARK SLOPE
HISTORIC
DISTRICT

Park Slope Historic District. Romanesque Revival double house at 803-813 Carroll Street/115-119 Eighth Avenue (C.P.H. Gilbert, 1888). Drawing: Robert Hartman and Harry Hansen

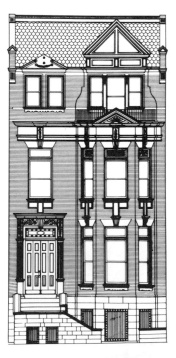

Park Slope Historic District. A Queen Anne house at 214 Lincoln Place (Charles Werner, 1883). Drawing: Robert Hartman

Synagogue (Eisendrath & Horowitz, 1908–10), and the architect Francis H. Kimball's spectacular Venetian Gothic Montauk Club (1889–91).

Pratt Institute. Pratt Institute was founded in 1884 by the wealthy Brooklyn manufacturer Charles Pratt as a school to train men and women in the manual arts. Pratt recognized the growing need for skilled industrial workers, and he believed that the best way to help people was to teach them to help themselves. The institute buildings were erected only a few blocks from Pratt's home on Clinton Avenue and originally faced onto city streets; the current campus environment was not created until the 1950s.

> **Library,** 224–228 Ryerson Street (William B. Tubby, 1896; north porch, John Mead Howells, 1936). As part of the institute, Charles Pratt organized Brooklyn's first free library, open to all citizens over the age of 14. Originally located in the Main Building (see below), the library received its own home in 1896. This transitional Romanesque Revival/Renaissance Revival structure is one of many designed by Tubby for the Pratt family.

> **Main Building Complex,** 215 Ryerson Street (Main Building, Lamb & Rich, 1885–87; porch, William B. Tubby, 1894; Memorial Hall, John Mead Howells, 1926–27; South Hall, William B. Tubby, 1891). Main Building is an imposing Romanesque Revival brick-and-stone structure that originally housed all institute functions. The bold arched entrance porch, perhaps the building's most striking feature, is an addition designed by Tubby in 1894. Tubby's South Hall is a modest Romanesque Revival work that was originally used as the Pratt Institute High School. The neo-Romanesque Memorial Hall, commemorating Charles Pratt's second wife, Mary Richardson Pratt, was planned as an assembly hall; the brick and stone building is adorned with sculpted figures by René Chambellan.

Pratt Row Houses, 220–234 Willoughby Avenue, 171–185 Steuben Street, and 172–186 Emerson Place (Hobart A. Walker, 1907). The Pratt family built a large number of row houses in the Clinton Hill neighborhood. These three rows, encompassing 27 houses, survive from an original complex of 38 houses that were planned for "people of taste and refinement, but of moderate means." Of Northern Renaissance–inspired design, the complex was built with rear service alleys and a central heating plant. The houses soon became popular with people affiliated with Pratt Institute; they are currently used as faculty housing.

🍎 **Prospect-Lefferts Gardens Historic District.** At the time when suburban development was sweeping through Flatbush, the northern edge of the area was built up primarily with blocks of modest row houses. This movement was initiated in the 1890s by James Lefferts, who subdivided eight blocks of his family's ancestral farm (see p. 172) into Lefferts Manor, a development with restrictive covenants that required the construction of single-family houses. Between 1897 and the mid-1920s row houses and a few freestanding houses were erected in Lefferts Manor and on some of the adjoining streets. Among the outstanding houses are the neo-Renaissance limestone rows on Maple and Midwood streets designed by Axel Hedman in the first years of this century and the Colonial Revival and neo-medieval brick houses from the 1920s that

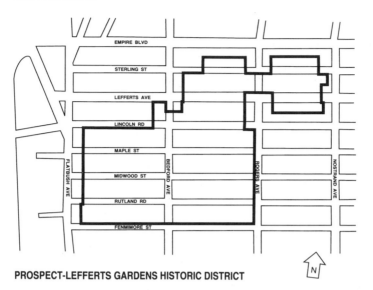

PROSPECT-LEFFERTS GARDENS HISTORIC DISTRICT

Slee & Bryson designed for sites on Fenimore and Midwood streets and Rutland Road.

Prospect Park Scenic Landmark, bounded by Flatbush Avenue, Parkside Avenue, Prospect Park West, and Prospect Park Southwest (Frederick Law Olmsted and Calvert Vaux, designed 1865; constructed 1866–73). Prospect Park is generally considered the masterpiece of designers Frederick Law Olmsted and Calvert Vaux. Planned as Brooklyn's counterpart to Central Park, Prospect Park is a milestone in the movement to create naturalistic parks in America's cities as a response to the increasing industrialization and congestion of the urban environment. A Brooklyn park was initially authorized in 1859, but the Civil War delayed work. In 1864 James S. T. Stranahan, later known as the "Father of Prospect Park," approached Vaux, who in turn persuaded Olmsted to assist with the design. Their plan, submitted in 1866, divided the park into three zones: meadows (notably the Long Meadow, which at 90 acres is the largest lawn in New York), forests, and water bodies. Vaux was responsible for a series of splendid structures, including several bridges, the Oriental Pavilion, and the terraces of the Concert Grove (designed in conjunction with Jacob Wrey Mould). The park's classical entrances, designed between 1889 and 1907 by McKim, Mead & White in conjunction with prominent sculptors (notably Brooklyn-born Frederick MacMonnies), reflect a late 19th-century shift in ideas about landscape design away from the picturesque in favor of increased formality. In addition to the gates, classical pavilions were erected within the park based on designs by McKim, Mead & White and the local architecture firm of Helmle & Huberty.

    Boathouse, Lullwater (Helmle & Huberty, 1904). As is appropriate for a building located at water's edge, this white terra-cotta-clad pavilion,

Prospect Park (Frederick Law Olmsted and Calvert Vaux, designed 1865; constructed, 1866–73). The lake with a rustic shelter. Photo: Landmarks Preservation Commission collection from the Long Island Historical Society

restored in 1984, was modeled on the Renaissance palaces that line the Grand Canal in Venice.

Croquet Shelter, Parkside Avenue (McKim, Mead & White, 1904). The Croquet Shelter, also known as the Grecian Shelter, is a beautifully proportioned Corinthian temple reminiscent of 18th-century French neoclassical garden pavilions.

 Prospect Park South Historic District. Prospect Park South, Brooklyn's most imposing suburban neighborhood, was a development scheme initiated by Dean Alvord, who sought "to create a rural park within the limitations of the conventional city block and city street." After purchasing approximately 60 acres of farmland in 1899, Alvord laid out all of the utilities, erected brick gateposts, planned lawns and malls, and hired the Scottish landscape gardener John Aitkin to supervise the plantings. Alvord also hired an architectural staff, which was headed by the talented John J. Petit, to design large, comfortable houses in a wide variety of styles. Petit was responsible for some of the finest houses in the district (as an alternative, owners could hire their own architects), including examples of the Colonial Revival, neo-Tudor, and Queen Anne styles, as well as several more uncommon examples, most notably a house modeled on a Japanese pagoda. Within a few years Alvord had created a community that, in his own words, was "acceptable to people of culture with means equal to some of the luxuries as well as the necessities of life."

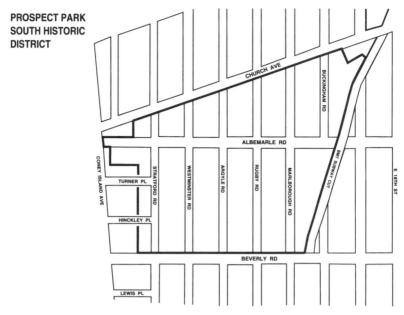

PROSPECT PARK
SOUTH HISTORIC
DISTRICT

Public Bath No. 7, 227–231 Fourth Avenue (Raymond F. Almirall, 1906–10).
Early in the 20th century New York City erected an extensive system of public
bath houses in neighborhoods where most of the residences lacked indoor
plumbing. The bath house on Fourth Avenue served the Gowanus community.
The building is faced in brick and terra cotta with glazed white surfaces that
connote cleanliness. Its ornamental forms evoke bathing and the sea. These
include fish, tridents, shells, and streams of water, many of them in polychromatic terra cotta. The building has been vacant for many years.

Public Schools. Public education began in Brooklyn in 1816 and, by the late
19th century, had grown to a point where Brooklyn had one of the most extensive systems of public education in the country. As the population of Brooklyn
increased and as more school buildings were needed, the office of superintendent of buildings was established. Samuel B. Leonard served as superintendent
from 1859 until 1879 and was responsible for the design of many of Brooklyn's
oldest surviving schools. He was succeeded by James W. Naughton, who
retained the position until the Brooklyn school system was merged into that of
the newly consolidated city in 1898 and New York's superintendent of school
buildings, C. B. J. Snyder, took charge of school design and construction
throughout the city.

> **Public School 9,** later Public School 111, now Public School 340, 249
> Sterling Place (Samuel B. Leonard, 1867–68; additions, James W.
> Naughton, 1887). This Early Romanesque Revival school was constructed
> in conjunction with the development of the surrounding Prospect Heights
> community in the 1860s. The focus of the building is a central gabled pavil-
> ion with fine brick arches.

Prospect Park South Historic District. A Japanese-style house, 131 Buckingham Road (Petit & Green, 1902). Photo: Caroline Kane

Public School 9 Annex, 251 Sterling Place (James W. Naughton, 1895). As the population of Prospect Heights increased in the late 19th century, P.S. 9 (see p. 180) became overcrowded and this handsome Romanesque Revival brick-and-stone annex with Renaissance-inspired detail was erected. The building has been converted into apartments.

Public School 34, also known as the Oliver H. Perry School, 131 Norman Avenue (Samuel B. Leonard, 1867; additions, Samuel B. Leonard, 1870, and James W. Naughton, 1887–88). One of the oldest schools in continuous use in New York City, Greenpoint's P.S. 34 is an Early Romanesque Revival building that is similar in design to P.S. 9 (see p. 180).

Public School 39, also known as the Henry Bristow School, 417 Sixth Avenue (Samuel B. Leonard, 1876–77). Located in Park Slope, this building in the French Second Empire style displays typically French features—the projecting central frontispiece and end pavilions, the crowning mansard roof with iron cresting—that were adapted by Leonard to the demands of public school design.

Public School 65K, 158 Richmond Street (Samuel Leonard, 1870; front facade, James W. Naughton, 1889). P.S. 65K, originally built in 1870, received the section of the building that fronts onto Richmond Street in 1889. Located in the Cypress Hills neighborhood, the school is a modest Romanesque Revival structure with striking Gothic-inspired detail.

Public School 71K, now the Beth Jacob School, 119 Heyward Street (James W. Naughton, 1888–89). This French Second Empire structure in

Williamsburg is one of the most beautiful schools designed by Naughton. The building is massed with projecting, pedimented end pavilions and a central frontispiece capped by a mansard roof, and it is articulated by large expanses of finely proportioned windows that permit a maximum amount of light to enter the classrooms. No longer owned by the city, the building now houses an Orthodox Jewish girls' school.

Public School 73, 241 MacDougal Street (James W. Naughton, 1888, and addition, 1895). The construction and rapid expansion of this school reflect the fact that the area where Bedford-Stuyvesant meets East New York underwent significant development following the opening of the elevated rail lines on Fulton Street and Broadway in the 1880s. The tall central tower of P.S. 73 is a focal point in the neighborhood; the school is ornamented with handsome terra-cotta detail.

Public School 86, also known as the Irvington School, 220 Irving Avenue (James W. Naughton, 1892–93). Naughton's creative use of Romanesque Revival forms is evident on this relatively small school in Bushwick, with its rough stone base, trios of arched windows, and large central gable articulated by a massive semicircular arch and flanked by pedimented dormers.

Public School 108, 200 Linwood Street (James W. Naughton, 1895). The imposing yellow brick Romanesque Revival mass of P.S. 108 in Cypress Hills rises from a rough stone base to a steeply sloping roof that is punctuated by gables and dormers.

John Rankin House, also known as the 440 Clinton Street House, now the F. G. Guido Funeral Home (c. 1840). This handsomely proportioned Greek Revival brick structure was erected for a wealthy merchant at a time when the area now known as Carroll Gardens was still largely rural. One of Brooklyn's largest residences of the 1840s, the house has an especially fine granite entrance surround and granite newel posts.

Reformed Church of South Bushwick, 855–867 Bushwick Avenue (Messrs. Morgan, 1853; chapel and Sunday school, J. J. Buck, 1881; church enlargement, 1883). This imposing church is unusual in its combination of austere Greek Revival forms, still popular in the 1850s in outlying areas such as Bushwick, with the type of Georgian-inspired tower and steeple that had gone out of fashion in most areas more than 25 years earlier. The church's records note that the design was "drawn up by Messrs. Morgan"; just who these men were is not known.

Renaissance Apartments, 488 Nostrand Avenue and 140–144 Hancock Street (Montrose Morris, 1892). The Renaissance was commissioned by the developer Louis F. Seitz, who was responsible for some of Brooklyn's finest late 19th-century apartment houses. The design of this pale yellow brick and terra-cotta structure is closely related to that of Morris's contemporaneous Imperial Apartments (see p. 172). The building has been vacant for several years.

Royal Castle Apartments, 20–30 Gates Avenue (Wortmann & Braun,

1911–12). One of the earliest apartment houses in Clinton Hill, the Royal Castle, faced in brick and limestone, is embellished by a series of fanciful corbels in the form of building masons. The building has a striking roofline with projecting arched gables.

Russian Orthodox Cathedral of the Transfiguration of Our Lord, 228 North 12th Street (Louis Allmendinger, 1916–21). The Greek cross plan and the impressive scale of the onion domes of this small yellow brick church typify design in the Russian Orthodox tradition. The cathedral itself stands as a symbol of the importance of Eastern European immigrants in the history of northeastern Brooklyn.

Elias Hubbard Ryder House, 1926 East 28th Street (1834). An extremely late example of a house designed in the Dutch Colonial style, the Ryder House displays such characteristic features as a sloping roof and deep projecting eaves. The house was slightly altered when it was moved to its present site in 1929.

St. Bartholomew's Church (Episcopal), 1227 Pacific Street (George P. Chappell, 1886–90). Chappell, one of Brooklyn's most creative late 19th-century architects, was responsible for this quirky English-inspired Queen Anne design. The asymmetrically massed church, with its richly textured stone-and-brick walls, tile cladding, and picturesque tower, is set behind a garden that creates the illusion of a rural church in this urban neighborhood.

St. George's Episcopal Church, 800 Marcy Avenue (R. M. Upjohn, 1887–88, and Sunday school, 1889). This late High Victorian Gothic design is a striking example of the vivid polychromy characteristic of the style. The building also reflects the idiosyncratic nature of R. M. Upjohn's work, notably at the entrance porch, with its stout dwarf columns, and the octagonal chimney tower.

St. Luke's Episcopal Church, now the Church of St. Luke and St. Matthew, 520 Clinton Avenue (John Welch, 1888–91). St. Luke's, built at the time when Clinton Avenue was Brooklyn's "gold coast," is one of the grandest 19th-century ecclesiastical buildings in Brooklyn. The design of the church and its adjoining chapel is loosely based on the Romanesque churches of Northern Italy. The building is faced with six different materials carefully modulated in color and texture to create a dramatic street facade.

St. Mary's Episcopal Church, 230 Classon Avenue (Richard T. Auchmuty, 1858–59). One of New York's most original but least well-known Gothic Revival churches, St. Mary's was designed by a partner in the firm of Renwick & Auchmuty. Executed in brownstone, the church was erected to minister to the population that settled near the bustling Brooklyn Navy Yard.

Sidewalk Clock, 753 Manhattan Avenue (early 20th century). This cast-iron sidewalk clock in Greenpoint is typical of the large clocks that were once commonly used to advertise jewelry stores and other businesses. (See p. 62.)

68th Police Precinct Station House and Stable, now the Sunset Park School of Music, 4302 Fourth Avenue (Emile Gruwé, 1891–92). This former police station is one of several station houses in Brooklyn designed late in the 19th

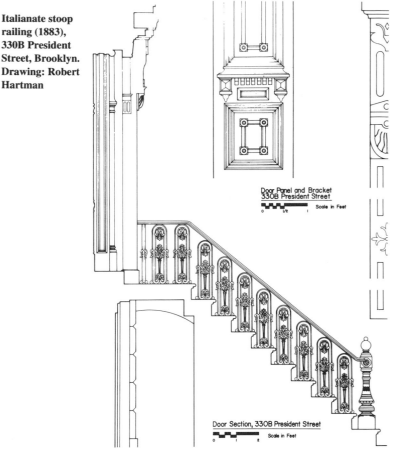

Italianate stoop railing (1883), 330B President Street, Brooklyn. Drawing: Robert Hartman

Door Panel and Bracket
330B President Street
Scale in Feet

Door Section, 330B President Street
Scale in Feet

century to resemble a medieval fortress. The impregnable quality is emphasized by the presence of a massive arched entry and a corner tower. The fortresslike design is offset by a use of such details as complex pointed-arched windows, exuberant iron tie rods, and fanciful carved heads. The stable has been converted into a school of music, and the main building is awaiting conversion to a new use.

Soldiers' and Sailors' Memorial Arch, Grand Army Plaza (John H. Duncan, 1889–92; alterations, McKim, Mead & White, 1894–1901). Designed in the tradition of Roman imperial arches, this Civil War memorial is the centerpiece of one of the finest formal civic design projects in the United States. The construction of Duncan's arch, the winning entry in a competition, was completed in 1892. Two years later Stanford White planned alterations to allow the addition of sculpture: heroic bronze groups representing the army and navy, as well as the arch's crowning Victory quadriga, all by Frederick MacMonnies; a pair of bronze relief panels depicting Lincoln and Grant on horseback (the horses were modeled by Thomas Eakins, the figures by William O'Donovan); and carved spandrel figures by Philip Martiny.

South Congregational Church Complex, 358–366 Court Street and 253–269 President Street (chapel, 1851; church, 1857; ladies' parlor, F. Carles Merry, 1889; rectory, Woodruff Leeming, 1893). Located on a prominent corner in the old neighborhood of South Brooklyn—now generally known as Carroll Gardens—South Congregational is a brick church articulated by a series of arches expressive of the finest Early Romanesque Revival design. To the rear are the chapel, the Romanesque Revival ladies' parlor, and the neo-Gothic rectory. The church congregation now worships in the former parlor, and the church and chapel have been converted into apartments.

State Street Houses, 291–299 and 290–324 State Street (1847–74). These 23 row houses between Smith and Hoyt streets reflect the development of this formerly rural section of Boerum Hill into a prosperous urban residential neighborhood in the mid-19th century. The brick- and brownstone-fronted houses are Greek Revival and Italianate in style.

Joseph Steele House, 200 Lafayette Avenue (c. 1850). Erected early in the 1850s, this frame house is a magnificent example of a residence in a transitional style, combining Greek Revival and Italianate elements. Of special interest are the handsome Greek Revival entrance and the Italianate cupola. The small wing at the east side of the house may date from as early as 1812.

👆 **Stuyvesant Heights Historic District.** This residential district is a part of the larger Bedford-Stuyvesant community. Early development in the district took place in the 1860s, when several freestanding suburban houses were erected on MacDonough Street. A few row houses were built in the early 1870s, but most of the district's row houses and mansions were built between c. 1880 and the first years of the 20th century. Within the district are fine examples of French Second Empire, neo-Grec, Romanesque Revival, and neo-Renaissance houses, all designed by local Brooklyn architects. As is true of most of Brooklyn's 19th-century residential neighborhoods, this district also contains several architecturally distinguished churches.

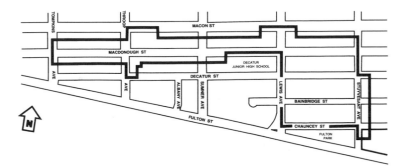

STUYVESANT HEIGHTS HISTORIC DISTRICT

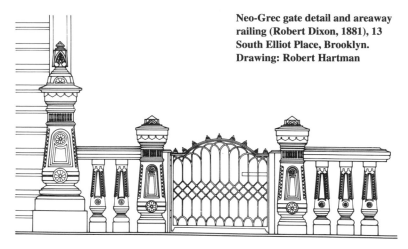

Neo-Grec gate detail and areaway railing (Robert Dixon, 1881), 13 South Elliot Place, Brooklyn. Drawing: Robert Hartman

20th Precinct Police Station House and Stable, later the 83rd Precinct Station House, 179 Wilson Avenue (William B. Tubby, 1894–95). Tubby, one of Brooklyn's most inventive late 19th-century architects, designed this fanciful police station as a mock-medieval fortress, complete with crenellations and a round corner tower; the building is entered through an eccentric Doric entrance porch embellished by a beautifully carved frieze.

23rd Regiment Armory, 1322 Bedford Avenue (Fowler & Hough and Isaac Perry, 1891–95). Designed to resemble a medieval fortress, the 23rd Regiment Armory is a vast and impressive example of late 19th-century military architecture. With its corner tower rising 136 feet, its great arched entrance, and its enormous drill shed, this building is the most imposing of Brooklyn's 19th-century armories. Fowler & Hough were local architects responsible for several important late 19th-century Brooklyn buildings; Isaac Perry was the architect for New York·State (the state financed the construction of most armories) and a specialist in armory design.

United States Post Office, Brooklyn Central Office, 271–301 Cadman Plaza East (Washington Street) (Mifflin E. Bell, 1885–91; extension, 1930–33). The office of the supervising architect of the U.S. Treasury was responsible for the design of many Romanesque Revival post offices in the United States. This Brooklyn building is one of the few such post offices still standing and still in use. The construction began during Mifflin Bell's brief tenure as supervising architect (1884–86); Bell's design was simplified following his resignation. The complementary Depression-era addition was designed during James Wetmore's term as acting supervising architect.

Johannes Van Nuyse House, also known as the Van Nuyse–Magaw House, 1041 East 22nd Street (1800–03). With its wide gambrel roof, this house is an especially fine example of a traditional Dutch Colonial farmhouse. Moved to

Weeksville Houses, also known as the Hunterfly Road Houses, 1698–1708 Bergen Street (1840–83). Photo: Caroline Kane

this site in 1916 from its original location several blocks to the south, the house was erected by Johannes Van Nuyse, the son of Joost Van Nuyse (see below), and his bride, Nellie Lott. Between 1844 and 1909 the house and its surrounding farmland were owned by Robert Magaw and his descendants.

Joost and Elizabeth Van Nuyse House, also known as Coe House, 1128 East 34th Street (before 1792). Joost Van Nuyse is recorded as having died in this building in 1792. With its characteristic Dutch Colonial design, the house is the sole remnant of Joost's 85-acre Flatlands farm.

Weeksville Houses, also known as the Hunterfly Road Houses, 1698–1708 Bergen Street (1840–83). These four small frame houses are all that remains of the 19th-century African-American community of Weeksville. Initially settled in the 1830s by free blacks, Weeksville grew by the 1870s into a community of several hundred, with its own public school, church, and other institutions. The surviving houses are located in the middle of a block, facing onto Hunterfly Road, a country road that predates Brooklyn's street grid. The old houses have been restored by Li-Saltzman Architects and serve as a living museum of African-American history and culture.

Weir Greenhouse, now McGovern-Weir Greenhouse, Fifth Avenue at 25th Street (G. Curtis Gillespie, 1895). Located across from the main entrance to Green-Wood Cemetery, this structure is a rare surviving example of a 19th-century commercial greenhouse. Erected by James Weir, Jr., a member of a Brooklyn family long involved in horticulture, the greenhouse is a wood-and-glass structure with projecting corner pavilions and an octagonal dome.

Williamsburgh Savings Bank, 175 Broadway (George B. Post, 1870–75; additions, Helmle, Huberty & Hudswell, 1905, and Helmle & Huberty, 1925). With its monumental arched entrance portico and towering dome, this early work by Post is one of the first conscious expressions of the Italian Renaissance style erected in America. Post's design anticipates the explosion of interest in Renaissance and classical architecture that culminated in the World's Columbian Exposition of 1893. The Williamsburgh Savings Bank was founded in 1851 to serve the rapidly growing independent city of Williamsburg. This building was the bank's third home and served as its headquarters until its new tower (see below) was completed in 1929.

Williamsburgh Savings Bank, 1 Hanson Place (Halsey, McCormack & Helmer, 1927–29). In 1929 the Williamsburgh Savings Bank moved its headquarters from Broadway in Williamsburg (see above) into Brooklyn's tallest building. The bank's new home consisted of a domed tower soaring 512 feet above Hanson Place. The skyscraper is famous for its monumental four-faced clock, the largest in the world at the time of the building's completion. At its base, the building is embellished with relief carving—much of it evoking themes related to saving and thrift, including figures of bees, pelicans, and squirrels—and metal grilles depicting four continents.

Winthrop Park Shelter Pavilion, now Monsignor McGoldrick Park, bounded by Nassau and Driggs avenues, Monitor and Russell streets (Helmle & Huberty, 1910). For this small park in eastern Brooklyn, Helmle & Huberty designed a curved pavilion that is reminiscent of such 17th- and 18th-century French garden structures as the Grand Trianon at Versailles. The use of Renaissance precedents can also be seen in other works by these architects, notably in the Brooklyn Central Office, Bureau of Fire Communications (see p. 157), and the Prospect Park Boathouse (see p. 178).

Wonder Wheel, 3059 West 12th Street (Charles Herman, inventor; and Eccentric Ferris Wheel Amusement Co, manufacturer, 1918–20). The Wonder Wheel is a variant of the typical Ferris wheel. The 150-foot-tall, 200-ton steel wheel has 24 passenger cars and can hold up to 160 passengers. While eight of the cars are stationary, the remaining 16 are swinging cars that slide along serpentine tracks. The Wonder Wheel has excited Coney Island visitors since the park opened on Memorial Day in 1920.

Henry and Abraham Wyckoff House, also known as the Wyckoff-Bennett Homestead, 1669 East 22nd Street (c. 1766). Originally built by Henry and Abraham Wyckoff, this house is generally considered to be the most beautiful of the surviving Dutch Colonial farmhouses in Brooklyn. During the Revolutionary War, Hessian soldiers were quartered on the premises. In 1835 the house was sold to the Bennett family, and it remained in their possession until the 1980s. The house has a long porch sheltered by a curved roof that rests on columns, and it retains its original double Dutch door. It was reoriented on the site in the 1890s.

Henry and Abraham Wyckoff House, also known as the Wyckoff-Bennett Homestead, 1669 East 22nd Street (c. 1766). Photo: Caroline Kane

Pieter Claesen Wyckoff House, 5900 Clarendon Road at Ralph Avenue (c. 1652; additions, 1740 and 1820). The Pieter Claesen Wyckoff House contains the oldest surviving built structure in New York State; fittingly, the house was the first New York City landmark to be designated after the establishment of the Landmarks Preservation Commission in 1965. The west wing of the Wyckoff House appears to have been built around 1652, with the main section added around 1740. The house was owned by Wyckoff descendants until 1901, repurchased by the Wyckoff Family Foundation in 1961, and donated to the city in 1970. It has been largely reconstructed and is now a museum.

QUEENS

Jacob Adriance Farmhouse, also known as the Creedmoor Farmhouse, now the Queens County Farm Museum, 73–50 Little Neck Parkway, Floral Park (1772; additions c. 1835 and later). The Adriance House is a rare example of a New York City farmhouse that is still set in a rural landscape. The original house, with its Dutch and English Colonial features, was greatly enlarged in the 19th century, giving the structure the Greek Revival character now evident.

Benjamin P. Allen House, also known as the Allen-Beville House, 29 Center Drive, Douglaston (c. 1848–50). Allen acquired property in Douglaston in 1847 and is thought to have erected this house shortly thereafter. The house, one of the few surviving 19th-century buildings in Queens constructed as a farm dwelling, was designed in a transitional style; the basic form is Greek Revival, but the cornices on the main house and its porches display Italianate brackets.

Louis Armstrong House, 34–56 107th Street, Corona (Robert W. Johnson, 1910). One of the world's most renowned jazz musicians and entertainers purchased this modest house in 1943 and occupied it until his death in 1971. Armstrong—or "Satchmo," as he was commonly known—gained world fame as a jazz trumpeter and bandleader on stage (notably at the Savoy Ballroom and other Harlem night spots), in recordings, and in Hollywood films. In 1983 Armstrong's wife, Lucille, willed the house and its contents to New York City for the creation of a museum and study center devoted to Armstrong's career and the history of jazz.

John Bowne House, 37–01 Bowne Street, Flushing (1661; additions, 1680, 1696, and c. 1830). The kitchen wing of the Bowne House is the oldest surviving structure in Queens and one of the oldest in New York City. The house is significant both as an example of 17th-century colonial construction and as a monument to religious freedom. John Bowne was arrested in 1662 for permitting the Quakers to hold meetings in the house. After appealing to the Dutch

Weeping Beech Tree, Weeping Beech Park,
 37th Avenue between Parsons Boulevard and
Bowne Street, Flushing (planted 1847). See p. 199.
Photo: Stephen Senigo

HUNTER'S POINT

QUEENS

government in Holland, Bowne was acquitted, thus establishing the right to freedom of worship.

Richard Cornell Graveyard, adjacent to 1463 Greenport Road, Far Rockaway (18th to 19th centuries). Named for the first European settler in the Rockaways, this small graveyard was established early in the 18th century and was used by the Cornell family into the 19th century.

Famous Players–Lasky Studio, later Paramount Studios Building No. 1, now Kaufman's Astoria Motion Picture and Television Center, 35–11 35th Avenue, Astoria (Fleischman Construction Company, 1919–21). Built at a time when New York City was a major center for motion picture production, the former Famous Players–Lasky Studio is once again one of America's most active film and television production centers. Between 1921 and 1927 more than 110 silent features were filmed here, including movies starring Gloria Swanson, Rudolph Valentino, W. C. Fields, and Dorothy Gish. Following the introduction of sound, films such as the Marx Brothers' *Animal Crackers* and Paul Robeson's acclaimed version of Eugene O'Neill's *The Emperor Jones* were shot at the studio.

Flushing High School, 35–01 Union Street (C. B. J. Snyder, 1912–15). Flushing High School, incorporated in 1875, is the oldest public secondary school in New York City. Its present home is an impressive Collegiate Gothic structure designed by the city's superintendent of school buildings. Like Snyder's earlier Curtis High School (see p. 222) on Staten Island, Flushing High School was given a campus setting. The choice of style and setting evokes the great Gothic colleges of Oxford and Cambridge.

Flushing Town Hall, later Flushing Municipal Courthouse, 137–35 Northern Boulevard, Flushing (1862). Before the consolidation of Greater New York in 1898, each town in the region had its own governmental center. This Early Romanesque Revival masonry building is one of the few such town halls still standing. The German-inspired design is striking in its use of round-arched forms for windows and doors, its entrance portico, and its corbelled cornice. The building is currently being rehabilitated for the use of the Flushing Arts Council.

Fort Totten, U.S. Government Reservation, Bayside. Between 1857 and 1863 the federal government purchased land in Queens for a fort that, along with Fort Schuyler (see p. 205) in the Bronx, would protect the mouth of the East River. In 1898 the fort was named for Joseph Gilbert Totten (1788–1864), the military engineer responsible for planning the nation's 19th-century seacoast defense.

> **Battery** (William Petit Trowbridge, engineer, 1862–64). This massive battery consists of two tiers of gun emplacements set into the hillside on the East River shoreline at Willets Point. The seaward wall is constructed of beautifully cut rough granite blocks with small square openings.

> **Officers' Club** (c. 1870; enlargement, 1887). Originally a one-story building, this picturesque Gothic Revival frame structure was enlarged in 1887. Its mock-medieval features include a crenellated roofline, a pointed-arched portico, and drip lintels.

Friends Meeting House, 137–16 Northern Boulevard, Flushing (1694; additions, 1716–19). The eastern third of the Friends Meeting House in Flushing is New York City's oldest structure in continuous use for religious purposes. In its proportions and framing system, this austerely simple wooden building offers evidence of the survival of medieval building techniques in the American colonies.

Grace Episcopal Church and Graveyard, 155–03 Jamaica Avenue, Jamaica (Dudley Fields, 1861–62; chancel, Cady, Berg & See, 1901–02; graveyard, c. 1734–). Grace Church was founded in 1702, and the congregation has worshiped at this site on the main street of Jamaica since 1734. The present church, a rough-cut brownstone Early English Gothic–inspired structure with a tall spire, is the third at this location. The early 20th-century chancel complements the design of the original building. Among those buried in the graveyard are Rufus King, whose house (see below) still stands a few yards to the west.

Arthur and Dorothy Dalton Hammerstein House, Wildflower, 168–11 Powells Cove Boulevard, Beechhurst (Dwight James Baum, 1924 and pre-1930). Although not as well known as his father, Oscar Hammerstein, or his nephew, Oscar Hammerstein II, Arthur Hammerstein was a successful theatrical producer who sponsored 26 Broadway shows, including works by Victor Herbert, George Gershwin, and Jerome Kern (see Hammerstein's Theater, p. 78). Following the success of the musical *Wildflower* in 1923, and his marriage to the actress and film star Dorothy Dalton, Hammerstein purchased a waterfront plot in Queens and erected this sprawling neo-Tudor house, which was enlarged prior to 1930. The house is one of many mansions erected along the north shore of Eastern Queens and adjacent sections of Long Island in the early decades of the 20th century. The building is currently vacant.

🍎 **Hunter's Point Historic District.** This district, extending along both sides of a single block, is an unusual example of 19th-century middle-class rowhouse construction in Queens. The urbanization of Hunter's Point followed the 1861 inauguration of ferry service between 34th Street in Manhattan and the nearby Long Island Railroad terminus. Development began in the historic district in the early 1870s and continued until 1890. Among the earliest houses are 10 faced with Tuckahoe (or Westchester) marble, a material rarely used for rowhouses.

Rufus King House, also known as the King Manor Museum, 150th Street and Jamaica Avenue, King Park, Jamaica (1733–55; additions, 1806, 1810, and c. 1830s). Rufus King—Massachusetts delegate to the Continental Congress, antislavery advocate, and three-term senator from New York—purchased a modest gambrel-roofed farmhouse and adjacent acreage in Jamaica in 1805. King immediately added a kitchen wing to the house; in 1810 he undertook major alterations, including the addition of a new dining room with chambers above and the construction of a new front elevation. Rufus King's heir, John Alsop King, was probably responsible for the Greek Revival additions, notably the front porch supported by four Doric columns. After 1896, when the last member of the King family died, the house became the property of New York City. In 1989–90 the city undertook a major restoration of the house's exterior and its **interior,** which features fine plasterwork, woodwork, and marble mantels.

Kingsland Homestead, 143–35 37th Avenue, Flushing (1785). Recent research has determined that this vernacular frame house, the second oldest in Flushing, was erected by Charles Doughty shortly after the Revolutionary War. The house is named for Doughty's son-in-law, Joseph King, who purchased the property in 1801. Moved to its current site in 1968, the Kingsland Homestead is now the headquarters of the Queens Historical Society.

J. Kurtz & Sons Store, 162–24 Jamaica Avenue, Jamaica (Allmendinger & Schlendorf, 1931). The former J. Kurtz & Sons furniture store is one of the finest examples of Art Deco architecture in Queens and a building of great prominence on the commercial thoroughfare of Jamaica Avenue. As one of the architects recalled, the brick building, with its black-and-white glazed tile pylons, polychromatic terra-cotta panels, and prominent vertical sign, was designed to be as "modern and colorful" as the contemporary furniture displayed inside.

Lawrence Family Graveyard, southeast corner of 20th Road and 35th Street, Steinway (1703–1975). This small private cemetery is the resting place of 89 members of the distinguished Lawrence family, including 12 high-ranking American military officers. Oliver Lawrence, who died in 1975, was the last family member buried at the site.

Lawrence Graveyard, 216th Street at 42nd Avenue, Bayside (1832–1925). The land on which this cemetery is located was given to the Lawrence family in 1645. Used for many years as a picnic grounds, the plot became a graveyard in 1832. Forty-eight members of the Lawrence family, including one mayor of New York, were interred at the site between 1832 and 1925.

Abraham Lent House, also known as the Lent Homestead, 78–03 19th Road, Steinway (c. 1729). One of the few surviving dwellings in Queens built in the Dutch Colonial tradition, the Abraham Lent House has walls of rough stone and contrasting wooden shingles and a steeply sloping roof with deep front and rear overhangs.

Marine Air Terminal, LaGuardia Airport (Delano & Aldrich, 1939–40). The Art Deco Marine Air Terminal evokes the glamour of early air travel. It was a principal feature of Mayor Fiorello LaGuardia's plan to build a major airport in New York City. North Beach Airport (as LaGuardia was originally called) was the largest single undertaking financed by the Works Progress Administration (WPA). The Marine Air Terminal was built for Pan American's luxurious trans-Atlantic seaplanes known as "clipper ships." The terminal is massed around a central circular core, with a rectangular entrance pavilion and two symmetrically disposed wings. Its exterior ornament includes a polychromatic terra-cotta frieze of flying fish. The **interior** consists of a small foyer and vestibule with stainless steel detail and a spectacular central rotunda encircled with James Brooks's *Flight*, a 12-foot-high, 237-foot-long mural commissioned by the WPA. The mural, which was painted over in the 1950s, was restored in 1980.

New York Architectural Terra-Cotta Company Building, 42-10–42-16 Vernon Boulevard, Long Island City (Francis H. Kimball, 1892). The New York Architectural Terra-Cotta Company was one of the leading manufacturers of ornamental terra cotta between 1886, when the firm was founded, and 1928, when it went bankrupt. The company manufactured the terra cotta for such landmarks as the Ansonia Hotel (see p. 120) and Carnegie Hall (see p. 70). This small office building displays the range and potential of the products

Marine Air Terminal, LaGuardia Airport (Delano & Aldrich, 1939–40). Photo: Carl Forster

manufactured by the company. Its architect was a pioneer in the use of ornamental terra cotta, as can be seen, for example, at his Montauk Club (1889–91) in Park Slope (see p. 175), with its Venetian-inspired terra cotta also fabricated by this New York firm. The building has been vacant for many years.

New York State Supreme Court, Queens County, Long Island City Branch, 25–10 Court Square, Long Island City (George Hathorne, 1872–76; reconstruction, Peter M. Coco, 1904–08). In 1870 the seat of Queens County was moved from Jamaica to Long Island City; shortly thereafter a new courthouse was erected. Following a disastrous fire in 1904 the building was rebuilt and enlarged in a Beaux-Arts manner by the local architect Peter M. Coco. A parking garage was built at the rear of the courthouse in 1988–90 (Skidmore, Owings & Merrill, architects), replacing two jail structures.

Benjamin T. Pike House, later the William Steinway House, 18–33 41st Street, Steinway (c. 1858). Pike, a manufacturer of scientific instruments, erected this magnificent Italianate stone villa, with its tall square tower and cast-iron porches, on what at the time was a beautiful riverfront site. The house was purchased in 1870 by William Steinway, whose piano factory is still located nearby.

Poppenhusen Institute, 114–04 14th Road, College Point (Mundell & Teckritz, 1868). The Poppenhusen Institute was established by the German-born Conrad Poppenhusen, founder in 1853 of the U.S. hard-rubber industry, as a vocational school for the workers in his nearby plant. What is thought to have been the first American free kindergarten for the children of working mothers

Prospect Cemetery, 159th Street at Beaver Road, Jamaica (c. 1668+). Early 18th-century headstones for members of the Ludlam family. Photo: Janet O'Hare

was housed in this French Second Empire structure. The building was designed by a Brooklyn architecture firm that specialized in institutional work. The institute, which still occupies the premises, continues to provide services to the community.

Prospect Cemetery, 159th Street at Beaver Road, Jamaica (c. 1668–). This 4-acre plot is the oldest cemetery in Queens. Established before 1668, the cemetery is the final resting place of many Revolutionary War veterans as well as members of such prominent Queens families as the Sutphins, Van Wycks, and Merricks. A small Romanesque Revival chapel was erected in 1857 by Nicholas Ludlum in memory of his three daughters.

Queensboro Bridge, spanning the East River between 11th Street and Bridge Plaza North and Bridge Plaza South, Queens, and East 59th Street, Manhattan (Henry Hornbostel, architect; Gustav Lindenthal, engineer, 1901–08). Inspired by the Pont Mirabeau in Paris, the Queensboro Bridge is a "through-type" cantilevered structure; that is, the roadway runs between the structure's piers and trusses. As the third bridge to span the East River and the first to connect Queens and Manhattan, it was a potent influence on the development of the borough of Queens. The heavy steel towers and frame rest on stone piers. Beneath the bridge are tall vaulted spaces clad with Guastavino tiles.

Reformed Dutch Church of Newtown and Fellowship Hall, 85–15 Broadway, Newtown (church, 1831; hall, 1860). This wooden church building displays a late use of the Georgian style; its cupola is a prominent feature of the Newtown community. Fellowship Hall, originally a chapel designed in the Greek Revival style, was moved to the site in 1906.

The Register, now the Jamaica Arts Center, 161–04 Jamaica Avenue, Jamaica (A. S. Macgregor, 1898). An excellent example of a public building in the neo–Italian Renaissance style, the former deeds registry, designed by a Queens architect, was erected in the year that Queens became a part of New York City.

Remsen Cemetery, adjacent to 69–43 Trotting Course Lane, Newtown (c. 1790–). The Remsens, among the earliest settlers of Queens, may have established this private cemetery in the mid-18th century, although the earliest extant gravestone dates from 1790. The main focus of the small plot is a World War I memorial with a flagpole and two statues of doughboys.

RKO Keith's Flushing Theater (interior), 135-29–135-45 Northern Boulevard, Flushing (Thomas Lamb, 1927–28). The ticket lobby, grand foyer, promenade, and lounges of the former RKO Keith's Flushing Theater, designed in a fanciful Mexican Baroque style, are a reminder of the grandeur of movie palaces in the 1920s. The space is currently vacant and deteriorated.

St. Monica's Church (R.C.), 94–20 160th Street, Jamaica (Anders Peterson, builder, 1856–57). This brick church has a distinctive central campanile that is reminiscent of the Romanesque architecture of northern Italy. Erected by the master mason Anders Peters under the supervision of the Rev. Anthony Farley, St. Monica's is one of the oldest surviving examples of Early Romanesque Revival architecture in New York, and one of the few Roman Catholic churches in the city executed in this style. Now located on the campus of York Community College, the building has been vacant since 1973 and is severely deteriorated.

Edward E. Sanford House, also known as the 102–45 47th Avenue House, Newtown (c. 1871). This small two-story house is one of the last intact 19th-century frame houses in Queens. Designed in a vernacular Italianate style, the house is especially notable for its decorative porch, gable, and fence, all of which display fanciful wooden detail.

Sidewalk Clocks. Many of New York's commercial streets were once graced by cast-iron sidewalk clocks generally erected as advertisements by local banks and stores (see p. 62). Two of these clocks survive in Queens.

> **161–11 Jamaica Avenue** (c. 1900). The handsome clock on Jamaica Avenue was probably erected by a jewelry store. The clock is crowned by a Greek-inspired acroterion.

> **30–78 Steinway Street** (1922). This cast-iron sidewalk clock was erected by Wagner's Jewelers in 1922. The clock was purchased secondhand by Edward Wagner and moved from Manhattan to its present site.

Cornelius Van Wyck House, 37–04 Douglaston Parkway (126 West Drive), Douglaston (c. 1735; addition, mid-18th century). Set at the edge of Little Neck Bay, this house, built by the farmer Cornelius Van Wyck in the traditional Dutch Colonial mode with hand-hewn scalloped shingles, is one of the finest residences of its type on Long Island. A Georgian-style extension was added to the west and south at some point before 1770. Additions were also made early in the 20th century when the structure served as a clubhouse, but these were removed during a restoration, early in the 1920s, by the architect Frank J. Forster.

Weeping Beech Tree, Weeping Beech Park, 37th Avenue between Parsons Boulevard and Bowne Street, Flushing (1847). This weeping beech was planted in 1847 by Samuel Parsons, owner of a large nursery in Flushing and supplier of original plant stock to both Central and Prospect parks. Intrigued by word of the existence of an exotic new variety of beech tree in Belgium, Parsons acquired a tiny shoot; the shoot has matured into this magnificent specimen. Parsons was one of several individuals who established Flushing as a mid-19th-century horticultural center.

THE BRONX

Robert and Marie Lorillard Bartow House, now the Bartow-Pell Mansion Museum, Shore Road, Pelham Bay Park (1836–42). Located near Long Island Sound, on land that was once part of the Manor of Pelham, this magnificent neoclassical country seat was built by Robert Bartow, who was descended from the Pell family. The house was purchased by the city in 1888 and, after several decades of neglect, restoration was undertaken in 1914 by the International Garden Club under the direction of the architecture firm of Delano & Aldrich. The elegant stone house faces a terraced garden dating from 1914–16. The exceptionally fine Greek Revival **interiors** were designed in the manner of Minard Lafever. The site includes an original stone stable/carriage house, later walled gardens, and a small family memorial plot.

175 Belden Street House (c. 1880). This small clapboard house, with its superb jigsaw-cut struts and brackets and a slate roof, is one of the finest picturesque cottages in New York City. Although the exact date of construction is not documented, the house was erected during City Island's heyday as a maritime community supported by fishing, shell-fishing, sail-making, and shipbuilding.

Bronx Borough Courthouse, East 161st Street at Third Avenue (Oscar Bluemner and Michael J. Garvin, 1905–15). The former Bronx Borough Courthouse was erected to serve the judicial needs of this rapidly growing borough. Garvin, a close political associate of the borough president, received the commission for the building, but he retained Bluemner to undertake the actual design work. Bluemner, who was trained as an architect in Europe and designed only a few buildings in New York, is best known as a pioneer of modern American painting. The Beaux-Arts courthouse is a massive granite structure embellished with overscaled French-inspired detail. The building has been vacant for many years.

52nd Police Precinct Station House, 3016 Webster Avenue (Stoughton & Stoughton, 1904–06). Detail of the clock tower. See p. 204. Photo: Caroline Kane

Bronx County Building, also known as the Bronx County Courthouse, 851 Grand Concourse (Max Hausle and Joseph H. Freedlander, 1931–35). Detail of *Victory and Peace* (Joseph Kiselewski, sculptor). Photo: John Barrington Bayley

Bronx County Building, also known as the Bronx County Courthouse, 851 Grand Concourse (Max Hausle and Joseph H. Freedlander, 1931–35). This monumental limestone-faced structure is an impressive example of the austere classicism popular for public edifices in the 1930s. Its sculptural program is especially striking. The carved detail includes Charles Keck's frieze of heroic figures symbolically engaged in various modes of productive employment (e.g., agriculture, industry, the arts). Eight freestanding groups of figures carved in pink Georgia marble (two flanking each of the four entrances) represent such themes as achievement, progress, and the majesty of law. The sculptor Adolph Weinman carved two of these compositions and also supervised the work of three other artists: Edward F. Sanford, George H. Snowden, and Joseph Kiselewski.

Bronx Grit Chamber, 158 Bruckner Boulevard (McKim, Mead & White, 1936–37). The Bronx Grit Chamber is a primary component of the Ward's Island Sewage Treatment Works, New York City's first major project to alleviate water pollution. The exterior of the building, a late work of McKim, Mead & White, is within the tradition of the monumental public buildings designed by the firm and is evidence of the fact that even the most utilitarian buildings were deemed worthy of impressive architectural expression.

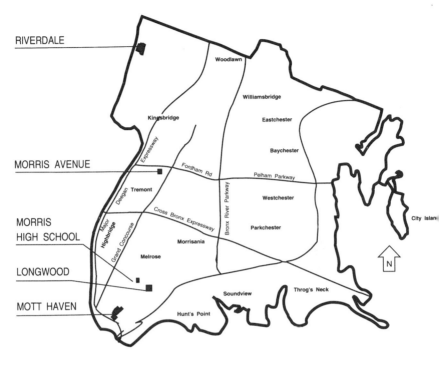

RIVERDALE

Woodlawn

Williamsbridge

Kingsbridge

Eastchester

Baychester

MORRIS AVENUE

Fordham Rd

Pelham Parkway

Tremont

Westchester

MORRIS
HIGH SCHOOL

Cross Bronx Expressway

Parkchester

Morrisania

Melrose

LONGWOOD

Throg's Neck

Soundview

MOTT HAVEN

Hunt's Point

City Island

N

BRONX HISTORIC DISTRICTS

Bronx Post Office, 560 Grand Concourse, at East 149th Street (Thomas Harlan Ellett, 1935–37). The Bronx Post Office, the largest of New York's 29 Depression-era post offices, was designed by Thomas Harlan Ellett as part of a Department of the Treasury program to employ out-of-work architects. Almost as soon as it was completed, the gray brick edifice was proclaimed a "significant example of an evolving American style, a new classicism free of dependence on the works of antiquity." Important works of art were commissioned for many of the post offices of this period. On the exterior of the Bronx Post Office are a pair of limestone panels, *The Letter* by Henry Kreis and *Noah* by Charles Rudy; the lobby contains a significant series of murals by Ben Shahn on the theme of America at work.

Christ Church (Episcopal), 5030 Riverdale Avenue (R. Upjohn & Son, 1865–66). As might seem appropriate for a church built in the suburban community of Riverdale, this High Victorian Gothic stone structure was designed to resemble a medieval English parish church. With its clearly delineated nave, transepts, chancel, and porch, its steep polychromatic slate roof (restored in 1991), its bell cote, diminutive crossing tower, and pointed-arched openings, Christ Church is among the most beautiful early designs of R. M. Upjohn, son of the better-known Richard Upjohn.

614 Courtlandt Avenue Building (1871–72). Erected by the saloonkeeper Julius Ruppert as a saloon and meeting hall serving the German community of Melrose South, this building is a simple French Second Empire structure with cast-iron window lintels and a handsome two-story mansard roof.

Eighth Coastal Artillery Armory, later the Eighth Regiment Armory, now the Kingsbridge Armory, 29 West Kingsbridge Road (Pilcher & Tachau, 1912–17). Pilcher & Tachau's design, centering on two tall round towers, was inspired by Viollet-le-Duc's mid-19th-century reconstruction of the great French medieval castle at Pierrefonds. At the time of its completion, the armory boasted the world's largest drill hall; measuring 300 by 600 feet, the hall is set beneath a vaulted roof supported by a double-truss steel frame.

52nd Police Precinct Station House, 3016 Webster Avenue (Stoughton & Stoughton, 1904–06). This romantic red brick police station was modeled on the Italian Renaissance villas of Tuscany, as is especially evident in the gabled roof slopes and the square four-faced clock tower. The modestly scaled civic structure gains stature from the architects' exploitation of inexpensive materials—brickwork laid in a diaper pattern, terra-cotta plaques, and blue tile window spandrels.

Fonthill, the Edwin Forrest House, now the Admissions Office of the College of Mount St. Vincent, West 261st Street at Palisade Avenue (1848–52). Located on a bluff overlooking the Hudson, Fonthill is a country house designed to resemble a medieval castle. The building consists of six interlocking octagonal units of varying height, which culminate in a tall, slender tower. Fonthill was erected for the famed Shakespearean tragedian Edwin Forrest (see Forrest Theater, p. 74) by a local builder, Thomas C. Smith, and was named for the English house Fonthill Abbey, built in 1796–1812. In 1856 Forrest sold the property to the Sisters of Charity of Saint Vincent-de-Paul, who have used the house at various times as administrative offices, a chaplain's residence, and a library. Fonthill's stone **carriage house/stable,** now Boyle Hall, and its **cottage** (c. 1848–52), combine Gothic and Italianate features in a manner representative of the finest in 19th-century rural design.

Fordham University, East Fordham Road at East 191st Street. Fordham University, originally known as St. John's College, received its first students in 1841. The campus is located on the former Rose Hill estate (see p. 214) of Horatio S. Moat, which was purchased by Bishop John Hughes (later New York's first Catholic archbishop) in 1839.

> **Outbuilding,** also known as Alumni House, now the Fordham University Housing Office (c. 1840). Although a stone plaque clearly dates this small fieldstone building to 1840, the exact date that construction began and the building's original use are not known. The austere rectilinear structure is a vernacular example of Greek Revival design, notable for the simplicity of its massing and fenestration.

> **St. John's Church,** now the Fordham University Chapel (William Rodrigue, 1841–45; enlargement, Emile Perrot, 1928–29). Rodrigue, a

Fonthill, the Edwin Forrest House, now the Admissions Office of the College of Mount St. Vincent, West 261st Street at Palisade Avenue (1848–52). Photo: Carl Forster

teacher at St. John's College, as well as the brother-in-law of Bishop Hughes, designed this Gothic Revival stone church with its tall pinnacled tower as the focal point of the campus of this new Catholic university. The chapel and nearby residence hall form the northern arm of the U-shaped complex known as Queen's Court (formerly the "Old Quad"). The chapel was enlarged in 1928–29 with the addition of the large transept.

St. John's Residence Hall (William Rodrigue, 1841–45). This fieldstone building was the first dormitory on the Fordham campus. It was designed in a Gothic Revival style that is reminiscent of English collegiate architecture.

Fort Schuyler, now the State University of New York Maritime College, east of the Throgs Neck Bridge (Capt. I. L. Smith, 1833–56). Fort Schuyler and its companion across Long Island Sound, Fort Totten (see p. 193) in Queens, were erected to protect the eastern entrance to New York Harbor. The massive fort, built of Connecticut granite, has walls up to 11 feet thick and once mounted more than 300 guns. The fort was abandoned in 1870. In 1934 the WPA rehabilitated the structure for use as a school. The architect William A. Hall converted the gun galleries into a library in 1966–67.

40th Police Precinct Station House, later the 50th Police Precinct Station House, 3101 Kingsbridge Terrace (Horgan & Slattery, 1900–02). This former police station is a small-scale Beaux-Arts structure with a dramatic curved corner and bold sculptural detail. It reflects the explicit intention of New York's leaders at the turn of the century to erect civic buildings throughout the five boroughs that would symbolize the importance of municipal government. The building is now a Parks Department community center.

Greyston, the William E. and Melissa Phelps Dodge House, 690 West 247th Street (James Renwick, Jr., 1863–64). In the 1860s Riverdale-on-Hudson became a popular country retreat for wealthy New Yorkers. William E. Dodge, Jr., who together with his father-in-law founded the mining firm of Phelps, Dodge & Co., was among the first to build here, commissioning this stone villa from the prominent architect James Renwick, Jr. The angular detail, quirky silhouette, and polychromatic slate roof mark this house as one of Renwick's earliest High Victorian Gothic designs and reflect Renwick's understanding of contemporary English design ideas. In 1961 the Dodge family gave the property to Columbia University Teachers College, which used it as a conference center until the late 1970s, at which time it was sold to a Zen Buddhist community. Having undergone extensive rehabilitation, the house is now once again a private home.

High Bridge. See p. 140.

High Pumping Station, 3205 Jerome Avenue (George W. Birdsall, 1901–06). The High Pumping Station, constructed as part of the Jerome Reservoir complex, pumped water to consumers throughout the Bronx, providing the necessary pressure to permit water to reach the upper floors of the borough's many new apartment houses. Birdsall, an engineer for the Department of Water Supply, Gas, and Electricity, was responsible for the station's construction; it is not known whether he actually undertook the design of the late Romanesque Revival structure. The building has a utilitarian form enlivened by expressive brick detail.

🍃 Longwood Historic District. The Longwood Historic District was almost entirely developed by George B. Johnson, who purchased the land in 1898. The cohesive character of the area can be traced to the fact that the majority of the houses were designed by the same architect, Warren C. Dickerson. These are semidetached two- and three-family neo-Renaissance brick structures. Among the distinctive features are the roofs with false mansards capped by polygonal or cone-shaped peaks. Also in the district are a series of simple single-family houses on Hewitt Place, designed by the Bronx architect Charles S. Clark, several apartment houses, a church, and a former synagogue.

Lorillard Snuff Mill, now the Snuff Mill River Terrace Café, Bronx River (c. 1840). One of the rare surviving examples of early industrial architecture in the city, this fieldstone-and-brick mill used the water power of the Bronx River to grind tobacco into snuff. The mill was in operation until 1870, when the Lorillard company moved to New Jersey. The building was rehabilitated in the 1950s and is now a public cafeteria located within the New York Botanical Garden (see p. 209).

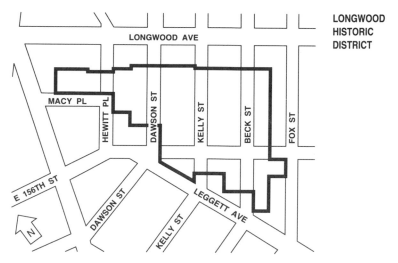

LONGWOOD HISTORIC DISTRICT

🍎 **Morris Avenue Historic District.** This one-block-long historic district is a notable example of a uniformly planned streetscape, developed by a single speculative builder working with one architect. In 1906–07 August Jacob purchased both sides of Morris Avenue between East Tremont Avenue and East 179th Street. John Hauser designed the two- and three-story, neo-Renaissance, two-family brick row houses with their projecting, full-height, angled or rounded bays; all of the houses were built before 1910. Hauser was also responsible for the pair of tenements at the Tremont Avenue end of the street.

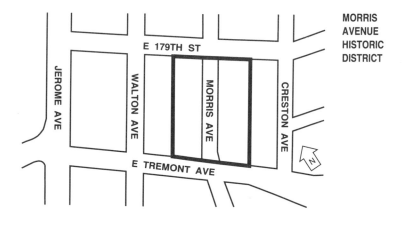

MORRIS AVENUE HISTORIC DISTRICT

Morris High School Auditorium (interior), East 166th Street at Boston Road
(C. B. J. Snyder, 1900–04; 1926). The Collegiate Gothic–style Morris High
School, located within the Morris High School Historic District (see below),
was the first major public secondary school in the Bronx and is one of the masterpieces of the New York City school architect C. B. J. Snyder. The auditorium
(now Duncan Hall), a high churchlike space with a balcony, is perhaps the
finest interior in any city school. The room contains elaborate Gothic plasterwork, steel-ribbed vaults set within Tudor arches, stained-glass windows, and a
series of organ pipes. It is decorated with several murals, most prominently the
French artist Auguste Gorguet's monumental 1926 World War I memorial entitled *After Conflict Comes Peace.* The New York City School Construction
Authority has undertaken restoration of the auditorium.

🍎 **Morris High School Historic District.** The Morris High School Historic
District focuses on the architect C. B. J. Snyder's masterful Collegiate Gothic
school building (1900–04) but also contains rows of neo-Renaissance houses
on Jackson and Forest avenues that were erected in this section of Morrisania
around the same time as Morris High. The population of the southwest Bronx
increased rapidly in the early 20th century as subway and elevated train lines
began to link this area to Manhattan. The district contains one survivor from the
area's rural past—the High Victorian Gothic red brick Trinity Episcopal
Church of 1874.

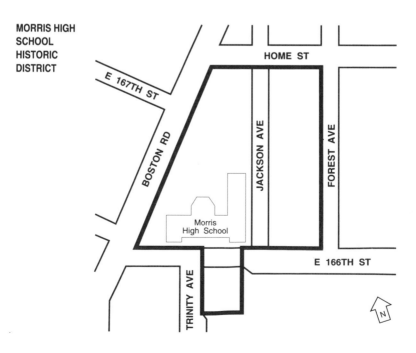

❧ **Mott Haven Historic District.** This district, named for Jordan Mott, who established the Mott Iron Works at East 134th Street and the Harlem River in 1828, contains the finest 19th-century row houses in the Bronx. Of particular note are two rows of brick houses on Alexander Avenue between East 139th and 140th streets: a 10-house unit on the east side, built in 1863–65, that is among the earliest row houses in the Bronx; and a 12-house row across the street, designed in 1881 by Charles Romeyn. The district also includes two imposing turn-of-the-century churches—St. Jerome's (Delhi & Howard, 1898) and the Third Baptist (Frank Ward, 1901)—a public library (Babb, Cook & Willard, 1905), and a police station (Thomas O'Brien, 1924).

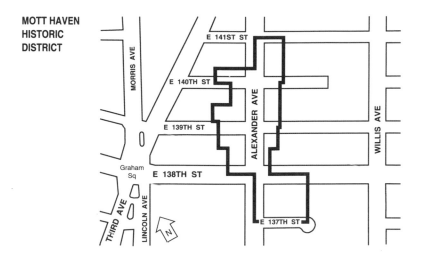

MOTT HAVEN HISTORIC DISTRICT

Mount St. Vincent Academy, now the College of Mount St. Vincent's Administration Building, West 261st Street at Palisade Avenue (Henry Engelbert, 1857–59; additions, 1865, 1883, and 1906–08). The main building on the campus of the College of Mount St. Vincent is dramatically situated on a hill commanding a sweeping view of the Hudson River and the Palisades. The site was acquired by the Sisters of Charity in 1856 when they purchased Edwin Forrest's Fonthill estate (see p. 204). With its complex round arches, tall tower, beautifully articulated brickwork, and two-story verandas, the building is a masterpiece of the Early Romanesque Revival. The expansive structure houses a wide variety of college activities.

New York Botanical Garden Conservatory, now the Enid A. Haupt Conservatory, Bronx Park, north of East Fordham Road (William R. Cobb of the firm Lord & Burnham, 1896–1902). The organization of the New York Botanical Garden in 1891 was inspired by the success of the Royal Botanic Garden at Kew, England. The garden and nearby New York Zoological Park

Mott Haven Historic District. Alexander Avenue between East 139th and 140th streets. Houses built in 1881 (Charles Romeyn, architect). Photo: Carl Forster

(see p. 211) were founded shortly after New York City acquired Bronx Park. The parkland had been part of the Lorillard estate, and the Botanical Garden incorporates the former Lorillard Snuff Mill (see p. 206). The 250-acre Botanical Garden was planned in 1895–96, but landscape and construction work did not actually begin until 1899. The magnificent conservatory consists of a central domed rotunda (known as the Palm House) and 10 connecting greenhouses. Cobb is credited with the design and with the structural system of steel, cast iron, wood, and glass, which was inspired by mid-19th-century exposition halls and horticultural structures, notably the Palm House at Kew. The conservatory was rehabilitated in 1976–78 under the direction of the architect Edward Larrabee Barnes and was renamed for the philanthropist who provided much of the funding.

New York University, now the Bronx Community College of the City University of New York, Hall of Fame Terrace at Sedgwick Avenue (McKim, Mead & White; plan, 1892–94; construction, 1894–1912). Dramatically sited on a terrace placed at the crest of a steep ridge overlooking the Harlem River, with the Hudson River and the New Jersey Palisades beyond, the former Bronx campus of New York University is a triumph of turn-of-the-century American architecture and a masterpiece of McKim, Mead & White partner Stanford White. In 1892 NYU decided to move its undergraduate school from its urbanized Washington Square site to a more rural location "suggestive of academic seclusion." White laid out the new campus and designed its classical and Renaissance-inspired buildings, all constructed of yellow Roman brick with terra-cotta and limestone trim.

Gould Memorial Library (1894–99). One of White's greatest buildings, this library is both the physical and symbolic center of the campus. The library, with its temple front and dome, was clearly modeled on the Roman Pantheon. Set at the edge of the terrace, the building was designed to blend with, rather than overpower, its spectacular site. The importance of this design in White's work was recognized in 1919 when his peers chose to create a pair of bronze doors for the library as a White memorial. The Gould Memorial Library contains monumental **interior** spaces. Richly detailed in marble, stone, mosaic, wood, and bronze, with Tiffany glass highlights, the interior was planned as a single unified whole. A long Renaissance-inspired staircase rises from the entrance to the rotunda of the library's main reading room. The rotunda has 16 columns of green Irish Connemara marble; sculpted, classically garbed figures; and a coffered dome. The building is no longer used as a library.

Hall of Fame (1900–01). White initially designed an ambulatory at the rear of the library that would take advantage of the superb views to the west; in 1900 the university chancellor, Henry MacCracken, suggested instead the creation of a Hall of Fame commemorating great Americans. White's magnificent colonnade was dedicated in 1901, although construction was not actually completed until 1912. The open terrace with Guastavino vaults and a tile roof contains the busts of noted scientists, writers, educators, and others who have made their mark on American culture.

Hall of Languages (1892–95) **and Cornelius Baker Hall of Philosophy** (1892–1912). Although completed 17 years apart, these twin classroom buildings, standing to either side of the library, complete the west range of White's 1892 campus plan. They are simpler than the library and serve as foils for that structure, accentuating its grandeur.

New York, Westchester & Boston Railroad, Administration Building, now the East 180th Street IRT Station, 481 Morris Park Avenue (Fellheimer & Long and Allen H. Stem, 1910–12). The short-lived New York, Westchester & Boston Railroad ran from Manhattan, through the Bronx, to White Plains and Port Chester, from 1912 until 1937. The stations, designed by a nationally known firm of railroad architects, were modeled after Florentine villas. The 180th Street building, which served as both station and offices, has an arcade, arched windows, and two square towers. In 1941 the section of "the Westchester" located within city limits was incorporated into the IRT system; it is now a part of the Dyre Avenue line.

New York Zoological Park, Bronx Park, south of East Fordham Road. The New York Zoological Park, better known as the Bronx Zoo, was founded in 1895. The New York Zoological Society immediately acquired a 250-acre site in Bronx Park and began the construction of the world's first zoological research center.

Paul J. Rainey Memorial Gates, park entrance at East Fordham Road (Paul Manship, sculptor, and Charles A. Platt, architect, 1929–34). This pair of monumental bronze gates is one of the finest examples of Manship's elegant public sculpture. The work consists of two gates with stylized plant and animal motifs. The gates were set within Platt's architectural framework. They were a gift of Grace Rainey Rogers in memory of her brother, Paul Rainey, a big game hunter and supporter of the zoo.

Rockefeller Fountain, park entrance at East Fordham Road (Heins & LaFarge, 1910). A gift of William Rockefeller, this 18th-century Italian fountain is set onto an exuberant basin designed by Heins & LaFarge.

Old West Farms Soldiers' Cemetery, 2103 Bryant Avenue (1815–). Situated in a modest, landscaped enclosure, this cemetery is the oldest public veterans' burial ground in the Bronx. It serves as the last resting place of veterans of four wars—the War of 1812, the Civil War, the Spanish-American War, and World War I.

Park Plaza Apartments, 1005 Jerome Avenue (Horace Ginsberg and Marvin Fine, 1929–31). As one of the first and most prominent Art Deco apartment houses in the Bronx, the Park Plaza ushered in the style that was to change the face of much of the borough. The facade was designed by Marvin Fine, who noted the direct stylistic influence of the new Chrysler and American Radiator buildings (see pp. 71 and 67). The orange brick structure contains fine terracotta ornament, including panels that depict an architect presenting a model of his building to the Parthenon.

Poe Cottage, Poe Park, 2640 Grand Concourse (c. 1812). In 1846 Edgar Allan Poe moved from New York City to this small cottage located in the village of Fordham. He lived here until his death in 1849, writing such masterpieces as "Annabel Lee" and "The Bells" while in residence. As development swept through Fordham later in the century, the house was slated for demolition, but a public outcry led to its preservation in 1902. In 1913 this shrine to one of America's great poets was moved by the city from its original location across the street to its present site at the north end of Poe Park.

Public School 15, 4010 Dyre Avenue (Simon Williams, 1877). At the time of its construction, Public School 15—a rare example in New York City of the rural, red brick schoolhouse—was surrounded largely by an undeveloped section of Westchester County. The Victorian Gothic building, with its paired gables supported by large brackets and its central bell tower, was designed by Simon Williams, who became the school's principal.

Public School 31, 425 Grand Concourse (C. B. J. Snyder, 1897–99). Public School 31 is one of a large number of schools erected in the Bronx around the turn of the century to accommodate the waves of people moving to the borough from other parts of New York City and from abroad. An early work of the school architect C. B. J. Snyder, Public School 31 was one of the first Collegiate Gothic public schools in New York, and it set the stage for Snyder's better-known examples of the style, including Morris High School (see p. 208).

Public School 91, now Public School 11, 1257 Ogden Avenue (George W.

Debevoise, 1889; additions, C. B. J. Snyder, 1905, and Walter C. Martin, 1930). As the population of the West Bronx rapidly increased late in the 19th century, the New York City Board of Education planned several new schools. Former Public School 91, one of the few surviving early school buildings in the borough, is a Romanesque Revival structure with a massive stone base, brick upper stories, and a mansard roof. The Ogden Avenue wing was added in 1905; the gymnasium/auditorium wing was built along Merriam Avenue in 1930.

Herman Ridder Junior High School, 1619 Boston Post Road (Walter C. Martin, 1929–31). Herman Ridder was the first "modernistic" Art Deco public school in New York City and one of the first schools erected specifically for use as a junior high. The building, faced with limestone and yellow brick enlivened by subtle polychromatic trim, has dramatically massed vertical buttresses and an entrance tower capped by setbacks modeled on the form of contemporary skyscrapers. The ornamentation incorporates abstract Art Deco elements and such iconographic features as stylized figures of male and female students, open books, and lamps of knowledge.

🍎 **Riverdale Historic District.** Encompassing approximately 15 acres of sloping land overlooking the Hudson River, the Riverdale district includes 34 buildings on landscaped sites. It is the nucleus of the parcel purchased in 1852 by five wealthy and influential businessmen who intended to create a suburban summer community named Riverdale. The district includes seven original estates linked by a carriage alley (now Sycamore Avenue) and one parcel subdivided from the adjacent Wave Hill estate (see p. 216). All of the estates, including that of William and Ann Cromwell (see Stonehurst, p. 215), were developed in the

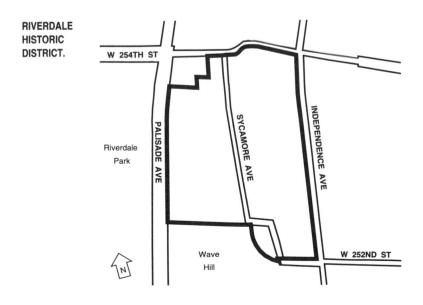

RIVERDALE
HISTORIC
DISTRICT.

1850s. Several early estate houses remain, as well as stables and carriage houses (now converted for residential use), stone walls, iron fences, and important landscape elements. Later buildings in the district illustrate the changing nature of suburbanization from the mid-19th century to the present.

Riverdale Presbyterian Chapel, now Edgehill Church of Spuyten Duyvil (United Church of Christ), 2550 Independence Avenue (Francis H. Kimball, 1888–89). The Edgehill Church, originally built as a chapel of the nearby Riverdale Presbyterian Church (see below), is a survivor from the period when Spuyten Duyvil was a sparsely populated area at the northern edge of New York City. Kimball's masterful design for this small, asymmetrical church nestled into a hillside combines elements from the Romanesque Revival, neo-Tudor, and Shingle styles in an extremely picturesque manner.

Riverdale Presbyterian Church and Manse, 4765 Henry Hudson Parkway (James Renwick, Jr., 1863–64). Renwick's English-inspired Gothic Revival stone church was built in 1863 with funding provided by local estate owners, including William E. Dodge, Jr., whose Renwick-designed house, Greyston (see p. 206), was under construction nearby. In the adjoining stone manse, now known as Duff House, Renwick combined Gothic Revival forms with a French-inspired mansard roof.

Rose Hill, the Horatio Shepheard Moat House, now the Fordham University Administration Building, East Fordham Road at East 191st Street (1836–38; additions, 1907). The central part of this fieldstone building was originally a freestanding country house erected on the Rose Hill estate by the Brooklyn merchant Horatio S. Moat. It is a superb example of the Greek Revival style, distinguished by a fine Ionic entrance portico and an octagonal cupola. The building became the nucleus of St. John's College, later Fordham University (see p. 204); the wings were added by the university in 1907.

St. Ann's Church (Episcopal) and Graveyard, 295 St. Ann's Avenue (1840–41). The oldest surviving church in the Bronx, St. Ann's was erected on the country estate of Gouverneur Morris, Jr., as a memorial to his mother. The Morrises, for whom the neighborhood of Morrisania is named, were a prominent colonial family (Gouverneur Morris, Sr., was one of the framers of the Constitution). The simple vernacular fieldstone church is articulated by Gothic windows and is capped by a Greek Revival steeple. The cemetery contains the graves of many members of the Morris family.

St. James Episcopal Church and Parish House, 2500 Jerome Avenue (church, Henry M. Dudley, 1864–65; parish house, Henry F. Kilburn, 1891–92). Designed for a rural parish in what at the time was part of Westchester County, St. James is a major work by Dudley, one of the leading Gothic Revival church architects of the mid-19th century. It is especially notable for its straightforward use of materials (fieldstone, red sandstone, wood, and slate) and for the clear delineation of interior spaces (nave, side aisles, transepts, chancel, and porch) on the exterior. The Gothic-inspired parish house complements the church building.

St. Peter's Church (Episcopal), Westchester, Complex and Cemetery, 2500 Westchester Avenue (church, Leopold Eidlitz, 1853–55; alterations, Cyrus L. W. Eidlitz, 1879; Sunday school and chapel building, Leopold Eidlitz, 1867–68; cemetery, 1702–). St. Peter's congregation was established in the village of Westchester in 1693. Leopold Eidlitz's impressive Gothic Revival stone edifice was the third church building on the site. In its straightforward use of materials and its emphasis on structural clarity, the building is characteristic of the work of Eidlitz, who was one of the most talented and influential American architects of the 19th century. After part of St. Peter's was destroyed by fire in 1877, the church was rebuilt and somewhat altered by Leopold's son Cyrus in 1879. Leopold's nearby Sunday school and chapel building (now called Foster Hall) is a superb example of High Victorian Gothic design. The cemetery contains many 18th-century gravestones.

Edwin and Elizabeth Shuttleworth House, also known as the 1857 Anthony Avenue House (Neville & Bagge, 1896). One of the few surviving suburban residences in the southern Bronx, this house was built for a prosperous stone dealer and his wife. While the firm of Neville & Bagge was responsible for the basic design, it is probable that Shuttleworth specified the use of one of the varieties of stone that he sold (stone houses were uncommon in the Bronx) and commissioned the sculpted detail from one or more of his most talented carvers. The idiosyncratic ornament, including male and female figures, marine elements, and portrait busts, survives as a monument to the anonymous stone carvers who created some of New York's finest architectural detail.

Spaulding Estate Coachman's House, 4970 Independence Avenue (Charles W. Clinton, 1880). This small Stick Style cottage was built as the coachman's residence for Parkside, the estate of the businessman Henry Foster Spaulding. Lively and varied textures are created by board-and-batten siding on the first floor, crossed sticks above, dormer windows with jigsaw ornament, and a slate roof with overhanging eaves.

Stonehurst, the William D. and Ann Cromwell House, later the Robert Colgate House, 5225 Sycamore Avenue (1856–58). The importer William Cromwell was one of the original investors who helped to establish Riverdale as a suburban enclave in 1852 (see Riverdale Historic District, p. 213). He sold his interest a year later, then purchased another plot of land in 1856 for the construction of this villa. After Cromwell's death in 1859, his widow sold the property to the paint manufacturer Robert Colgate. Stonehurst is one of the most elegant mid-19th-century country houses along the Hudson and is unusual within the Italian villa tradition for its classical symmetry. The house derives its name from the beautifully dressed gray stone used in its construction.

Sunnyslope, the Peter S. Hoe House, later Temple Beth Elohim, now the Bright Temple A.M.E. Church, 812 Faile Street (c. 1860). This picturesque Gothic Revival villa is an extraordinary survivor from the mid-19th century. Built for Peter S. Hoe, a member of the firm of R. M. Hoe & Co., manufacturers of printing equipment, Sunnyslope was part of a 14.6-acre estate in rural West Farms. Although the architect is not known, this compact, asymmetrical stone house is in the style of Calvert Vaux and may have been inspired by one of the designs Vaux published in his 1857 book *Villas and Cottages.* Most of the other country houses in West Farms were destroyed as the area was urbanized after 1900, but Sunnyslope was saved when it was converted into a synagogue in 1919.

University Heights Bridge, spanning the Harlem River between West Fordham Road, the Bronx, and West 207th Street, Manhattan (William H. Burr, consulting engineer, with Alfred P. Boller and George W. Birdsall, 1893–95; relocation and expansion, Othniel F. Nichols, chief engineer, 1905–08; enlargement and reconstruction, 1987–92). The University Heights Bridge is a steel-truss structure consisting of a central revolving swing span, three masonry piers, and steel approach spans. The central span and two flanking approach spans were originally located at Broadway (at the northern tip of Manhattan Island) and comprised the Harlem Ship Canal Bridge. In 1905–08 the bridge was floated south to its present location and a second west approach span was constructed. The bridge is especially notable for the aesthetics of its design, a particular concern of the engineer Alfred Boller. It has a graceful curved profile, two stone pavilions, four sidewalk shelters with cast-iron piers, and ornate iron railings. As part of a reconstruction project in 1987–92, the entire structure was widened.

Isaac Valentine House, now the Valentine-Varian House, 3266 Bainbridge Avenue (1758). This pre–Revolutionary War vernacular Georgian house, constructed of fieldstone, was built for the blacksmith and farmer Isaac Valentine and was sold in 1791 to Isaac Varian. Saved from demolition when it was moved in 1965 onto city-owned property, the house has been restored for use as a museum and as the headquarters of the Bronx County Historical Society.

Frederick and Frances Jay Van Cortlandt House, also known as the Van Cortlandt Mansion, Van Cortlandt Park, Broadway at West 242nd Street (1748–49). Solidly built of locally quarried fieldstone with contrasting brick trim, Frederick Van Cortlandt's mansion is one of the handsomest Georgian manor houses of the era. The formidable size of the house and the quality of its interiors are evidence of the great wealth amassed by a few prominent 18th-century New York families. The **interior** combines the formal elegance of the Georgian style with features typical of the older, more conservative Dutch Colonial tradition. The mansion was saved thanks to the creation of Van Cortlandt Park, and it has been maintained since 1896 by the Society of Colonial Dames.

Washington Bridge. See p. 151.

Wave Hill, William Lewis Morris House, 675 West 252nd Street (1843–44; later additions). This imposing stone mansion, the focus of a magnificent estate overlooking the Hudson, is operated as part of the Wave Hill Center for Environmental Studies, an educational-cultural center with an arboretum, greenhouses, art galleries, and a sculpture garden on the grounds. The original (central) section of the house was built for the jurist William Lewis Morris in

1843–44 using locally quarried Fordham gneiss. In 1866, following Morris's death, the house was sold to the publisher William Henry Appleton. George W. Perkins, one of America's leading financiers, purchased the property in 1893. Between the time of his acquisition of Wave Hill and his family's donation of the estate to New York City in 1960, the side wings and main entrance enframement were constructed and the grounds relandscaped. In 1932 Perkins's tenant, Bashford Dean, built the armor hall at the north end of the house (Dwight James Baum, architect); Dean's armor collection is now at the Metropolitan Museum of Art.

Richmondtown Restoration, Richmond Road, Richmondtown. Voorlezer's House (c. 1695). See p. 230. Photo: Carl Forster

STATEN ISLAND

Asbury Methodist Church, now Son-Rise Interfaith Charismatic Church, 2100 Richmond Avenue (1849; remodeling, 1878). This church was named for Francis Asbury, a preacher sent to America by John Wesley, the founder of Methodism. Asbury, who was consecrated in 1784 as the first bishop of the American Methodist Episcopal Church, preached on Staten Island for 45 years. This simple vernacular brick church building, constructed by a mason named Riker and the carpenter J. L. Richards, follows in the traditions of Federal architecture. The front was rebuilt and the tower added in 1878.

Alice Austen House, 2 Hylan Boulevard (c. 1700–50; remodeling, 1846, c. 1852, and 1860–78). This picturesque house overlooking the Narrows was the home of Alice Austen (1866–1952), one of America's outstanding early photographers. The original one-room Dutch Colonial house was erected in the early 18th century and gradually enlarged. In 1844 Alice Austen's grandfather purchased the property, renamed it Clear Comfort, and remodeled it in the Gothic Revival style. The house has been restored by New York City and is now a museum commemorating Alice Austen's artistry.

Stephen D. Barnes House, 2876 Richmond Terrace (c. 1853). One of the few survivors on "Captain's Row," which runs along the shore road opposite the Kill van Kull, this large Italianate brick house was erected by Stephen D. Barnes, a prosperous oysterman. It has been damaged by fire and is now vacant.

Henry Hogg Biddle House, 70 Satterlee Street (late 1840s). The Biddle House, overlooking the Arthur Kill, exemplifies an unusual aspect of vernacular design on Staten Island—the combining of Dutch Colonial–style spring eaves with Greek Revival columned porticos. This structure is the only extant local house with two-story porticos and spring eaves on both the front and rear elevations. These elements add a sense of grandeur to the relatively small waterfront dwelling.

Pierre Billiou House, also known as the Billiou-Stillwell-Perine House, 1476 Richmond Road (c. 1660s; additions, c. 1680 to c. 1830). The original stone section of this house was erected by Pierre Billiou in the 1660s, shortly after

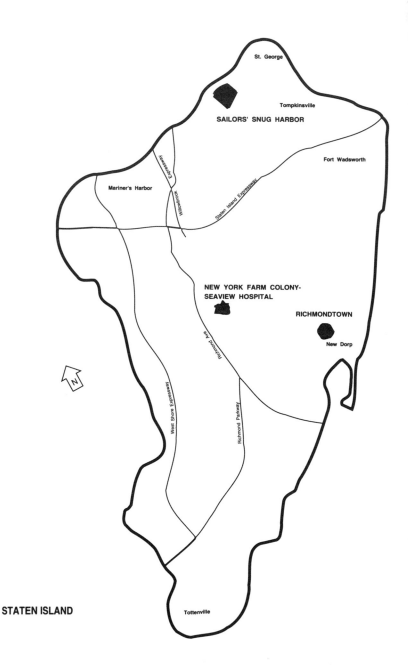

St. George

Tompkinsville

SAILORS' SNUG HARBOR

Fort Wadsworth

Mariner's Harbor

Expressway

Willowbrook

Staten Island Expressway

**NEW YORK FARM COLONY-
SEAVIEW HOSPITAL**

RICHMONDTOWN

Richmond Ave

New Dorp

N

West Shore Expressway

Richmond Parkway

STATEN ISLAND

Tottenville

Alice Austen House, 2 Hyland Boulevard (c. 1700–50; remodeling, 1846, c. 1852 and 1860–78). The family home as photographed by Alice Austen. Photo: Staten Island Historical Society

the first permanent settlement was founded in the region known as Olde Dorp. Constructed according to medieval building traditions, the house is the oldest surviving building on Staten Island. Billiou's daughter married Thomas Stillwell, and they built the first of several additions to the house. For 150 years, beginning in 1764, the house was owned by members of the Perine family. In 1919 this became the first site on Staten Island to be acquired by a historical society for use as a house museum.

James R. Boardman House, also known as the 710 Bay Street House (1848). Dr. Boardman, the resident physician at the nearby Seaman's Retreat Hospital (see p. 234), built this wood-frame Italianate house atop a steep bluff overlooking the Narrows. In 1894 the house was purchased by Capt. Elvin Mitchell with money received from the Cunard Lines in recognition of his heroism in saving the lives of all 176 people aboard the SS *Oregon,* which sank off Fire Island.

Brighton Heights Reformed Church, 320 St. Mark's Place, at Fort Place (John Correja, 1863–64). When the Reformed Protestant Dutch Church in Tompkinsville outgrew its original building, it acquired this property in nearby Brighton Heights and commissioned the Manhattan architect John Correja to design a stone structure. The cost of building the Gothic Revival design proved high, and Correja eventually adapted the form to allow for the construction of a less expensive wooden building. With its prominent spire, the church is highly visible along the northeast shore of Staten Island.

Conference House, also known as Bentley Manor, the Christopher Billopp House, Hylan Boulevard (c. 1675). This house is famous as the site of a conference on September 11, 1776, among three delegates of the Continental Congress—Benjamin Franklin, John Adams, and Edward Rutledge—and the British Admiral Lord Howe that proved an unsuccessful effort to avert the Revolutionary War. The house was erected by naval captain Christopher Billopp, who was granted a patent on 1,600 acres of southern Staten Island in 1676. Because of its historical importance, efforts were made to preserve the site as early as 1888, but it was not until 1926 that it was acquired by the city and restoration began.

The Crimson Beech, William and Catherine Cass House, 48 Manor Court (Frank Lloyd Wright, 1958–59). The only residence in New York City designed by Frank Lloyd Wright, this house is an example of the prefabricated houses Wright initially designed in 1956 for the builder Marshall Erdman of Madison, Wisconsin. These prefabs were the last of Wright's many attempts at designing moderate-cost housing. The components were shipped from Madison and assembled on Lighthouse Hill under the supervision of Wright's associate Morton H. Delson.

Curtis High School, Hamilton Avenue at St. Mark's Place (C. B. J. Snyder, 1902–04; additions, 1922, 1925, and 1937). Staten Island's first secondary school building, Curtis High School was built following the consolidation of Greater New York. It was part of a plan to erect a major high school in each of the outlying boroughs—Erasmus Hall, Morris (see p. 208), and Flushing (see p. 193) high schools were the other three. The school is named for the nationally prominent writer and orator George W. Curtis, who lived nearby. The Collegiate Gothic school is situated in an appropriate campuslike setting.

Decker Farmhouse, 435 Richmond Hill Road (c. 1810; expansion, c. 1840). This simple clapboard building is typical of the small farmhouses that once dotted Staten Island. The modest, early 19th-century house was expanded in 1840 when the front porch and other additions were constructed. The building is now a farm museum operated by the Richmondtown Restoration (see p. 229).

752 Delafield Avenue House, also known as the Scott-Edwards House, 752 Delafield Avenue (early 18th century; remodeling, 1840). The original one-story brownstone house on this site was probably erected in the first part of the 18th century, possibly by Capt. Nicholas Manning. At a later date the second story was added; the Greek Revival portico was most likely placed on the building in the 1840s, perhaps by Ogden Edwards, the first New York state supreme court justice from Staten Island, shortly after he purchased the house.

69 Delafield Place House, also known as the Samuel MacKenzie Elliott House (possibly Calvin Pollard, c. 1850). This beautifully proportioned stone house was built as a real estate investment by Samuel MacKenzie Elliott, a prominent oculist and eye surgeon and a vocal abolitionist. Elliott, who began purchasing property in northern Staten Island in 1839, built so many suburban houses in the vicinity that the area became known as Elliottville. The Scottish-born doctor/developer is known to have commissioned several designs from the prestigious New York City architect Calvin Pollard, and this Gothic Revival house may be one of them.

Edgewater Village Hall, Tappan Park and Canal Street (Paul Kühne, 1889). This Romanesque Revival brick building with a square central tower was erected to house the civic functions of the village of Edgewater. It is one of only two village halls built on Staten Island (see New Brighton Village Hall, p. 226).

Ernest Flagg Estate, Stone Court, now the Scalabrini Fathers of St. Charles and the Copperflagg Residential Development, 209 Flagg Place (Ernest Flagg, 1898 to c. 1917). Stone Court was built as the country estate of the prominent American architect Ernest Flagg. Flagg was introduced to Staten Island in 1897, and a year later he began to purchase land in a section of Todt Hill with splendid ocean views. Here he erected a large house that was indebted to the form of Staten Island's early Dutch Colonial–style dwellings, with their steep, sloping gambrel roofs and deep eaves (the roof slope was somewhat altered when the house was enlarged in 1907–09). Flagg extensively landscaped his grounds and also erected a series of other structures, including the extant gatehouse, stable, water towers, retaining wall, gardener's cottage, palm house, garage, and storage house, all of which were originally faced with whitewashed fieldstone. Much of the estate is now occupied by a complex of large suburban houses designed by Robert A. M. Stern and built in the 1980s.

Ernest Flagg Estate Cottages. Flagg not only built his own large estate on Todt Hill, but he also used the area to experiment with the construction of innovative low-cost dwellings of modular design that embodied his pioneering vision of affordable middle-class housing. Although Flagg erected only a few cottages, his ideas were widely disseminated through popular magazines and his book *Small Houses*. Three of the houses are landmarks.

Bowcot, 95 West Entry Road (Ernest Flagg, 1916–18). Bowcot was the earliest of Flagg's experimental stone cottages. Built into a curved section of the stone wall of his estate (thus the name Bowcot—a diminutive for "bowed cottage"), the small house is carefully integrated with its setting. Among Flagg's innovations were the use of "mosaic rubble," a technique of setting rubble stone into a concrete wall.

McCall's Demonstration House, 1929 Richmond Road (Ernest Flagg, 1924–25). In 1924–25 Flagg built a model house for the benefit of the readers of *McCall's* magazine. A series of articles detailing the construction of this cottage served to popularize Flagg's ideas on residential design. When the house was completed, Flagg leased it to his secretary.

Wallcot, also known as House-on-the-Wall, 285 Flagg Place (Ernest Flagg, 1918–21). Wallcot is a simple dwelling erected in conjunction with flanking walls. Both the cottage and walls were built of Flagg's mosaic rubble. The house has the picturesque sloping roofs and dormers that Flagg favored for their evocation of "home."

Fort Richmond, now Battery Weed, Fort Wadsworth (Joseph G. Totten, 1845–61). Built at a crucial site on the edge of the Narrows at the entrance to New York Harbor, Fort Richmond was designed in 1845 by the army's chief engineer, but construction did not begin until two years later. Due to inadequate funding, work dragged on until 1861. The trapezoidal granite building, named for Gen. Stephen Weed after his death at Gettysburg in 1863, is a magnificent example of military architecture.

Fort Tompkins, Hudson Road, Fort Wadsworth (1858–76). Fort Tompkins, a pentagonal granite structure, is set on a hill above Fort Richmond. The fort contained gun emplacements that were burrowed into the hill.

Garibaldi-Meucci Museum, 420 Tompkins Avenue (c. 1845). This small house is preserved by the Sons of Italy as a memorial to two great Italians. Giuseppe Garibaldi, the liberator of Italy, lived in the house in 1851–53 while in exile in the United States. Garibaldi was a guest of Antonio Meucci, one of the early developers of the telephone.

Hamilton Park Cottages. Hamilton Park (originally known as Brighton Park) was probably the earliest suburban residential park on Staten Island and one of the first self-contained, limited-access suburban subdivisions in the United States. Laid out c. 1851–52 by Charles Hamilton, Hamilton Park had dwelling sites set on curving drives amidst a naturalistic landscape. Development proceeded slowly; only three or four houses were erected in the 1850s, but in the 1860s the German-born architect Carl Pfeiffer designed 12 additional residences.

105 Franklin Avenue House, also known as Hamilton Park Cottage (Carl Pfeiffer, c. 1864). The Hamilton Park cottages were among Pfeiffer's first American commissions. Somewhat simpler and less picturesque than the earlier Harvard Avenue House (see below), this Italianate brick building has a magnificent arcaded loggia.

66 Harvard Avenue House, also known as the Pritchard House (c. 1853). This Italianate stuccoed house, with its stone trim and its notable wooden porch, balcony, and projecting window hood, is the only intact survivor of Hamilton Park's original suburban residences.

Peter Housman House, 308 St. John Avenue (c. 1730; addition, c. 1760). The small one-room stone wing of this 18th-century vernacular house was erected c. 1730 on the Dongan estate. (Shortly after his appointment as royal governor of New York in 1683, Thomas Dongan acquired approximately 5,100 acres on Staten Island.) Thirty years later Peter Housman, a prosperous millwright, erected a large clapboard extension. With its steep roof and unusually deep overhang the addition matches the architectural form of the original building.

Charles Kreischer House, 4500 Arthur Kill Road (attributed to Palliser & Palliser, c. 1888). In 1854 Balthasar Kreischer established the Kreischer Brick Company in southwestern Staten Island. Balthasar built a villa at the top of a hill overlooking his factory, and around 1888 a pair of houses were erected at a lower elevation for his two sons, including this exuberant Stick Style house for Charles Kreischer. The Kreischer Brick Company was an important late 19th-century Staten Island industry, producing a variety of architectural materials, including terra-cotta ornament and many types of bricks.

Cornelius Kreuzer House, also known as the Kreuzer-Pelton House, 1262 Richmond Terrace (1722; additions, 1770 and 1836). Three construction phases are clearly visible on the exterior of this house. Cornelius Van Santvoord, minister of the Dutch Reformed Church in Port Richmond, erected the original one-room section in the Dutch Colonial tradition. The steep-roofed central wing was added by Cornelius Kreuzer, and the two-story brick end section in the Federal style was built by Daniel Pelton.

Lane Theater (interior), 168 New Dorp Lane (John Eberson, 1937–38). Designed by one of the preeminent theater architects of the 20th century, the foyer, lounge corridor, and auditorium of the Lane Theater comprise one of the last surviving historic theater interiors on Staten Island. The Lane is among the few largely intact Art Moderne theaters in New York City, although a conversion to discotheque use is planned.

David Latourette House, now the Latourette Park Golf Course Club House, Latourette Park, Richmond Hill Road (c. 1836; alterations, 1936). The Latourette House, an especially imposing example of a Greek Revival residence, is one of the few early 19th-century brick country houses on this scale to survive in New York City. In 1928 the Latourette farm was sold to the city for use as a park and golf course. The Parks Department subsequently undertook a series of alterations that included the removal of dormer windows, the reconstruction of the four tall chimneys, the replacement or reconstruction of the floor, cornice, and railings at the original front porch, and the extension of the porch along the south elevation.

Henry McFarlane House, later the New York Yacht Club, also known as the McFarlane-Bredt House, 30 Hylan Boulevard (c. 1841–45; additions, c. 1860, c. 1870s, and c. 1890s). The site of this villa adjoining the Alice Austen House (see p. 219) property enjoys commanding views across the harbor. The house has had many owners and has been substantially enlarged since the original cottage was constructed, apparently by the merchant Henry McFarlane. The earliest addition was built around 1860 when the dry goods merchant Henry Dibblee doubled the size of the dwelling, copying the original detail so that the house appeared to be a single structure. Between 1868 and 1871 the house served as the headquarters of the New York Yacht Club (see p. 86); it was during its tenancy that the club first successfully defended the America's Cup.

Abraham Manee House, also known as the Manee-Seguine Homestead, 509 Seguine Avenue (late 17th to early 19th centuries). Located on Prince's Bay near the southern tip of Staten Island, this house has a complex building history that may extend back to the construction of a one-room dwelling by Paulus Regrenier in the late 17th-century. A major rubble-stone addition was constructed early in the 18th century by Abraham Manee. Further additions were made early in the next century by the Seguine family, who acquired the property in the 1780s.

Gustave A. Mayer House, originally the David R. Ryers House, 2475 Richmond Road (1855–56). With its boxy massing, arcaded porch, deep bracketed eaves, round-arched openings, and square cupola, this house, built for David R. Ryers, epitomizes the Italian villa form that became popular in the United States in the 1850s. In 1889 the property was purchased by Gustave A. Mayer, the confectioner who invented the Nabisco sugar wafer. Mayer used the basement of the villa as a workshop to experiment with novelties for his business. The house was occupied by members of the Mayer family for 100 years.

Memorial Church of the Huguenots, now the Reformed Church of Huguenot Park, 5475 Amboy Road (Ernest Flagg, 1923–24; assembly hall, James Whitford, Jr., 1954–55; library, 1903–05). Dedicated in 1924 as the National Monument of the Huguenot–Walloon–New Netherlands 300th Anniversary of Religious Freedom, this stone church is both a testament to a significant aspect of Staten Island's early history and an important late work by Flagg. The design, reminiscent of the vernacular Norman architecture of England and northwestern France, offers evidence of both Flagg's interest in medieval design and his experimentation with economical means of construction. Like the Ernest Flagg Estate Cottages (see p. 223), the building is a concrete structure set with rubble stone (quarried on Flagg's nearby estate) and built on the modular system first used at the estate cottages. The site also includes an assembly hall that was added to the west side of the church in 1954–55 and a small wooden public library built in 1903–05 and moved to this site shortly thereafter. The former library was once the smallest branch of the New York Public Library system.

Rev. David Moore House, also known as the Moore-McMillen House, 3531 Richmond Road (1818). This frame farmhouse with a gambrel roof and an elegant entranceway is one of the few buildings in the Federal style on Staten Island. The house was built by nearby St. Andrew's Church (see p. 233) for its minister, David Moore. Moore served the church for 48 years and was eventually given the house; his descendants occupied the premises until 1943. In the following year the prominent Staten Island historian Loring McMillen purchased the property, living here until his death in 1990.

New Brighton Village Hall, 66 Lafayette Avenue (James Whitford, 1868–71). This small but impressive French Second Empire brick building was erected at a time when the northern Staten Island village of New Brighton was the suburban home of many prominent New Yorkers. Whitford was a local architect who arrived in Staten Island from England in 1852. The building has been vacant since 1968.

New Dorp Light, 25 Boyle Street, New Dorp Heights (c. 1854). Now converted into a residence, this vernacular clapboard cottage with a tall square tower served for almost 90 years as a beacon to ships entering New York Harbor.

🍎 **New York City Farm Colony–Seaview Hospital Historic District.** Staten Island's only historic district, consisting of the buildings and grounds of two municipal institutions, recognizes the commitment made by New York City at the turn of the century to improve social and health-care services for the needy. The New York City Farm Colony was organized in 1902 to house the able-bodied indigent. Construction began in 1904 on a series of striking Colonial Revival dormitories and other structures built of local rubble stone. The first Farm Colony building, designed by Renwick, Aspinwall & Owen, set the style for buildings by other architects erected during the following ten years. Between 1930 and 1934 the capacity of the farm colony was doubled with the construction of a series of Colonial Revival brick buildings designed by Charles B. Meyers. The entire complex is bordered by fields that were farmed by the colony's residents. Separated from the farm colony by Brielle Avenue, Seaview Hospital was founded in 1905 for the treatment of tuberculosis. The architect

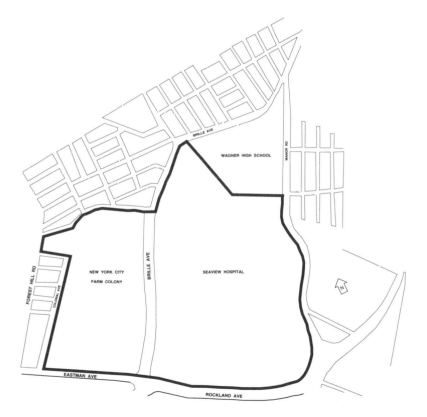

NEW YORK CITY FARM COLONY–SEAVIEW HOSPITAL HISTORIC DISTRICT

Raymond F. Almirall conceived the plan for the hospital and designed the original facility. Later additions include Renwick, Aspinwall & Tucker's two groups of small open-air pavilions designed in 1917 for ambulatory patients. The hospital buildings are all set within a therapeutic environment that provided abundant fresh air and landscaped vistas. Most of the buildings are no longer in use.

Northfield Township District School 6, now Public School 20 Annex, 160 Heberton Avenue (1891; addition, James Warriner Moulton, 1897–98). This structure is among the most impressive of the public school buildings erected on Staten Island before its consolidation with New York City. The Romanesque Revival school, which has a wealth of sculptural ornament, was built in two sections, each with a tower that is visible throughout the neighborhood.

Frederick Law Olmsted House, also known as the Poillon House, 4515 Hylan Boulevard (early 18th century; additions, 1830s). The high stone base of the present house was probably erected in the early part of the 18th century and used as a barn. The building appears to have been converted into a residence by the addition of the frame upper stories in the 1830s. In 1839 the house and surrounding land were purchased by Samuel Akerly, a renowned agricultural reformer. Nine years later the young Frederick Law Olmsted bought the property; over the next few years he relandscaped the site and undertook a variety of agricultural experiments. In 1853 Olmsted moved to Manhattan, where he would eventually embark on a career as America's first landscape architect.

22 Pendleton Place House, also known as the W. S. Pendleton House (attributed to Charles Duggin, c. 1855). This Gothic Revival house—with its tower, projecting oriel, varied windows, and steeply pitched gables—commands a high elevation above the Kill van Kull. The house was one of a number of suburban dwellings in New Brighton built as rental units by William S. Pendleton. Several of these houses are known to have been designed by the English-born and -trained architect Charles Duggin, and although there is no specific documentation for this house, it is probably one of his buildings.

Poillon-Seguine-Britton House, 361 Great Kills Road (c. 1695; additions, c. 1730, c. 1845, and 1930). Like many rural dwellings of its kind, this farmhouse on Great Kills Bay has undergone many changes in its more than two-hundred-year existence. In the late 17th century Jacques Poillon erected the original stone structure. His son, Jacques Poillon II, enlarged the house around 1730. More than a century later Joseph and Sara Seguine added a clapboard second floor and colonnaded veranda and attached an earlier building to the side of the house for use as a kitchen. In 1930 Richard Britton created a sunroom by enlarging and enclosing a part of the porch. The building has been badly damaged by fire.

Richmond County Courthouse, Richmond Terrace (Carrère & Hastings, 1913–19). Shortly after Staten Island became a part of New York City, a new civic center was planned. This impressive temple-fronted L-shaped limestone courthouse and the Staten Island Borough Hall (see p. 234) are the only two major features of the plan that were erected. Carrère & Hastings, one of the pre-eminent early 20th-century American architecture firms, received the commission for both civic center buildings, probably because John M. Carrère was a resident of Staten Island.

Richmondtown Restoration, Richmond Road, Richmondtown. Due to its central location, the town of Richmond became the seat of county government on Staten Island in 1729. Richmondtown's importance declined after Staten Island joined New York City in 1898, although its courthouse remained in use until the Richmond County Courthouse (see p. 228) opened. In 1939 the Staten Island Historical Society inaugurated the preservation of Richmondtown, including the restoration of historic village buildings and the relocation of endangered buildings from other Staten Island sites. The museum village, which is owned by New York City and operated by the historical society, recalls three centuries of life on Staten Island. The names and dates given below are those currently used by the Richmondtown Restoration historic village and museum complex.

Basketmaker's Shop (c. 1810–20). Originally located in New Springville, this modest clapboard Dutch Colonial cottage was erected for the basketmaker John Morgan.

Bennett House (c. 1839; addition, c. 1854). This clapboard house with Greek Revival elements is located on its original site. Built as a residence with a cellar bakery, the house belonged to the shipping merchant John Bennett and his family from the late 1840s through the early 20th century.

Boehm House (c. 1750; addition, c. 1840). This extremely simple pre–Revolutionary War clapboard house, the home of the teacher Henry M. Boehm from 1855 to 1862, was moved to this site from Greenridge.

Britton Cottage (c. 1670; additions, c. 1755, c. 1765, and c. 1800). Built in four stages, this wood-and-stone farmhouse was moved from New Dorp Beach in 1967. The central stone section, which was probably built around 1670, may have served as Staten Island's first government building. The Britton family owned the house from 1695 to 1714 and again from 1895 to 1915.

Christopher House (c. 1720; addition, 1730). Originally a one-room-and-attic structure on the Dongan estate (see Peter Housman House, p. 224), this vernacular stone house was the home of the patriot Joseph Christopher during the Revolutionary War and is said to have been the meeting place of the American Committee of Safety. It was moved to Richmondtown in 1969.

Eltingville Store (c. 1860). This modest board-and-batten commercial building was originally a one-room grocery store in the village of Eltingville.

Guyon-Lake-Tysen House (c. 1740; additions, c. 1820 and c. 1840). A superb Dutch Colonial–style house erected in the New Dorp–Oakwood area by the Huguenot settler Joseph Guyon, this building was moved to

Richmondtown in 1969? The gambrel roof, spring eaves, and front porch are especially notable. The kitchen wing was added around 1820 and the dormer windows 20 years later.

Historical Museum, originally the Richmond County Clerk's and Surrogate's Office (1848; additions to c. 1918). This simple brick building, constructed in the tradition of the Federal style, served the county government until around 1920, when civic functions moved to St. George. The building was converted into a museum in the 1930s.

Kruser-Finley House (c. 1790; additions, c. 1820 and c. 1850–60). Endangered by the construction of the Willowbrook Parkway, this modest clapboard building was moved from Egbertville in 1965. Originally a one-room house, the structure was extended around 1820 and again around 1850–60, when a shop, thought to have been used by a cooper, was added.

Parsonage (c. 1855). Located on its original site, this vernacular Gothic Revival clapboard building with gingerbread detail was originally the parsonage of the Reformed Dutch Church of Richmondtown.

Rezeau–Van Pelt Cemetery (1780s to 1860s). A rare surviving 18th-century private graveyard, this cemetery was used by two families who occupied the Voorlezer's House (see below) in the 18th and 19th centuries, after the house ceased to be used as a school.

Stephens-Black House (c. 1838–40). Stephen D. Stephens erected this simplified Greek Revival house, and his family lived here until 1870, operating the one-story general store (reconstructed in 1964) that was added to the rear at some point after the main house was completed.

Third County Courthouse, now the Visitors Center (1837). With its Doric portico and square cupola, this Greek Revival courthouse was the centerpiece of Richmondtown during its period as a governmental center. The courthouse remained in use until 1919.

Treasure House (c. 1700; additions, c. 1740, c. 1790, and c. 1860). Still on its original site, this modest clapboard building was the house and workshop of Samuel Grasset, a tanner and leatherworker. The Treasure House derives its name from the local legend that a $7,000 cache of British coins was found hidden in its walls around 1860.

Voorlezer's House (c. 1695). Built by the Reformed Dutch Church as a school, church, and home for the "voorlezer," or lay reader and teacher, this two-story clapboard structure is the oldest surviving elementary school in the country and the oldest surviving building from the settlement of Richmondtown. Its restoration in 1939–42 was Richmondtown Restoration's first project.

Rossville A.M.E. Zion Church Cemetery, Crabtree Avenue (1852–). This cemetery is a major surviving element of Sandy Ground, a 19th-century settlement of free black oystermen and their families who moved to Staten Island

Sailors' Snug Harbor, now the Snug Harbor Cultural Center, 1000 Richmond Terrace. Administration Building, also known as Building C (Minard Lafever, 1831–33). Photo: Carl Forster

from Maryland. The cemetery contains the burial sites of members of at least 34 African-American families, some of whose descendants still reside in the area.

Sailors' Snug Harbor, now the Snug Harbor Cultural Center, 1000 Richmond Terrace. Sailors' Snug Harbor was established with an 1801 bequest from the merchant Robert Randall, who left a large plot of land north of Washington Square in Manhattan for the establishment of an institution for the care of "aged, decrepit and worn-out sailors." Randall's bequest was challenged in court, and it was not until 1830 that the case was settled, by which time the Washington Square area was being developed as a prestigious residential neighborhood. Realizing that their Manhattan property was extremely valuable, the trustees of Sailors' Snug Harbor leased the land and in 1831 purchased a large farm on the north shore of Staten Island, where they proceeded to erect a complex of buildings. Sailors' Snug Harbor housed retired seamen at this location until 1972, when it moved to North Carolina. Following a series of court challenges that upheld the validity of landmarks regulation and devised tests to determine its effects on property devoted to charitable purposes, the Sailors' Snug Harbor facility was sold to New York City. The complex is now a cultural center.

Main Buildings, Buildings A through E (Administration Building, Minard Lafever, 1831–33; interior renovation, 1884; dormitories, Minard Lafever,

1831–41, and Richard P. Smyth, 1879–81). The centerpiece of the Sailors' Snug Harbor complex is the former Administration Building (Building C), Minard Lafever's earliest surviving work. This magnificent Greek Revival structure, with its monumental Ionic portico, was constructed of Westchester marble. It originally housed all of the institution's functions except for cooking. The plan of the **interior** is Lafever's, but the rectangular hall, second-floor gallery, and elliptical dome were redecorated in 1884 with stained glass, murals, and other painted details in the neo-Grec style. As the number of residents at Sailors' Snug Harbor increased, new dormitory buildings were erected. The pavilions (Buildings B and D) that flank the main building were designed by Lafever in 1831 in a simplified Greek Revival style, but were not built until 1839–41. The end pavilions (Buildings A and E), designed by Richard Smyth, echo the form of the central building. Together the buildings form a masterpiece of the Greek Revival.

Chapel, now Veterans Memorial Hall (James Solomon, 1854–56; interior renovation, 1873; addition, 1883). The Manhattan builder James Solomon erected this Italianate chapel in 1855–56; the bell tower that he had recommended was not built, however, until 1883. The chapel was an important aspect of life at Sailors' Snug Harbor, since daily attendance was mandatory for all residents. The **interior** of this deconsecrated chapel has a simple rectangular layout with three aisles, a raised platform and shallow apse, and a balcony supported by cast-iron columns. In 1873 the decorator Charles Berry refurbished the chapel, adding *trompe l'oeil* architectural elements that include the recently restored pilasters and entablature.

Fence (Frederick Diaper, 1841–45). This monumental iron fence, erected to keep residents from unauthorized excursions, extends for more than a third of a mile along Richmond Terrace. The fence was designed by the British-born Diaper, who derived inspiration from the Cumberland Gates in Hyde Park, London; the fence was fabricated by William Alexander of Manhattan.

North Gatehouse (Richard P. Smyth, 1873). The Italianate gatehouse, with its arched central tunnel and diminutive cupola, gave access to the main building complex from Richmond Terrace. It was one of four gatehouses erected in an effort to prevent liquor from being brought onto the property illicitly.

St. Alban's Episcopal Church, originally the Church of the Holy Comforter (Episcopal), 76 St. Alban's Place (R. M. Upjohn, 1865; enlargement, R. M. Upjohn, 1872). St. Alban's in Eltingville, a rare example of board-and-batten construction in New York City, is one of the city's finest rural Gothic Revival wood-frame buildings. The church was erected in 1865; in 1872 it was moved to its present site and enlarged by the insertion of transepts between the nave and chancel. In 1951 the Holy Comforter parish merged with St. Anne's, Great Kills, to form St. Alban's. In 1990 the church completed a restoration (Li-Saltzman, architects) that included repainting in historically accurate colors.

St. Alban's Episcopal Church

St. Andrew's Church (Episcopal), Old Mill Road at Arthur Kill Road (attributed to George Mersereau, 1872). This stone edifice housing Staten Island's oldest Episcopal congregation is located just outside the Richmondtown Restoration (see p. 229). Construction of the original church began in 1709. This structure burned in 1867 and again in 1872; surviving sections of the original walls are encased in the present stonework. With its rounded windows and carefully delineated nave, tower, and entrance porch, the church resembles the Norman parish churches erected in 12th-century England.

St. John's Church (Episcopal), 1331 Bay Street (Arthur D. Gilman, 1869–71). Arthur Gilman's Gothic Revival granite structure, whose tall spire serves as a prominent landmark to ships arriving in New York Harbor, was planned to resemble a medieval English parish church. The design reflects 19th-century theories of Episcopal church architecture, especially in its clear delineation of such building parts as nave, side aisles, transepts, chancel, and tower. Gilman was a well-known architect in Boston before moving to Staten Island and receiving the commission for this church, which replaced an 1844 wooden church building.

St. Patrick's Church (R.C.), 53 St. Patrick's Place (1860–62). Located across the street from the Richmondtown Restoration (see p. 229), St. Patrick's is an integral part of the old community of Richmondtown. The church is a dignified example of the Early Romanesque Revival style.

St. Paul's Memorial Church (Episcopal) and Rectory, 225 St. Paul's Avenue (Edward T. Potter, 1866–70). St. Paul's Memorial Church and Rectory form one of the finest High Victorian Gothic religious complexes in New York

City. The noted architect Edward T. Potter created a dynamic work using a dark gray stone with lighter-colored Connecticut brownstone banding and polished granite dwarf columns on the entrance porch. The church was damaged by fire in 1940 and again in 1985; restoration took place following both fires. The two-and-a-half story rectory, resembling a rural English parish house, complements the church.

Seamen's Retreat, now Bayley-Seton Hospital, 131 Bay Street. The Seamen's Retreat was founded by the New York state legislature in 1831 to care for sick and disabled merchant seamen. The institution served seamen for 150 years. Run by the state until 1883, the facility became a U.S. Marine Hospital, then a U.S. Public Health Service Hospital until 1981. As befits a hospital for sailors, the Seamen's Retreat enjoys a waterfront location with fine harbor views. The retreat's physicians were in the forefront of medical research and reform, campaigning for improved conditions for sailors on ship and in port and undertaking bacteriological research that laid the groundwork for the public health endeavors later carried out by the National Institutes of Health.

> **Main Building** (Abraham P. Maybie, builder, 1834–37; additions, 1848, 1853, and 1911–12). This imposing Greek Revival hospital, constructed of granite ashlar, originally consisted of a central pavilion (with Doric entrance portico) projecting forward from flanking wings with two-story porches. As the hospital expanded, matching end pavilions were constructed in 1848 and 1853, and an additional story was added to the flanking wings in 1911–12.

> **Physician-in-Chief's Residence** (Staten Island Granite Company, builder, 1842). Designed to harmonize with the nearby hospital building, this house is a severe granite structure in the Greek Revival style.

Joseph H. Seguine House, 440 Seguine Avenue (1837). This sophisticated Greek Revival country house is located at the highest point on the Seguine family's ancestral farm. The farmer, shipping merchant, and industrialist Joseph Seguine, born in the nearby Abraham Manee House (see p. 225), belonged to the fifth generation of his family to live on Staten Island.

Sleight Family Graveyard, also known as the Rossville or Blazing Star Burial Ground, Arthur Kill Road at Rossville Road (1750–1850). This small graveyard, which served the village of Rossville, is one of the earliest community cemeteries on Staten Island.

John Frederick Smith House, later the Dorothy Valentine Smith House, 1213 Clove Road (1893–95). The prominent local banker and insurance dealer John F. Smith erected this house in a restrained version of the Queen Anne style. The house was the lifelong home of Smith's daughter Dorothy, the author of several books and articles on Staten Island's history and a founder of Richmondtown Restoration.

Staten Island Borough Hall, Richmond Terrace (Carrère & Hastings, 1904–06). Borough Hall is the most prominent feature of Staten Island's governmental center and one of the great early 20th-century civic monuments of

Staten Island Borough Hall, Richmond Terrace (Carrère & Hastings, 1904–06).
Photo: Carl Forster

New York City. The noted firm of Carrère & Hastings (John M. Carrère lived on Staten Island) designed Borough Hall in a style reminiscent of the brick-and-stone châteaux erected in France during the early 17th century. This is especially evident on the east elevation, facing New York Harbor, where the facade consists of a central pavilion flanked by projecting wings, all crowned by a mansard roof. The massing creates a courtyard reached by a long flight of stairs. A tall clock tower, visible from the harbor, rises from the center of the west elevation.

Staten Island Lighthouse, Edinboro Road (1912). This octagonal brick tower rising from a rusticated limestone base houses a 350,000-candlepower beacon that guides ships into New York Harbor.

Julia Gardiner Tyler House, originally the Elizabeth Racey House, also known as the Gardiner-Tyler House, 27 Tyler Street (c. 1835). This Greek Revival mansion with a portico supported by four Corinthian columns was purchased by Juliana and David Gardiner and given to their daughter Julia, the wife of President John Tyler. Julia did not occupy the house until 1868, after her husband's death, when she moved to Staten Island with her seven stepchildren.

Tysen-Neville House, also known as the Neville House and the Old Stone Jug, 806 Richmond Terrace (c. 1800). The builders of this exceptional farmhouse of rough sandstone (now whitewashed) were probably Jacob and Mary Tysen.

Recent rehabilitation work on the facade has revealed that the unusual two-story veranda, which was added at an unknown dated, perhaps in the late 19th century, assumed its present configuration around 1910, and that the hexagonal cupola was added at that time. Through part of the 19th century the house was used as a tavern, known as the Old Stone Jug, which was frequented by residents of Sailors' Snug Harbor (see p. 231). The building is often referred to as the Neville House, after Capt. John Neville, a retired naval officer who purchased the property in the 1870s.

U.S. Light-House Service, Third District, Staten Island Depot Office Building, later the U.S. Coast Guard Station Administration Building, 1 Bay Street (Alfred B. Mullett, c. 1865–71; wings, 1901). The relatively small but boldly detailed granite-and-red-brick office building (now painted) is one of the few surviving examples of the French Second Empire buildings designed by A. B. Mullett during his tenure as supervising architect of the Treasury. The Staten Island lighthouse depot complex was established for the storage of materials destined for East Coast lighthouses and as an experimental station for the testing of new materials and methods of lighthouse operation. The office building was constructed, beginning in 1868, as a fireproof facility for the storage of the depot's records.

John King Vanderbilt House, 1197 Clove Road (c. 1836). A representative example of Greek Revival design on Staten Island, this house reflects the transition of the northern part of the island from a rural area into a region of suburbs and villages. The building was restored in 1955 by Dorothy Valentine Smith, who lived next door (see p. 234) and who was a descendent of the house's original owner.

364 Van Duzer Street House (c. 1835). This house is a fine example of Staten Island vernacular construction that combines the traditional curved overhanging eaves of the Dutch Colonial style with a two-story Greek Revival portico. It is one of three dwellings erected by Robert M. Hazard, an early Stapleton developer, shortly after he purchased the site in 1834.

390 Van Duzer Street House. This house of indeterminate history no longer occupies its original site. The house is thought to be an 18th-century structure onto which a Greek Revival porch, possibly salvaged from another house, was added.

Caleb T. Ward House, 141 Nixon Avenue (Seth Geer, c. 1835). Located at the crest of Ward's Hill, with a magnificent view of New York Harbor, this monumental mansion is the finest Greek Revival country house surviving in New York City. The house has brick walls stuccoed to simulate stone and an impressive two-story portico. Geer, the builder of Colonnade Row (see p. 48) in Manhattan, has recently been identified as the architect.

Abraham J. Wood House, also known as the 5910 Amboy Road House (c. 1840). This house was erected by the farmer and oysterman Abraham Wood shortly after he purchased the property in 1840. The main section of Wood's new Greek Revival house may have been an addition to an earlier building (now part of the west wing). The house, which has many features typical of vernacular Greek Revival design on Staten Island, is especially notable for its entranceway.

Woodland Cottage, also known as the 33–37 Belair Road House (c. 1845; addition, c. 1900). In the 1830s Staten Island's farms began to undergo suburban development. Woodland Cottage, which was built as a rental unit, is one of the few surviving examples of the picturesque Gothic Revival houses that were quite common in Clifton in the early years of the area's suburbanization. The original cross-gabled section has steep roof slopes outlined by bargeboards; the house features diamond-paned casement windows with drip moldings. Between 1858 and 1869 the cottage served as the rectory of St. John's Church (see p. 233).

Woodrow Methodist Church, 1109 Woodrow Road (1842). This simple Greek Revival country church was erected in 1842 on the site of Staten Island's first Methodist church. The tower was added in 1876.

GOVERNORS, LIBERTY, AND ROOSEVELT ISLANDS

Governors Island. Located in Upper New York Bay, at the entrance to the East River, Governors Island—which early Dutch settlers of the area called *Nooten Eylandt*—is now under the jurisdiction of the U.S. Coast Guard. Early in the 18th century British funds were allocated to fortify the strategically sited island, but this money was diverted by Lord Cornbury for the construction of a mansion to house New York's colonial governors. Troops were first stationed on Governors Island in 1755; the island served as an army base until 1966, when it was turned over to the coast guard.

> **Block House** (Martin E. Thompson, 1843). This austere Greek Revival brick building with a fieldstone base and a finished-stone entrance enframement was built as a prison and has been used as a military headquarters building, a hospital, and officers' quarters.

> **Castle Williams** (Lt. Col. Jonathan Williams, 1807–11). Castle Williams is a massive stone bastion that once boasted more than 100 cannons. It is one of a series of forts, including Castle Clinton (see p. 15) just across New York Harbor, built to fortify New York as tensions rose between America and the British in the early 19th century. Constructed of red Newark sandstone, the two-story circular fort is a military installation of imposing proportion.

> **Commanding General's Quarters,** now the Admiral's House (1840). The former home of the army's Commanding General is an extremely late New York example of a residence in the Federal style. The two-story brick house has a typical Federal doorway and a portico supported by six attenuated double-height columns.

> **Fort Jay** (1798; reconstruction, 1803–06). The original fortification at the north end of Governors Island was completed in 1798 and named for John Jay, who at the time served as secretary of foreign affairs. Extensively

Statue of Liberty, Liberty Island (Frédéric Auguste Bartholdi, sculptor, and Gustave Eiffel, engineer, 1871–86), before restoration. Photo: Jet Lowe, Historic American Engineering Record, National Park Service rebuilt in 1806 as a star-shaped stone structure with an impressive French-inspired entrance, the fortification was renamed Fort Columbus. The original name was restored in 1904.

Governor's House, now the Commanding Officer's Residence (c. 1708). This large brick house in the Georgian style is one of the oldest residences in New York City. The house, which has a Greek cross plan, was supposedly built by Lord Cornbury, the first British governor of the colony of New York. Since 1740 the house has undergone many alterations.

Liberty Island. Known as Bedloe's Island until 1956, this island was the site of Fort Wood, a structure in the shape of an 11-pointed star, erected in 1806–11 to fortify the entrance to New York Harbor. The fort was incorporated into the plans for the base of the Statue of Liberty. Although located within New Jersey's territorial waters, the island itself has since the late 17th century been considered a part of New York City. An agreement of 1834 provides that the island is in New York above the mean low-water mark and in New Jersey below it.

Statue of Liberty (Frédéric Auguste Bartholdi, sculptor, and Gustave Eiffel, engineer, 1871–86; base, Richard Morris Hunt, 1881–86). This portrait of Liberty, famed the world over as a symbol of the United States of America, was a gift from the people of France. The idea for the statue was initiated by a group of French intellectuals who advocated republican rule in France during the Second Empire. These individuals hoped the ideals inspired by the construction of the statue would lead to greater democracy in France. It was not until 1903, when Emma Lazarus's famed poem "The New Colossus" was inscribed on a tablet at the base of the pedestal, that the Statue of Liberty became the symbol of American immigration. The Alsatian sculptor Frédéric Auguste Bartholdi started work on the statue in 1871 and by 1875 was ready to begin actual construction. Money was raised in France for the casting of the colossal piece. The beaten copper exterior was placed on a wrought-iron armature designed by Gustave Eiffel to support the statue's weight and to provide bracing against the winds that would batter the statue when erected at the mouth of New York Harbor. Construction of the base was the responsibility of the United States. Appropriately, the design was undertaken by the French-trained architect Richard Morris Hunt, with money raised through contributions encouraged by Joseph Pulitzer in his newspaper, the *New York World*. In 1885 the statue arrived from France in hundreds of crates, and was erected under the supervision of Gen. Charles P. Stone, an army engineer. A major restoration of the statue was completed in time for its centennial in 1986. This work was directed by Swanke Hayden Connell, architects, with the engineering firm of Ammann & Whitney; the French metalworkers of Les Metalliers Champenois also contributed their expertise.

Roosevelt Island. The six landmark structures on Roosevelt Island, dating from the late 18th century to the early 1890s, illustrate the transformation of this 107-acre island from a farm to the home of several large institutions. In 1676 the Blackwell family took possession of the island, and it remained in their hands until purchased by the city in 1828 for the construction of hospitals, asylums, and a prison. Long known as Blackwell's Island, the name was changed to Welfare Island in 1921 and to Roosevelt Island in 1973. The island now houses several institutions as well as a planned residential community that opened in 1975. In conjunction with the residential development, several of the older buildings were restored or stabilized by Giorgio Cavaglieri.

James Blackwell House (between 1796 and 1804). This simple Georgian-vernacular clapboard farmhouse, the oldest building on the island, was erected by descendants of the island's original European settlers.

Chapel of the Good Shepherd, now Good Shepherd Community Ecumenical Center (Frederick Clarke Withers, 1888–89). Withers's design for this late Victorian Gothic chapel combines the traditions of English parish churches with the demands of an unusual commission. The chapel was a gift of the banker George M. Bliss to the Episcopal City Mission Society and was intended for use by inmates of the nearby city institutions. The stone building has a clearly delineated nave, chancel, and tower, as well as a pair of entrance porches—for male and female inmates, respectively.

Lighthouse (James Renwick, Jr., supervising architect, 1872). The 50-foot-tall lighthouse was erected on what was once a separate tiny island. The octagonal shaft, faced with rough stone blocks of gray gneiss quarried on the island by convict labor, is enlivened by Gothic detail, notably a gabled entrance and a band of foliate ornament.

New York City Lunatic Asylum, now Octagon Tower (A. J. Davis, 1835–39; alterations, Joseph M. Dunn, 1879). The Octagon Tower—the sole surviving portion of the city's lunatic asylum—was originally the central section of a larger structure planned by Davis in 1835–36. As completed in 1839, the complex consisted of the octagon and two patient wings. In 1879 the wings were enlarged and a dome was added. The building is now badly deteriorated, but a restoration is planned.

Smallpox Hospital (James Renwick, Jr., 1854–56; south wing, York & Sawyer, 1903–04; north wing, Renwick, Aspinwall & Owen, 1904–05). Now a picturesque ruin that was stabilized in the 1970s, this Gothic Revival stone structure was built for the treatment of smallpox patients. In 1903–05, by which time the hospital served as a nurse's residence, the facility was enlarged to form a U-shaped structure.

Strecker Laboratory (Withers & Dickson, 1892; third floor, William Flanagan, 1905). This small, Romanesque Revival, gray-stone-and-orange-brick building was originally a pathology laboratory for the nearby Charity Hospital. The building is now in ruinous condition.

INDEX

This index contains the names and alternate names for all entries listed in the guide. In addition, addresses are included for properties with names that are not readily identifiable by the passerby on the street. Entries for properties outside Manhattan are identified by borough: Bronx (Bx), Brooklyn (Bklyn), Queens, and Staten Island (S.I.), unless the name of the entry includes the borough; for example, Bronx County Building.